Aldous Huxley

Aldous Huxley
A Critical Study

by Laurence Brander

Rupert Hart-Davis LONDON 1969

©Laurence Brander 1970
First published 1970

Rupert Hart-Davis Ltd
3 Upper James Street
Golden Square, London W1

Printed in Great Britain by
C. Tinling & Co. Ltd
London and Prescot

Cased ISBN 0 246 63963 6
Paper ISBN 0 246 64014 6

To B.D. and M.G.D.

Acknowledgment

The author acknowledges with many thanks the kindness of Mrs Laura Huxley and Messrs Chatto and Windus Limited in allowing him to quote extensively from the published works of Aldous Huxley.

Contents

A•

Introduction

THE WORK OF Aldous Huxley developed through four of the most interesting decades in the history of Western Man and he responded all the time to what was going on around him: the breaking of Europe, the knowledge explosion with its technological revolution, the population explosion with the appearance of Mass Man, the economic revolution with its tantalising promise for poor men everywhere. During these decades violent oppositions came into being. It became possible for whole populations to be properly fed, clothed and housed; it became possible for them all to be destroyed together in a few minutes. The aeroplane and mass communications developed until what seemed a spacious world became a confined space in which the multitudes jostled one another. For the first time, on the other hand, it became possible to relieve mankind of its secular pain and anxiety.

Huxley was always sensitive to these oppositions, the eternal balance between good and evil in nature and in human societies. He was prepared to take a full look at the worst; but he spent more time in exploring the new possibilities of advantage to man. He believed in the individual, and he saw the possibilities of greater awareness for the individual. He believed that the balance could only come right if a sufficient number of individuals acted with steady good purpose. It is the Existentialist reaction in a time of flux, the Stoic attitude modified for the times. The unbelievably wonderful possibilities for good were frightening because they could become equally powerful possibilities for evil. But they had to be faced.

To all this Aldous Huxley reacted sensitively and energetically. He could not escape from his heredity, on the one side the Huxleys, on the other the Arnolds, two of the great intellectual families of the nineteenth century, when the responsible use of knowledge seemed to be replacing religion in the control of human societies. When Huxley was a boy, men believed in the steady progress of human betterment. The belief was based on the stability of society and it foresaw our knowledge explosion but not the breaking up of European societies. With his family background and the educational advantages of Eton and Balliol, Huxley could feel he inherited this world of progress. But he was born in 1894, and would have gone to war if he had not been nearly blind. The rich creative years of early manhood were spent in a society which was trying to forget the horrors of war, and the social earthquakes it had brought. He began with books of verse and intellectual satirical novels. The verses showed promise but never said much; a characteristic of most verses in England ever since. The prose was witty and ran clearly and nimbly. He discovered immediately a gift of style, which is a gift frequently denied English novelists.

Any creative act is pleasure and in his first novels creation must have been wholly agreeable for this young Edwardian out of Late Victorians speaking to Georgians. But even in that first decade, with its first flush of stories and novels, there are essays which show him the typical twentieth-century cultivated man, a product of the great explosion of knowledge, troubled by the use to which so many of our discoveries are put in our irresponsible and acquisitive societies.

That was the first decade of his writing, and the second, the thirties, was the decade of anxiety. We could foresee another breaking of nations and as the years went by, the doom became as inevitable as tragedy. The pursuit of pleasure in writing gave way to the search for sanity in human affairs. In the novels, the lighter play of the intellect was enriched by a serious search for truth in human affairs which would make stable belief in human ideals possible. The wit and the comic situations were still there and the sex play was more sophisticated than before. But the other side, the skull beneath the beating temple, the anxiety in the eyes, were now evident. And the essays became the expository prose of 'An Enquiry into the Nature of Ideals and into the Methods employed for their Realization' called *Ends and Means*.

The transformation from the 'amused Pyrrhonic aesthete' (his own description of himself up to the time of *Brave New World*) to the dedicated preacher was gradual, and he never entirely gave up the lighter pleasures of prose fiction. But the joys of creating amusing sexual situations and agreeable conversation between exciting people gave way to studies of the mental and spiritual conflict in people who were at the mercy of the times. By the forties, the natural passage of the years and the stresses of the times brought the preacher forward. In the face of gigantic and inescapable calamity he turned to what could be salvaged, and that was the individual mind. The fifties were clouded for us all. We could not believe that the bomb would not explode over us; and though we knew that every human life must some day end, we could not reconcile ourselves to simultaneous destruction. No one pointed out the advantages, with no one to mourn and the planet healthier and more lovely without the human race or at any rate without Western Man. Huxley's imaginative reaction in *Ape and Essence* was as tortured as a fine mind could make it.

He did not live to see our present accommodation with the nuclear threat. With the usual resilience of the human mind, we neglect to visualise what can happen. He had found another way to deal with horror too horrible to be faced: the mystical realisation of the foundation of existence. The seeds of all his thinking are apparent in the twenties; so we find in *Proper Studies* the idea that we are essentially fragments of the Whole. A decade later, in *Eyeless in Gaza*, he says: 'In time, it might be possible to establish a complete and definitive *Ars Contemplativa*.' The fragments could learn to realise the Whole. Just after the war, in *The Perennial Philosophy* he quotes a saying of Jacob Boehme's which will often appear again in his writing. It is in answer to the question, where does the soul go when the body dies: 'There is no necessity for it to go anywhere.' It is the same answer as the Sanscrit offers, again frequently quoted: *tat tvam asi*, meaning 'that art thou', the immanent eternal self.

Realisation of that sort can be pursued with the energy that goes to the discovery of priceless treasure, so we find Huxley constantly seeking greater awareness, constantly trying to push further back the frontiers of mystical experience. Eventually, he was ready to experiment with drugs under strict medical supervision. The two short pieces he wrote about his experiences, *The Doors of Perception* and *Heaven and Hell*, have become very well known and, as they are written with all his grace and persuasiveness, they have encouraged young people to experiment. Nothing could be more dangerous, as Huxley argued forcibly in an Appendix to *The Devils of Loudun*. But not many read that, and eager young experimenters forget that you can only discover what is ready to be discovered from your inner self and so, until the strenuous studies and exercises of religious experience have been undertaken, any experience of transcendence is not likely to be permanently rewarding.

What is rewarding is indicated in *Time Must Have a Stop*, when Malpighi says: 'There's only one corner of the universe you can be certain of improving, and that's your own self.' That was written just a year before Huxley published *The Perennial Philosophy*, his handbook for those who wished to discover themselves. He had come to the position every man arrives at if he is intelligent and retains his integrity. He concentrated on the individual. It is the answer to all the turbulence of a world which has been broken and can destroy itself. It is the answer to the problem of Mass Man, from whom it has become so difficult to escape, whom it is so difficult to help. In the East, the contemplative emanates an influence which strengthens the mass of men. In the West, individual intelligences filter good sense through the mass. In the end, we all put our hope in the individual. In the East, it is the achieved individuality which is fit to become part of the One. In the West, it is the individual, who finds there is no necessity to go anywhere because he is already part of Existence.

We can trace very easily in Huxley's writings the development of his sensibility of the power of the spirit, in our Manichean world of vigorous evil. In *Beyond the Mexique Bay* he met a doctor who had consciously developed the spiritual side of his nature. In *Eyeless in Gaza* a Scots doctor turns up in Central America who had developed his powers in the same area of existence. Huxley's contribution to the rehabilitation of western man was the anthology of perennial philosophy. In the fifties, in *Adonis and the Alphabet*, he says: 'Understanding comes when we liberate ourselves from the old and so make possible a direct, unmediated contact with the new, the mystery, moment by moment, of our existence.' Or that wonderful expression of reconciliation with our condition and with all existence at the end of *The Doors of Perception*: 'To be enlightened is to be aware, always, of total reality in its immanent otherness—to be aware of it and yet to remain in a condition to survive as an animal, to think and feel as a human being, to resort whenever expedient to systematic reasoning. Our goal is to discover that we have always been where we ought to be.' In the end he gathered up all the ideas in these late essays in a final imaginative statement in his last novel, *Island*, written when he knew he was dying and might not be able to address us again. He introduced another medical man of Scottish descent, to instruct us in the conduct of the compassionate spirit in our world of good-and-evil, and to express his final assuring view of a future life; death is the moment of transition into the Clear Light. The expression of this simple faith in *Island* is the most eloquent writing that Huxley has left us.

In all this, he was committed to the human situation in the years and decades, moment by moment, through which he was living. He was concerned for his fellow existences, so it will be useful to have a preliminary look at one part of his background, and what other men on the same quest were saying at that time. It was realised right at the beginning of the century by perceptive spirits like H. G. Wells and by the time the 1914–18 War was over it was generally recognized that our century was beginning to enjoy one of the great knowledge explosions. As we all now know, that has meant on the one hand, previously unimagined explorations through time and space as well as into the human body and the human mind. On the other hand, because so much of the new knowledge has been successfully applied to the physical problems of human existence, it has produced great wealth and on that great wealth the masses have risen.

But the mass defeats itself and for decades it has been swamping order, producing disorder and at times revolution. For masses find leaders who lead them astray and carry us all with them. In the intellectual world, there is a Manichean nightmare, knowledge used for good and evil to bring us, on the one hand to the verge of universal destruction, and on the other to the possibility of a humanity intellectually enriched beyond the wildest dreams of

the nineteenth century. The possibilities before the human race
have never been so dark or so bright, and the greatest strain on
the intellectual life of western man has been in retaining a sense
of order. Our knowledge in the worlds of chemistry and physics,
biology and psychology is increasing with such overwhelming
rapidity, and is being applied with such skill that the old social
orders are becoming inadequate before we have any idea of what
to put in their place.

The rise of the masses and the dangers that has brought has
been eloquently described in Ortega y Gasset's *The Revolt of the
Masses*, which opens forthrightly: 'There is one fact which,
whether for good or ill, is of the utmost importance in the public
life of Europe at the present moment. This fact is the accession of
the masses to complete social power', and he goes on to say that,
as the masses can never direct themselves, this has brought to
Europe the greatest crisis that can affect a civilisation. That was
published in 1930, bringing together papers he had published
through the previous decade. The twenties was a tumultuous
decade, the first after the war which we used to think was the
first move in the suicide of Europe, but which we begin to hope
was the first move in sweeping away old and otiose orders, in
order to allow Europe to reconcile itself to its own knowledge
explosion.

Something of our present reaction was caught by Paul Valéry
in 1922 in an essay he called 'The Europeans'. His refreshing
French rhetoric is a herald of our present state: 'Man is that
different animal, that bizarre living creature who has set himself
off from all others, who stands above them by virtue of his—
daydreams—the intensity, continuity, and diversity of his daydreams! And by their extraordinary consequences, which go
even so far as to modify not only his own nature but also the
very Nature around him, which he strives indefatigably to
dominate with his daydreams.'

That was the twenties and in that decade Huxley began writing,
giving us all his short stories, many of his novels and a few books
of essays. They show little of the concern that Ortega expresses
so eloquently, or of the world view which Valéry speaks of with
such élan. They reflect the febrile gaiety of the decade, which was
in part an unconscious effort to return to a social order which the
war had shattered for ever. The book in that decade which adum-

brated his concern about what was happening to western civilisation, *Proper Studies*, is the first of his discussions of the human
condition and it opens appropriately with an essay called 'The
Idea of Equality'.

The next decade in Europe was blighted by the shadow of
coming war, the clash of mass against mass in fratricidal insanity.
But towards the beginning of it, in Easter 1933, another Spaniard,
Salvador de Madariaga, wrote a long letter to his friend Paul
Valéry expressing the high purposes of the European intellect at
that time. He too felt the power of the masses, 'the sense of being
swallowed up, as if drawn down by nameless forces in a yawning
gulf'. But he also had a vision of a new society taking shape. As
Ortega had a vision of a united Europe, Madariaga had a vision
of a world order, whose 'constituents are men, races, and nations;
its creative moral force is culture; its creative natural forces are
place and climate; its guide is reason; its faith is the intuition of
order—which is to say, the relatively modest dogma that God is
not crazy'. This makes the role of mind clear to him: 'Its task
therefore is to discover and define the order sensed by our faith
and felt as a necessity by the mind itself.' In times of disorder
and the threat of anarchy he expresses eloquently the intense
intellectual desire for order.

During that decade, Huxley became committed to social and
political affairs. In 1932 he published *Brave New World*, a fable
about social and intellectual order in a mass society, the social
and intellectual order of hell, with every action of body and mind
predetermined, manipulated, controlled. His best novel in the
decade was *Eyeless in Gaza*, and the essence of that book is the
'Diary of Anthony Beavis' as he indicated by choosing it for the
Everyman Library anthology of his writings. Beavis is an intellectual, but he has nothing of the virile optimism which enabled
European intellectuals at that time to see a tolerable and possibly
illuminating future for Europe. Beavis begins his diary with:
Video meliora proboque, deteriora sequor ('I see and approve the
better way but in fact I follow the worse'), the words of a Roman
poet conscious of the revolting masses around him and sunk in
the pessimism which coloured Huxley's outlook, that pessimism
which is an occupational disease of intellectual life at any time.

But in the following year Huxley displayed the intellectual
sturdiness of his forebears, and less of the melancholy he had

inherited from the Arnolds. In *Ends and Means* he argues forcibly
for right living, which for him was a sensible and courageous
search for ideals. There is still an element of Stoic fortitude in his
approach, like that expressed by Jung about the same time in his
essay on 'The Spiritual Problem of Modern Man': 'The man
whom we can with justice call "modern" is solitary. He is so of
necessity and at all times, for every step towards a fuller consciousness of the present removes him further from his original
participation mystique with the mass of men—from submersion
in a common unconsciousness.' That was precisely the situation
of Anthony Beavis, who lived with the shadow of the masses
clouding his mind, a shadow which Huxley lived to expel in his
last novel, *Island*. But in the thirties Huxley had nothing of the
splendid hope expressed by Jung a little later in the same essay.
Jung describes how a truly modern man must detach himself
from the masses, and even then: 'He is completely modern only
when he has come to the very edge of the world, leaving behind
him all that has been discarded and outgrown, and acknowledging
that he stands before a void out of which all things may grow.'
Only much later did Huxley arrive at this confidence in the
individual.

It is well to remind ourselves from time to time of the courageous
thinking which quickened in Europe during these apparently
desolating years. They were also the years of the third great
European age of scientific discovery. It is a part of our inheritance, but for most imaginative writers it is the other culture
which is an unknown world. Not so for Huxley, whose own
training was not scientific but who shared the family freedom of
the world of science. He also made himself familiar with the
world of philosophy—among our modern novelists he is the
nearest counterpart in our second Renaissance to the *uomo
universale* of the first.

It is his philosophical preoccupations which appear to most
advantage in the forties, the most difficult decade in our century
for European man. When it opened we were returning to absolute
barbarism and when it ended we were beginning to fear imminent
and total destruction. Not for centuries had it been so difficult to
see any light in our future. And yet there were still philosophers
in Europe who could see more clearly than the rest of us, who
could see not only the necessity for hope but its validity. As

Valéry had addressed Europeans in 1922, Karl Jaspers addressed them in 1946 in an essay which he called 'The European Spirit'. In that essay he sought to steady his fellow Europeans after the nations had been broken again. He had an inkling of a great future: 'Europe seems to be in a critical moment of preparation. In the breaking-up of everything that has hitherto been solid the European is set free for ways of which we have an inkling but no knowledge. What makes us afraid is our great freedom in face of the emptiness that has still to be filled.' All through his essay the refrain is: 'The way to the future leads through the individual, through each individual.' In that same year, 1946, Huxley made his contribution. He published his *Perennial Philosophy*, a handbook for the individual who is intent on developing his own social and spiritual usefulness to his society.

Very soon, another Existentialist philosopher followed Jaspers by writing an exhortation to the ordinary European, and followed Ortega by facing the problem of the masses. Gabriel Marcel, in his *Man against Mass Society* recognised that the current threat to European culture is the financial and social power which Mass Man has been given. It is the duty of the individual—the human being who has been able to rise out of the mass and discover his own integrity—to combat these mass values. To do so we must measure ourselves against universal values, which is to fall back on Matthew Arnold's touchstones of taste. But individual excellence is not enough and Marcel's argument is worth following here, because it adumbrates what Huxley said in *Island*. Indeed, in one sentence he expresses the whole spirit of that ideal island society. 'We shall act with calm and constancy in the world around us, showing in our everyday life the spirit that works within us and opposing ourselves to every spirit that is not entirely reasonable and entirely generous.'

Reasonableness and generosity are not distinguishing characteristics of the masses and in his Conclusion Marcel reminds us that it is difficult for the individual also to sustain them alone. So he holds that we must rehabilitate an aristocracy, just as E. M. Forster wanted a democracy of the aristocrats of the intelligence. They have been discredited by the false leaders of the masses, and they must come back; for egalitarianism means levelling down. 'The mass itself is a lie, and it is *against the mass* and *for the universal* that we must bear witness.' Only his aristocrats can do so, for only they 'can be vitally connected with that universal purpose, which is the purpose of love and truth in the world'.

All this the Huxleys and Arnolds of the nineteenth century would have applauded. In their time the mass had not been given power and their efforts were directed against the political parties of the day when they failed to act or followed wrong courses of action. It was the presence of this intellectual aristocracy in Victorian England that made 'democratic rule' tolerable. They were all middle class together and the appeal to reason and good faith was possible. The Huxleys of our time have lived with us through our social revolution and our knowledge explosion, and their efforts have been directed towards sustaining those universal values of which Marcel writes, so that eventually a new aristocracy of the mind and spirit will emerge to direct our affairs.

When we read Aldous Huxley we watch the development of a considerable creative gift from the youthful irresponsibility of the 'amused Pyrrhonic aesthete', to the wholly committed intellectual and creative force at the service of his fellow men. In the first novel, the swift flash of Peacock wit; in the last, that light which Marcel said we must radiate 'for the benefit of each other, while remembering that our role consists above all and perhaps exclusively in not presenting any obstacle to its passage *through us*'. It was that spirit which made Huxley concentrate more and more on becoming aware, of realising to the utmost the possibilities of the mind and the spirit and advancing wherever he could the frontiers of human knowledge.

He has left a very considerable oeuvre, novels, short stories, essays, anthologies, travel books, biographies and in them all he has left strong impressions of his own spirit. His sense of style never deserted him and we see him in all his writings as clearly as through a windowpane. His work has that double interest we expect in any writing worth studying; it is by an interesting and powerful individual, and it has something unique to say. Huxley in his life and in his writing demonstrates an admirable way of coping with our extraordinary world.

The Novels 1

Crome Yellow

OUR WORDS give us away and never more than in fiction. Nothing shows the size and nature of a man's mind and spirit more clearly than a novel. Nothing fails more obviously than a design for a fiction which is too big for the author. A natural novelist will keep his designs within his powers and young novelists will be content with modest beginnings. Aldous Huxley published his first novel when he was twenty-seven, and he had no trouble in completing his design.

He takes us, like so many English novelists before him, to a country house and there the characters talk to one another just as Peacock's did. The characters are sketches, caricatures, characters in the old literary sense rather than people who react upon one another. There are young people, so there are love affairs but they exist only to be thwarted in an entirely comic atmosphere. There are old people, typed and true to their types, and they talk and do nothing. It is all very agreeable, for the scene unfolds in unnoticeable prose and it is intelligent and amusing, with no thought of stresses or clashes or vulgarity or anything disagreeably real. The young novelist has lived a little and read a great deal and he relies on his reading and his sense of comedy to carry him through. There is no criticism of life, because life does not intrude on this fantasy, but there is a good deal of criticism of literature in the pleasant and precise way of parody.

There is no hero, we need another word for the character at the

centre whom we follow all the way, who is just an ordinary like-
able young man. Denis Stone has published a book of verse. He
is going to spend a few weeks at Crome, a large country house that
had sheltered ten generations, and there he will meet Anne, with
whom he is in love. Anne, who is four years older than Denis,
thinks he is a nice boy but never becomes aware of his feelings for
her. His hostess, Priscilla Wimbush, has all the makings of a
managing character but she manages nothing at all. We learn
eventually of a very gay past but she hardly affects our present
concerns. Her husband, Henry Wimbush, is more interesting. He
has written and printed the family history and regales his guests
with passages which make us long for the whole work. There is
nothing like an inset in a flimsy tale to vary the entertainment.
The passage about the dwarfs is amusing, the one about the three
lovely daughters with souls above food and drink, who apparently
deny their bodies food and drink as well, is even better. Brief
comic sketches like these release the young author's abundant
energies and compensate for lack of a plot.

A sketch of Mr Bodiham, the rector, is good for a chapter. Mr
Bodiham is a brown thought in a brown shade, a picture case of
some of the clerical occupational diseases. Where would comic
fiction be without its clerics? But the chief supporting characters
are Mr Scogan, like an extinct saurian, and Gombauld, who
provides a shimmer of action by seducing the earnest Mary on
the roof. Anne is unattainable, beautiful and unaware, Jenny is
unattainable because she is deaf and Mary is sympathetic and has
a great capacity for earnestness and love.

It is Scogan who makes us think of Peacock, but in chapter
twenty-seven Scogan becomes the fortune-telling gypsy woman
at the Fair and gives us a comic scene the equal of vintage
Wodehouse. The Fair itself, like the earlier visit to the piggery, is
very much in the Wodehouse vein, but while in Wodehouse the
comic creations exist only by impinging on one another, in Huxley
the energy is intellectual and exerts itself in the literary joys of
parody and pretended quotations and conversation. If there is a
hint of action, it is among the young people and is therefore of
dalliance and courtship, but the reader is allowed to glance only
shyly and his gaze is soon diverted. Early in the book Denis
found that: 'In the world of ideas everything was clear: in life all
was obscure, embroiled.' In his first novel Huxley easily avoids

obscurity by keeping to the world of ideas which his precocious and extensive reading had created for him, and he gave us a gay little sketch which we still read with undisturbed amusement.

Antic Hay

'My men, like satyrs grazing on the lawns,
Shall with their goat feet dance an antic hay.'
MARLOWE   *Edward II*

IN THE last long scene when Gumbril and Myra Viveash are
together he says: 'And here I am left in the vacuum', and she
replies: 'We're all in the vacuum.' The novel is part of Huxley's
portrait of the twenties, a gentle aphrodisiac compounded of
people who were concerned with the strenuous business of idling.
Leisure for them had become phrenetic. There was too much to
remember. When Mrs Viveash walked out one morning along the
sunny side of the King's Road, Chelsea, she remembered she had
done so on a similar morning with Tony Lamb, who a week later
was dead, shot through the head. She remembered his eyes and
that they had turned to dust. It is the only time such memories
are mentioned but they lay upon the early twenties like a doom.

Young Gumbril is too young for such memories and he is
concerned to get away from the odious business of teaching. In
the opening scene he is in the school chapel, decides he can bear
it no longer and has the inspiration which will give him financial
release. We shall never know how many of their best ideas came
to our forebears under the inspiration of the church. Where the
seats were hard, Gumbril's idea was for patent small clothes with
an insertion on the seat of the trousers, which could be inflated
to make sitting tolerable. Gumbril's father is an architect and he
knows someone who can help to market the youthful idea. Young
Gumbril goes home to his father's house in a dilapidated London
Square and finds his father talking to his friend Porteous, a
scholar of 'Late Latin'. Huxley has always been good with old

men, especially scholars, and these two old gentlemen are about the only charming people in the book. Later on, they produce the only charming gesture. It concerns old Gumbril's model of London according to Wren, that London of Should-Have-Been which we are again failing to realise. He is very proud of it but when Porteous's son gets heavily into debt and Porteous has to sell even his precious library to pay the debt, old Gumbril sells his model and buys back the more precious books.

There is the ghost of another gesture, a moment of the still submerged world of the poor, a gesture so slight, so toneless, that it is hardly even a faint foretelling of Huxley's later preoccupation with social problems. A group of the central characters, the artists who make the group, have been dining in Soho, and they go out into the streets and stop at a coffee stall at Hyde Park Corner. Myra Viveash suddenly appears and there, against her beauty and her so expensive clothes, we begin to sense the presence of the poor. They are very like the traditional poor in *Punch*, there to be funny or pathetic.

At the beginning of the story we have had other distractions from the solemn or enraptured pursuit of bed. Young Gumbril has sympathetic views on education—why keep the uneducable at school at great expense and make them miserable when they could be happily continuing their education in charge of an adult on the factory floor? He is especially severe on the teaching of history, which rots the minds of the young with a diet 'of soft vagueness'. There is a good deal that is amusing about archi-tecture and music, favourite subjects for the little essays Huxley offers in and out of his novels.

Very soon young Gumbril goes out in pursuit of sex and gets his girl by transforming his personality. He buys himself a great big beard and disguised in that he has cheek enough for anything. First time out he picks up a charming girl who eventually takes him home with her. It is charming comedy, for she has to pretend she is somebody grand and apologises for the wretched furniture— 'ours is in store on the Riviera'—and both are so innocent of the art of seduction that it takes them some time to get where they want to be. They will meet again but he must know who she is so that he can ring her up. She gives him her card: she is the wife of the physiologist in our set. Her affaires run in parallel with those of Myra Viveash, who is much sought after but is bored and sated and only makes love because there is nothing else to do. Lypiatt the painter wants to shoot himself, his exhibition a failure, his love for Myra so consuming. Shearwater, our physiologist, is in almost worse case. He ends up in his laboratory pedalling a captive cycle mile after mile, day after day, not in the name of science but for hopeless love of Myra.

We visit the right restaurants in this novel, go to the right picture dealers, listen to the right music in the right concert halls. We are admitted to studios and laboratories, to the private lives of our set as well as to the pleasures of their conversation. Huxley fulfils the traditional obligation of the London novelist so well fulfilled by Thackeray in his grandfather's time, to take us to places most of us would never otherwise see and to introduce us to people we should never meet. Huxley, in the twenties, was allowed to show us a side of life that the English novelist had not been allowed to show us for a very long time.

In the beginning of the novel there is instruction on education, architecture, politics and music, but that mood soon gives way to the absorbing topic of bed and how to fill in the hours between. Jazz, restaurants, taxis and the lights of London. At the end, a long taxi ride to and fro in the West End, while Myra and Gumbril visit their friends and particularly the men who would like to have her or die. *Antic Hay*, when it was published, was a very daring novel. It was a stronger piece of writing than either *Crome Yellow* or the early short stories. Its blatant decadence was exacerbated by the brief early passages in a serious reforming mood. Our tastes on the main theme are coarsened now, but *Antic Hay* is amusing still, because it is witty and it has style. Our emotions are never involved except in that one scene when old Gumbril has to confess to his son that his beloved model has gone. In the twenties people wanted to be very daring and to shock one another. Huxley succeeded, and he will do so again but with much more sophistication.

Those Barren Leaves

'Enough of Science and of Art;
Close up those barren leaves;
Come forth, and bring with you a heart
That watches and receives.'
WORDSWORTH   *The Tables Turned*

THE NOVEL follows the poem. There are the oppositions on
which Huxley based his later fiction, the physical and the intellectual, the healthy and the decadent, the illusion and the reality.
He has gone back to the formula of *Crome Yellow*, a houseparty
with love affairs and conversation. The 'heart that watches and
receives' will appear at the end. The house is a palazzo, the hostess
the rich and possessive Lilian Aldwinkle. She possesses the palace
and the Cybo Malaspina who had owned it. She possesses the
scenery all round, from the mountains to the waters of the Mediterranean where Shelley drowned. She possesses Italian painting
and literature: all, all, for herself and for her guests; so she feels
she possesses her guests. She is particularly possessive of her
niece, Irene, and one of the lighter joys of the novel is the escape
of youth from a smothering possessiveness.

Irene's affaire with Lord Hovenden is as gay and innocent as
something in P. G. Wodehouse, and told very much in his spirit.
At the other extreme, there is the sophisticated affaire between
Mary Thriplow and Calamy. Considerable skill is shown in keeping the other affaires within comic limits. Otherwise, Lilian
Aldwinkle's urgent feeling for the handsome young Chelifer would
be unpleasant, and the calculated pursuit of the moron heiress by
old Cardan would be completely out of tune.

The comic atmosphere is sustained against a magnificent background. Huxley had discovered by this time in his short stories

and his essays a gift for description which he had exercised on
Italian scenes. He exploits it to the full, from the opening descriptions to the sustained passage when the whole party is driving
down to Rome, and finally in the closing dialogue which is placed
against an appropriate natural background in the classical spirit.
When they go to Rome, we are dazzled with erudition, for we
drive through centuries of civilisation while the young lord plucks
up courage to ask Irene to marry him. That is an entirely charming
episode, the youth of the world in a novel where the other characters are tarnished with experience and age.

There are natural descriptions in a different mood when Cardan
pursues a report of a bit of ancient sculpture which he hopes to
pick up cheap and falls in with Grace Elver and her brother. The
pursuit of the sculpture is a comic short story in itself, with
Cardan's vivid imaginings of its antiquity and value, when fore-
seeably it turns out to be a stock product of the 1830s. Cardan
always lost, as we shall see. The 'Elver' story is from the *Purga-
torio*, used by Stendhal, translated by Hazlitt and used again by
Somerset Maugham in *The Painted Veil* (published in the same
year as *Those Barren Leaves*), the story of the beautiful Siennese
heiress who was taken by her jealous husband to the malarial
swamps where she mysteriously died. Some commentators had
suggested she was purposely exposed to malaria and died of it;
and it was in this same hope that Elver brought his moron sister to
live there so that he could succeed to her fortune. Cardan outwits
him and supplants him and brings her as a guest to the palace,
hoping eventually to marry her. Poor Cardan. He is haunted by
poverty and reckons that £25,000 in Hungarian 'seven per cents'
will see him through. Alas for his hopes; in that splendid motor
trip to Rome the gluttonous moron insists on eating fish from one
of the lakes and dies of food poisoning.

Lilian Aldwinkle's pursuit of Chelifer is again squalor tempered
by comic presentation. He is introduced by long quotations from
his autobiography and we wonder, as we do elsewhere in this
strangely lengthened novel, why Huxley padded out with so much
irrelevant material. This digression carries us back to London for
nearly a hundred pages, giving us Chelifer's meditations at the
office desk of the *Rabbit Fancier's Gazette*, which are amusing; a
glimpse of life at his boarding house, which is not; and a long-
short story of his disappointment in a love affair, which is equally

unamusing; and samples of his verses, which are no better than Huxley's own. Certainly the rather cumbrous digression explains why Lilian pursued him—he was a personable young love poet—and why he was at such pains to elude her, and once again the comic mood is sustained.

The affaire between Calamy and Mary Thriplow is central and realistic, and it develops the more interesting theme in the book, the search for the freedom of the spirit which is necessary for the pursuit of truth. The later Huxley is first seen in Calamy. He is, at the beginning of the novel, an experienced amorist who wants no more of it but Mary Thriplow has only to play upon his weakness intelligently. She is the only available woman for him and he will fall if she makes herself attractive. She quickly senses that she must be demure and her intelligence at every stage leads her to success. At the end of the affaire she writes it down for future reference from notes she made as it went along.

Novelists can't waste time. Calamy retires to a cottage up the mountain to contemplate and in the final chapter Cardan and Chelifer find him there so that we can have the dialogue about the nature of reality. Huxley's powers are concentrated in the opening of this final chapter to provide an appropriate setting and, when all has been said, to give a natural symbol of hope to Calamy in his search. The bare rocks of the mountain that catch the rays of the sun above the mists reassure him.

For those who are interested in Huxley's ideas this is a most rewarding novel. He is accepting a challenge to his technical ability to cover the extremes of the range of human thought and feeling. It means that he is writing at two speeds, the even, rapid narrative speed, best illustrated in that afternoon drive when Hovenden proposes to Irene; and the slower speed necessary for the intellectual probings and questionings. He changes speed frequently in these early novels and short stories, often more successfully than here, where the transitions are sometimes abrupt. But it is all well done and the essay writing and dialogue is interesting not only in itself, but because there are first statements of themes to which Huxley will return all through his life.

There are suggestions of themes which will be developed in *Brave New World*. Chelifer composes a little catechism in his autobiography which provides echoes:

Q. On what condition can I live a life of contentment?
A. On the condition that you do not think.
Q. What is the function of newspapers, cinemas, radios, motor-bikes, jazz bands, etc.?
A. The function of these things is the prevention of thought and the killing of time.

This carries us forward to *Brave New World Revisited*; but we may ask what else better the human animal is expected to do with leisure, except try to kill time gracefully.

A little later, when Cardan and Falx, the labour leader, are together, Falx confesses he feels 'a certain moral laxity, a certain self-indulgence' around him in Mrs Aldwinkle's house party. Cardan reminds him of the moral laxity and self-indulgence of those politicians, like himself, who pursue power: 'people who have tried both, have told me that the joys of power are far more preferable, if only because they are a great deal more enduring, to those one can derive from wine and love.' The argument will be carried further in *Ends and Means* and *The Perennial Philosophy*. In the twenties we were just beginning to realise what a frightening amount of power modern societies develop and must give to their politicians, who can not be expected to use it efficiently. Later on, Cardan speaks to Falx about the ordinary people and we sense a much stronger reaction than the sentimental treatment in *Antic Hay*. 'There are a few choice Britons who will never be slaves, and a great many who not only will be slaves, but would be utterly lost if they were made free.'

In the final dialogue Cardan and Chelifer discuss our modern society again. Most people live as part of the tribe. Few are individuals. But education has unsettled the tribe, and they are 'too conscious of themselves to obey blindly, too inept to be able to behave in a reasonable manner on their own account'. Cardan puts his hope in the mass media to produce a new settled tribalism. But we still prefer to conduct our affairs by cheating and in anger, dividing ourselves into two tribes or more on every question, not for complementary and constructive partnerships but to squabble and hinder progress.

The introduction of these themes as well as the treatment of the characters and the management of the story shows a considerable advance in technique and power over the two previous novels. His world and his characters are much more three dimensional. He creates Calamy to express his own favourite ideas, Calamy who from the beginning wants to give up love affairs and be a contemplative. In the final dialogue Calamy is expressing ideas to which Huxley will give the most devoted attention: 'If one desires salvation, it is salvation here and now. The kingdom of God is within you... The conquest of that kingdom, now, in this life—that's your salvationist's ambition.' Then the hope that dominates Huxley's later years: 'Perhaps if you spend long enough and your mind is the right sort of mind, perhaps you really do get, in some queer sort of way, beyond the limitations of ordinary existence.' And later: 'I begin to feel in myself a certain aptitude for meditation which seems to me worth cultivating.' Then more strongly: 'There is a whole universe within me, un-known and waiting to be explored; a whole universe that can only be approached by way of introspection and patient uninterrupted thought. Merely to satisfy curiosity it would surely be worth exploring. But there are motives more compelling than curiosity to persuade me. What one may find there is so important that it's almost a matter of life and death to undertake the search.'

That is the modern theme, and it is very much Huxley's. Following it from these beginnings is one of the great attractions of his work. Calamy has one more attempt to resolve his own difficulty, to reconcile the unquenchable amorist in himself and the thirst for the contemplative life. In the end he decides that every part of our nature is true and we must reconcile them. In the physical world we accept time and space and we are condi-tioned to accepting them in three dimensions. The fourth dimen-sion—we heard plenty about that in the twenties—completes the continuum of unknowable reality, which 'is the same for all observers'. The pictures drawn of this unknowable reality by the best observers, Gotama, Jesus and Lao-tsze resemble one another very closely. Returning to physical life, Calamy decides that the natural sexual instincts have nothing to do with morality. We accept relativity, the existence of good-and-evil. And sex becomes evil only when it interferes with the freedom of the mind 'to contemplate and recollect itself'.

The Edwardians expressed the interfering power of sex by writing about Pan. In the twenties, discussion became more open and Huxley was intrigued to express each extreme of human excitation. It required great skill and he was successful. He brought life to the barren leaves and brought Wordsworth's spirit to his novel. We have seen that 'Our meddling intellect Misshapes the beauteous forms of things' and that 'Sweet is the love which Nature brings' to natural pleasures. At the end, in that splendid dialogue between the three men against the background of the woods and the hills, the speakers 'Close up those barren leaves' and 'Come forth' and discover 'a heart that watches and receives'.

Point Counter Point

'All you need is a sufficiency of characters
and parallel contrapuntal plots.'
Philip Quarles's Journal

POINT COUNTER POINT is almost a novel without a story.
There is a world of characters and we are given short stories about
them, moving through time and place, to make them alive in
depth. But there is no general movement of the characters towards
tension. It opens with a depressing situation between Marjorie
Carling and Walter Bidlake. They live together, they cannot
marry, she is with child by him and he is in love with someone
else. He is going to a party to meet the other woman.

For seventy pages we are taken to an evening party in Tantamount House. We begin to meet the characters. The older Bidlake,
the painter, and his erstwhile mistress, the hostess, are described
and set in motion with gusto. Lord Edward, the host, is described
with affectionate detail. He is a scientist and not very aware of his
wife's social world. Unlike his Communist assistant, Illidge, who
has all the sensitivity of the inverted snob. Everard Webley,
eventually the Communist's victim, is allowed to express his views
as leader of the British Fascists. The four chapters describing the
people at the party are a sketch of Vanity Fair in the twenties. We
are as indebted to Huxley for his portraits of the twenties as we
are to Thackeray for his conversation pieces of the 1850s. The
focus changes at the end of the fifth chapter and we are brought
back by a simple device to the wretched Marjorie Carling, followed
by the simplest of bridges to carry us from Tantamount House to
the western shores of India in the next chapter. So far, Walter has
hardly met Lucy Tantamount, whom he loves so madly and so

B

much against his will. Nor has there been the least hint of a story. One-sixth of the book gone and we have characters in plenty, but we are called away to India and we leave them all.

We stay in India for less than twenty pages, long enough for a tepid caricature of an Indian politician and to enjoy a detailed analysis of a new character, Philip Quarles, the husband of old Bidlake's daughter. It begins with a conversation between them in which we sense that here may be a parallel to her brother's situation, the fatigue of living with someone who has become boring. But it is different. Her life is to care for her writer husband, and that is not easy: 'All his life long he had walked in a solitude, in a private void.' That analysis continues what seems to be a self-portrait. Philip is seen sympathetically through the eyes of his wife: 'A kind of Pyrrhonian indifference, tempered by a consistent gentleness and kindness... and finally his intelligence —that quick, comprehensive, ubiquitous intelligence that could understand everything, including the emotions it could not feel and the instincts it took care not to be moved by.'

We turn the page and we are back in Tantamount House, and this time Bidlake does meet Lucy. Spoilt child as she was— though already thirty—her one desire was to leave her mother's party and go to a Soho restaurant. They go off together while we are left to meet another character who has no part to play and is created in her own carefully rehearsed conversation. Molly d'Exergillod is regaling Burlap with the conversation she pre-pared for a recent luncheon. 'Like all professional talkers Molly was very economical with her wit and wisdom. There are not enough *bons mots* in existence to provide any industrious con-versationalist with a new stock for every social conversation.' Huxley often drew maliciously from the life at that time, but it is unnecessary to disturb skeletons. Characters and conversation; anything, it would seem, to avoid a story. But then we have a little action in a taxi-cab when young Bidlake kisses Lucy. She is masterful and his passion has made him abject. The relationship is hardly likely to prosper. Her whim is to have supper among friends, so we meet Spandrell the artist, and Mark Rampion the writer and his wife.

We overhear their talk for a few pages, and then a new chapter begins and we have the love story of Mark and Mary Rampion. It is told tenderly, with the greatest sympathy, but it is never

sentimental and at the end it explodes into comic laughter. It is
the story of the poor boy and the rich girl falling in love and
overcoming all the barriers which existed then between rich and
poor. It is the story of young people marrying and meeting all
the troubles of learning to live together. It is is so much more
agreeable than the other sketch of D. H. Lawrence, the 'Kingham
story'. It is an accomplished portrait of a genius who was a
friend. Lucy and Walter arrive and the restaurant becomes a
pandemonium of the twenties, which, as Rampion has just said,
was 'the golden age of guzzling, sport and promiscuous love-
making'. We are by this time almost a third of the way through
the book and we continue to exist on animated scenes.

We follow Lucy and Walter, then Burlap, then Lord Edward
and are switched with increasing velocity between them. It is a
fair example of the jazz-prose of the twenties. There is no narrative, only people and their talk. The talk is clever, a reflection of
the popular intellectual interests of the decade, and it proceeds
with the speed of chatter at a cocktail party. When it is over, we
have met Rampion, and we know a little more about a few of the
characters, especially old Bidlake. We have had an impression of
London night life and we are brought full circle to the depressing
situation between Marjorie Carling and Walter Bidlake. We are
into the second third of the novel and we are still waiting for a
story; not impatiently, for the people and their talk are amusing
enough to keep our attention. The night ends with Lucy and
Spandrell together and there is an unstressed discussion of Illidge
in their talk which will echo later.

Next day the characters begin to look more black and white.
Burlap is more obviously a double thinker: 'She watched him
living his life of disguised and platonic and slimily spiritual
promiscuities.' The observer is a new character, his secretary,
Miss Cobbett. A novel exists on characters and story and if we
have no story we are likely to have more characters. We have
new places too, with a satirical sketch of the editorial offices of a
literary weekly in Fleet Street in the twenties. We sensed in the
last novel, when we went to the *Rabbit Fancier's Gazette*, that
Huxley did not find Fleet Street the most sympathetic of places.
Then at last, a fragment of narrative comes to a climax. Walter,
who begins the day with resolutions of being loyal to Marjorie and
never seeing Lucy again, ends it by making Lucy his mistress at last.

Immediately that is achieved we are taken off to Spandrell and learn more about him. Characters are creatures of time rather than space and Huxley provides one character after another with a past. The technique is as simple as possible. Without any explanation or machinery we slip back in the character's mind to former days. There is no strain, as there is for a moment when we turn the page to a new chapter and find a nanny and some children at their lessons. They are the children of old Bidlake's daughter, and we are at ease in our own world again when Mrs Bidlake comes to walk in the garden and admire the flowers. We have Miss Fulke and the children and only a row of dots between them and the ship in the Red Sea with Elinor and Philip Quarles aboard. Why fling us again and again into the far flung Empire away from these fascinating people in London?

A novel is a structure in time and it is natural to criticise it in time as well as place, as each scene modifies the last. In *Point Counter Point* we have no story when we are half way through, practically no pointing or countering, but still only characters and conversation. The characters sometimes become a short story as we meet them in depth and their conversation becomes a mirror of the times or of the author. By this time, we also know what will happen when two characters are juxtaposed, so the pointing and countering is beginning. When Burlap goes to see Rampion in his studio to buy some drawings cheaply we know how each will behave and how they will talk.

When we are more than half-way through the novel we still have no story and a whole chapter is given to creating an entirely new character. If we have any more characters, how can we have a story? How can so many be involved in a situation? How can we possibly have tension with our interest spread among so many? This is more like life than fiction; meeting or jostling, rather than pointing and countering. But at any rate this new character, Mr Quarles, father of Philip, becomes a short story; a grubby little story, a caricature of a pseudo-writer, a collector of card indices, dictaphones and special pens. The story is that he makes love inelegantly to his Cockney secretary who goes to bed with him at a price.

In the long chapter twenty-one we feel that we were not taken to Bombay in vain. Elinor and Philip Quarles had to be brought home to waken the plot. Things begin to look as if there is going to be movement. Up to now, nearly all the movement has been into the past. Short stories moving backward instead of a plot moving forward. Even now, when Philip lunches Spandrell at his club, we move backward to Spandrell's earlier years. Even now, the only perceptible movement is towards another love affair, between the bored Elinor and the ever-ready Webley.

The next brief chapter uses the quotation-from-notebooks technique which Huxley favoured so much, probably because he was so sufflaminated with ideas that he had occasionally to pour them out neat to get them all expressed. But there is more than that in these extracts, which echo Gide: 'There is an explanation of this almost storyless, plotless novel, this magnificent weight of character and period colouring doing so very little.' Quarles is developing the idea of the musicalisation of fiction, which we know was in Huxley's mind. 'The changes of moods, the abrupt transitions.' A little later: 'In sets of variations the process is carried a step further. Those incredible Diabelli variations, for example. The whole range of thought and feeling, yet all in organic relation to a ridiculous little waltz tune. Get this into a novel. How? The abrupt transitions are easy enough. All you need is a sufficiency of characters and parallel, contrapuntal plots.' Huxley makes characters with amusing characteristics and often with ideas, all of them described in prose as refreshing as white wine on a spring morning. And when he preaches he does not labour, like his friend D. H. Lawrence.

The ideas presented next are political. On the one hand the Fascist leader fighting the Communists in the streets, bullying his aide; on the other Rampion discussing industrial civilisation and what it does to human beings. 'It'll be a very long time before decent living and industrial smell can be reconciled. Perhaps, indeed, they are irreconcilable. It remains to be seen.'

Little episodes in the series of short stories follow glimpses, vignettes: the lecherous old Quarles and his pert mistress; young Quarles with his wife and son; a satirical page on modern medicine; old John Bidlake in abject fear of death, visited by Lady Edward. A last sentence link with the next chapter, in which Lucy is writing letters. Letters have been used to develop characters in the novel, ever since it was invented. Lucy is a selfish rich young woman creeping towards middle age, and these letters give her away. They are part of the mental putrefaction which lingers about the novel.

Troubled once again by an excessive rush of ideas, Huxley takes refuge in pouring them out in the notebook of Philip Quarles. The entries this time are concerned with the preoccupations of Huxley's thinking; people in society and the effort to be individual. 'People want to drown their realisation of the difficulties of living properly in this grotesque contemporary world, they want to forget their own deplorable inefficiency as artists in life. Some drown their sorrows in alcohol, but still more drown them in books and artistic dilettantism; some try to forget themselves in fornication, dancing, movies, listening-in, others in lectures and scientific hobbies.' Anything to fill the hours, anything to avoid tedium, anything to avoid ourselves and the emptiness of our being. Quarles rejects the Search for Truth; it is just an amusement, a distraction. Huxley will regain confidence there.

Another chapter in the lives of John and Janet Bidlake follows. It is as though Huxley were determined to offer examples of excellence in many kinds of prose; and what better sample of undulating narrative could we have than this chapter? The more ample rhythms are in agreeable contrast to the terse journal writing of the previous chapter. Sheer style is carrying us along.

We are moving now towards the melodramatic crime story and point and counter clash more quickly. In chapter twenty-nine we watch Everard Webley reviewing his troops, a splendid mockery of a Hyde Park Review, and for counter we watch Spandrell mocking Illidge. A glimpse of Elinor, and finally she and Webley drive down to the country and wander like lovers among the flowers, followed by the harsh, hurting counter of Spandrell taking an old prostitute to the country and driving her to tears by smashing the foxgloves. Scene and counter scene follow one another with quickening interest.

Point and counter begin to drag each other down towards pain and savagery and death. The exaggerations become macabre. In the twenties they liked to pretend things were worse than they were to make them endurable. Huxley begins to hurt his readers. From now on there is only one flicker of sanity, Rampion and all he says, and that only serves to increase the effect of horror by contrasting it with grace. Old Bidlake is the first victim of the mood. 'It was as though some part of him obscurely desired to accept defeat and misery, were anxious to make abjection yet more abject.' His counter, the little boy who was his grandson, falls ill.

Then Lucy Tantamount plumbs the degradations of lust and
almost destroys Edward by writing a scarifying description of her
concupiscence. Old Quarles can evade reality no more when his
mistress beards the cowardly old lecher in his den to tell him she
is going to have a baby, his baby. Mrs Quarles as usual does what
she can to efface the squalor and cover up the shame. But his
pretences have been battered down and old Quarles is broken.

Elinor decides to take Webley for her lover and that goes as
wrong as can be, for Spandrell turns up at her flat when she is
waiting for Webley. She is summoned by telegram to her sick
child and Spandrell is able to seize the chance to eliminate the
absurd Fascist leader. He involves Illidge and together they kill
him. The twisted little Communist and the perverted intellectual
have done a public service.

It is at this point that we get the final scene for Rampion. It
amounts to a statement of the humanist position, the engagement
of the whole man in the search for the completely satisfying life
in the completely satisfying society. 'The only truth that can be
of any interest to us, or that we can know, is a human truth. And
to discover that, you must look for it with the whole being.' The
counterparting of that is the illness of the child, Phil Quarles. He
dies of meningitis, a horrifying death, faithfully described. In this
Mystery Play of the twenties, death is reserved for the huge
athletic figure of Webley and for the child. In Huxley's philosophy,
old age was sufficient punishment in itself.

The last dramatic scene is Spandrell's, with the Rampions as
witnesses. He invites them to hear a recording of Beethoven's
A Minor Quartet. We enjoy the fine critical phrases but they cannot quite raise the scene above melodrama. Huxley's essay on the
'archaic Lydian harmonies' is managed with the greatest care,
fine writing with a vengeance followed by the countering so carefully arranged by Spandrell; his own execution by Webley's
followers. Two characters in particular counter one another and
stand out in this great concourse of the twenties, Spandrell and
Rampion. Spandrell is said to be modelled on Baudelaire, and if
we turn to Huxley's essay on Baudelaire, written about the same
time as the novel, we find phrases which describe Spandrell. 'Even
the sublimest of the Satanists are a little ridiculous. For they are
mad, all mad; and, however tragical and appalling their insanity
may be, madmen are always ridiculous.' There is similarity in his

absorbed affection for his mother and in his horrified reaction when she remarries. And he shares the hell of the satanist, who knows that compassionate regard is the only way to look at humankind but he can only satanically reject it.

Rampion was conceived at the richest time of Huxley's friendship for Lawrence, and we can go to the later 'Introduction' to Lawrence's letters for phrases which describe Rampion. He dwells on Lawrence's 'terrifying honesty' and his concern with 'the mystery of the world'. He says that Lawrence 'could never forget, as most of us almost continuously forget, the dark presence of the otherness which lies beyond the boundaries of man's conscious mind'. He could only create Rampion in his own image, and he was not yet ready to create a character concerned with 'the dark presence of otherness'. He was ready for 'terrifying honesty' and this is exploited in Rampion as counter to Spandrell's satanism. In the essay we are reminded of Lawrence's preoccupation with sex. In the novel we are spared that; it is full of sex, but Rampion has another function. He is sensitively creative in the sense that he is curiously aware of what is going on in other characters' minds. He knows that something is seriously wrong with Philip Quarles in that last meal in Soho and when Spandrell comes in Rampion quickly senses that there is something seriously wrong with him. He is sensitively compassionate in contrast with Spandrell's violence against the characters of his friends. As so often, when we look back on the performance, the evil character seems the greater achievement; but Rampion is among the most agreeable characters in Huxley's novels.

Gide's *The Counterfeiters* was published three years before *Point Counter Point*. There, the novelist in the story is asked about the subject of his novel: 'It hasn't got one... Let's say, if you prefer it, it hasn't got one subject... "a slice of life"... I should like to put everything into my novel.' Huxley did that as far as he could in *Point Counter Point*. He could give us one little London group, which lives within itself, and there is no attempt to include any other. That gives him as big a slice as he could attempt. The territory is big enough. It takes us from London to Bombay, from Pall Mall to country houses. But the true place of this novel is the country of the mind of artistic and literary people in London in the twenties. The idea, as Gide's character states it, is to get away from naturalistic fiction into the nature of man, away from the limiting time dimension of story-telling, and attempt depth. It is not new. Huxley found it in Dostoevsky's *The Possessed*. It is an answer to Forster's cry in his Clark lectures, just a year earlier: 'Yes—oh dear yes—the novel tells a story... and I wish it was not so.' The idea was in the air. The novel should be like life, and most lives do not provide stories. They are a set of characteristics which sometimes accrete into characters; which mix or clash; point and counter point; and then it is all over.

At the beginning Huxley prints Fulke Greville's stanza, 'Oh, wearisome condition of humanity'; and when he does so in *Texts and Pretexts*, it is just after a quotation from Walter Bagehot which helps us in understanding the idea behind this novel. Bagehot says that the necessary ignorance of man 'shows us that a latent Providence, a confused life, an odd material world, an existence broken short in the midst are not real difficulties, but real helps; that they, or something like them, are essential conditions of a moral life to a subordinate being'.

The Short Stories

HUXLEY took to the short story naturally and wrote it with gusto. He would set himself a theme—take the Dr Jekyll and Mr Hyde idea but make one of the personalities female; discover a painter who has been forgotten for forty years; draw a picture of D. H. Lawrence and make him in love with a middle-class English mother; cozen an oil millionaire with an enigmatically simple girl and see what can be made of the juxtaposition; have a young girl fall in love with a middle-aged novelist and embroider the situation with thought and emotion. Huxley accepts every challenge with zest. He gives himself plenty of room and enjoys himself to the full. In the Jekyll and Hyde story the male edits a serious review and the female is a successful popular writer. The forgotten painter offers splendid comic possibilities, for he can talk excitedly about his master, Benjamin Haydon, and quote Darwin as if *The Origin* had been published the other day. The merciless sketch of Lawrence can be set in a conversation piece of the twenties and the venomous sketch of the oil millionaire and his unlikely mistress can be put in a frame of which any storyteller could be proud. Develop the collision between the girl and the novelist against a Roman background and produce a little masterpiece.

All of them are the work of a young man and they all belong to the twenties. They supplement the early novels to give us a picture of that exotic decade, all jazz and high thinking. A hectic, macabre death dance, flushed with fever, an anxious prelude to the following decade of fear and shame; and, at the same time, obvious aftermath of the war. A decade in which Europe began to realise it had been destroying the social processes of many centuries, but was not yet aware that more action in that tragic sense was doomed to follow. For the young it was a decade like all the others; some had a good time, noisy, silly, feverish; others looked forward to making the world more sensible and bringing to flower in England a society which would be sane and compassionate.

With that thin silver trail of thought these stories have little to do. There would be plenty of it in Huxley's work but in other forms. The stories appeared in five volumes between 1920 and 1930, and they develop from a first collection in which there is little merit and not much amusement to a final volume which contains a minor masterpiece.

Limbo

The first volume, *Limbo*, opens with a prototype of the long-short form in which Huxley found room to develop any amusing idea or situation that occurred to him. The 'Farcical History of Richard Greenow' is the Jekyll and Hyde story in which Richard Greenow has an *alter ego*, Pearl Bellairs, who writes popular fiction. We are given examples, amusing parodies of the sentimental commercial work popular then. But there is all the time and space in the world, which is the impression any professional short story writer will give even if he has only two thousand words to do it in. So we begin with sketches of public school and undergraduate life. At school Greenow has a crush on a handsome young aristocrat. Then quite suddenly he realises that the handsome boy is an ox, and much later the reader sees that this crush was Pearl Bellairs'.

Thirty pages of agreeable padding before the hilarious-horrible theme begins. With a little experience he drops the padding and makes everything relevant to his tale. The split personality is an intellectual male of the twenties, interested in philosophy and mathematics and a gushing female personality who pours out best-selling fiction and patriotic journalism at ever-increasing speed. At first by night, while the male part is completely detached and unaware; but when he wakes in the morning and finds four

thousand words of a novel, he is very disturbed. A relapse to the
schoolboy crush brought on by a fatiguing evening among the
Fabians? But morning after morning he wakes to find pages more
of the novel; and in five weeks it is completed. He is hard up, so
he sends it to a literary agent. The crazy logic of the situation unfolds. A woman's magazine with a huge circulation snaps up the
novel. Jarred, the young man goes for a long solitary walk and
before he gets home faces the fact that he must be a herma-
phrodite. He refuses to let it worry him. If the woman in him
keeps herself to herself, she will support him so that he can
continue his philosophical and mathematical studies.

The gusto is sustained for another seventy-five pages before it
dissolves in dust and ashes. Dick goes down from college the
most brilliant man of his year, and we meet his sister, a rebel at
college and a manly English girl, very intelligent, very efficient,
and a particularly handsome young woman. She will represent the
normal reaction as her brother's dilemma develops. Meanwhile,
Dick has to decide what he is going to do, and as he is 'a real
Englishman' he compromises. He continues his studies and he
puts money and articles into a weekly which will preach the
reforms England so obviously and so urgently requires. The
amusing theme is unfolding very much in the spirit of Max
Beerbolm. Hitherto, Pearl has worked by night but now she takes
over five days. Dick sits down on 7 August at his desk to write
and he comes to in Regent Street and finds 12 August on his
evening paper. Worse, instead of his writing articles for his
weekly, Pearl has been writing jingo articles; there is one in his
evening paper with promise of more.

An inevitable quality is just as necessary in a comic story as in
a serious theme; crazy themes must have their logic as much as
any other, and anyone who follows stories on television will know
how difficult it seems to be to develop a story with probability
and consistency. In this story the reader feels that nothing could
have happened otherwise. Pearl seizes on him whenever he is
tired or below par and writes recruiting articles and patriotic
songs; and when he is fit again he writes another article against
conscription. Dick now has to decide whether he will become a
martyr and go to prison as a pacifist. We are given a desolating
description of a Tribunal for conscientious objectors. Fortunately
for the story, Dick eludes martyrdom and goes to work on the

land. Pearl is able to write articles about being a land-girl. She might have suffered extreme frustration in prison. The young aesthete is very uncomfortable with his workmates and the villagers. Huxley might have remembered that in later years, when he advocated the smallholding life. After three months on the land Dick sums it up: 'That bloody old fool Tolstoy!'

His sister Millicent and his editor, Hyman, do not neglect him. She tidies up his cottage and Hyman comes down to upbraid him. These two visitors have much in common and their creator has his revenge on them by marrying them to one another. That disposes of the main supporting characters and the story now approaches the macabre ending which is inevitable in any Jekyll and Hyde *dénouement*. Dick declines as Pearl becomes the dominant partner and takes over the management of their life. It is nimbly done. There is one more extravagance; Pearl wants the vote and Dick is impelled to ask for it. He wakens in a lunatic asylum, in acute mental and physical decline. The two personalities have worn out the body, comedy has turned sour, and the horror story ends with his death.

This opening long-short story indicates the talent which will go to the fine stories he will write before he leaves the form. He can find a good idea and he can develop it with fertile zest. He has strong views on various subjects and there is room for them to be touched on in these stories. But they cannot be sustained and developed; and that may be why he eventually abandoned the form. The simpler explanation is that the market for the short story disappeared. The rush of progress made printing too expensive; only cheap commercial material could find a market. But obviously Huxley was an intellectual rather than a storyteller; in a previous incarnation in an eastern bazaar he would not have been a storyteller but an ascetic, exhorting the people in parables. To avoid that, he left the short story altogether.

The next long-short is 'Happily Ever After', a manufactured product which lacks life. The story is a study of the thoughts of a young man who is sent to war and expects to be killed. It is not successful but it is a contribution, very minor, to the literature of our European distress.

'Eupompus Gave Splendour to Art by Numbers' is a phrase in

Ben Jonson's *Discoveries* which amused Huxley because no scholar
had been able to explain it, so he wove a fantasy round it. The
story is set in a frame which is another of those friendly sketches
of a scholar which it amused Huxley to draw. The story is a brief
anecdote about a fashionable portrait painter in ancient Alexandria
who suddenly shut himself away, refusing all commissions, and
giving all his energies to 'giving splendour to art by numbers'.
The only thing worth doing was counting 'because it was the one
thing you could be sure of getting right'. So he painted a picture
of 33,000 black swans, and a school of admirers who called themselves the Philarithmics sat counting the swans day by day. It is
a vigorous little fantasy, built round a baffling phrase, but the
prose still lacks life and magic. There is no resonance, no individuality. We notice this deficiency in the prose still more in the
three short commercials which end the book. The prose is like
an empty, unfurnished room, without personality.

Mortal Coils

Mortal Coils was published only two years later but it is worlds
away from *Limbo*. The apprentice has become a skilled craftsman
whose technique we enjoy, whose anecdotes are apt to his purpose,
whose prose is no longer an echo in an unfurnished room but a
lively vehicle with pace and power.

The first story in this collection, 'The Gioconda Smile', is
a good anecdote, well worth working on and Huxley fashions
every detail skilfully. The characters in it are of necessity; conceived and developed as they are necessary to the tale. Janet
Spence would have to be as she is to play her part and so would
Mr Hutton and his wife and the wretched little Doris. So the
mean little suburban anecdote which could be told in a couple
of hundred words is worked out over sixty pages, so that an
intensity of passion can be injected into it as well as a feeling
that every action leads inevitably to the next, right to the final
outcome.

The story is well known. Mr Hutton has a valetudinarian wife
and amuses himself with a vulgar little mistress, Doris, whom he
carefully and successfully conceals from his suburban friends.

Among them is Miss Spence, a spinster in the late thirties, with whom he is vaguely philandering. She is a passionate woman, able to conceal her feelings until she has poisoned the wife. She then offers herself quite pitifully to Hutton. He learns with embarrassment that many innocent remarks and actions have been interpreted by her as signs of desire in him as great as her desire for him. It is clear to her that only his fine sense of honour prevented him having an affaire with her. Hutton extricates himself and flies from this desperate female whom he cannot placate by marriage as he has already married Doris. He takes Doris off to Italy. He is bored with her by the time they get to Florence and when his sister tells him in a letter that Janet Spence is putting it about that he poisoned his wife he laughs at the idea that he should have murdered anyone to marry this stupid little girl. Almost immediately his weakness overcomes him again for he goes into the garden to enjoy a girl who is working there. He realises that he is in the net; he cannot escape from his nature. He has played into the hands of Janet Spence; the moves are inevitable and he is hanged.

That is the strength of the anecdote Huxley hit upon. It had inevitability; the classical feeling of fate and nemesis. Given the situation and the characters who made it, nothing else could happen. There is classical feeling in the way we are shown Hutton watching fate overtaking him; and in the glimpse at the very end of fate overtaking the woman who murdered him; and of the old doctor who rescues Doris and prescribes for Janet Spence. Not a great story; but a thoroughly efficient performance.

'Permutations among the Nightingales' may be looked on as a light-hearted parody of a Renaissance drama of passion and fortune hunting. The experienced fortune hunter gets 170,000 francs from a middle-aged Jewess and immediately turns his skilled attention to an American heiress with two hundred million dollars. Among the lovers, the most pathetic are the magnificent Lucrezia and the mean little Alberto, who are so interested in describing their unhappiness to one another that they end up in bed together; much to Lucrezia's disgust next morning. A light-hearted bit of froth with no unpleasant aftertaste.

'The Tillotson Banquet' is another amusing absurdity in which the storyteller exerts himself to exploit every aspect of fun in his idea. Suppose that a forgotten mid-Victorian painter is suddenly found to be alive. What can be made of that idea by the comic spirit? There will have to be something dramatic in it, something with colour in it. Huxley immediately invents a young art critic and a noble lord, patron of the arts, who wants early nineteenth-century frescoes by the painter. The young man must find him. He does so but finds the old man so feeble he cannot possibly paint. The noble lord loses interest but the young man is touched by the miserable condition of the old painter, almost blind and penniless in a slum basement. Something must be done. Nobody will give money, says the noble lord, unless they get something for it. So they decide to run a Banquet and invite people who detest one another so that they get some fun for their pains. Huxley is a generous storyteller; he offers these additional piquancies all the time. All the possibilities are enjoyed to the full in a vivacious account which proceeds at high speed without any faltering in the enjoyment of all the fun that can be extracted from the situation.

'Green Tunnels': first the story has to come and then the storyteller's mind plays upon it. Here is a story about youth and age, a theme which he will develop into a minor masterpiece in his last short story. Here, none of the characters are developed and no sympathy is aroused. They are three ageing people and a girl, living in what Karl Jaspers has called the European Museum. No interesting characters or sharp story interest; just a blurred image of a bored young girl, whose youth is being wasted. But it is the beginning of a talent Huxley developed; of portraying girls in their innocence, just as they were trembling on womanhood.

'Nuns at Luncheon'. The final story is all vivacity and it is made of a simple anecdote set in a frame which is more interesting than the anecdote. A young German nun is a nurse, famous for her conversions of the sick, for who could resist a nun who was so beautiful and so charming? One day she is no longer a nurse but a cleaner who has just been forced to attend her own burial service. She is observed by the English woman journalist who is a patient in the hospital and who later tells the tale, sitting at lunch in a London restaurant with the narrator. Miss Penny, the

journalist, is loud, brassy, out for any copy at any price. When
she sees the nurse disgraced she pursues the story as soon as she
is well enough, finding out the girl's family and gradually getting
the whole story. Everyone but Miss Penny is rather dim, the
narrator, the nun and the Italian thief who seduced her. The
picture is ordinary, but the frame is glittering.

The prose in *Mortal Coils* is lively and entertaining. There is
nothing of the gawkiness and general lack of tone so apparent in
Limbo. This is the prose of a storyteller, not yet distinguished but
adequate. The stories are about betrayal, of a man and an old
maid betrayed by their natures in 'The Gioconda Smile', of an
old man betrayed by time in 'The Tillotson Banquet', of a young
girl betrayed by older people in 'Green Tunnels' and of a nun
betrayed by her natural affections in 'Nuns at Luncheon'. There
is a mortal coil in a central character, some emotional disturbance
over which the character can have no control, 'the pangs of dis-
prized love' and 'the whips and scorns of time'. So the stories are
beginning to enjoy the piquancy we expect in Huxley, and there
is much entertainment to come. He is using his brains to make
amusing embroideries round anecdotes of a very simple character;
and his stories are told in the ambience of disillusion which
suffused the decade.

Little Mexican

The first story in the *Little Mexican* collection returns to the
theme of an old man falling in love with a young girl. It is always
happening; old men's minds are young. It is the theme of Huxley's
last, best short story. Here, it makes a very long story because the
first half is not a story at all, but a long prose diversion in the
style of Henry James. The prose proceeds with the speed of a
huge prehistoric lizard, moving with melodious friction into his
theme. It reads like a parody of the later James mannerism; the
involutions evolve out of one another until collapse seems inevitable and then, suddenly, they are brought safely to rest. There
is a long paragraph of involved embarrassment about the nature
of some local Flemish sweetmeat. What could be more exquisitely
palpitating and refined? After nearly seventy pages of this it begins
to look as if there might be a story coming. Huxley has in fact

been recalling the lost world before the war; the placid continuity
of life, for ever lost.

The story is about a man who was growing old when the war
broke out and what the war did to him. It is very definitely in
two parts; the pre-war world and the shattered world after the
war. The high Jamesian prose suitably gives the atmosphere of
the earlier world, and as soon as action comes, that prose disappears and a narrative prose takes its place which not only has
pace, but carries those nuances and reflections which made story-
telling worth while for Huxley.

In 'Little Mexican' he is back in rollicking comedy related with
smooth but ebullient sophistication. He will draw a mildly
Rabelaisian Italian count, old, worldly, cunning; who will devote
himself to arranging his life round his leisure and his lechery. To
get the best out of him he must have a butt, and a son and heir
will do, who will always serve his father's purposes, doing all the
work and earning all the money. To arrange that is easy; he
marries the lad to a worthy woman, religious and fertile, so that
very soon the young Count has hostages to fortune and however
much he may long to escape, he is tied to his family and to making
money for his father. The young man's situation is ludicrous and
the situation is developed hilariously. Huxley enjoys it so much
that he becomes openly the narrator.

'Hubert and Minnie' is a sad story of first love. The boy is
nineteen, the girl twenty-eight, and the result can be foreseen.
The story is told round a married woman, Helen Glamber, whose
spirit was very much of the twenties: 'I think one ought to rush
about and know thousands of people, and eat and drink enormously, and make love incessantly, and shout and laugh and
knock people over the head.' Minnie idolises her and takes her
advice about a love affair, for she is desperately in love with
young Hubert and would like to give herself to him. So it is
arranged; but alas, on the day before the assignation, he meets a
young girl with red hair and some association with the musical
comedy stage. The quality of his short commercials has improved very much.

'Fard' is brutal and short. Sophie is the ageing servant of a very selfish Parisienne who has quarrelled with her husband and is preparing to leave him. Sophie is desperately tired and looks it, which offends Madame: 'She hated having old, ugly people near her.' But she cannot think of getting rid of such an efficient maid. As the frantic packing goes on, Sophie becomes more and more a death's-head. Madame has an inspiration. She tells Sophie to use a little rouge. It transforms the old woman and Madame is happy and full of energy again.

'The Portrait' is a study of an art dealer, whose business Huxley says in *Those Barren Leaves* 'has the charm of being more dishonest than almost any other form of licensed brigandage in existence'. He goes on to summarise this tale almost exactly: 'You take advantage of the ignorance or abject poverty of the vendor to get the work for nothing. You then exploit the snobbery and the almost equally profound ignorance of the rich buyer to make him take the stuff off your hands at some fantastic price.'

'Young Archimedes'. It is a favourite plan when beginning a short story just to talk about something of great interest to yourself. As, for instance, the house you hired in Italy, where the landlady cheated you outrageously. If you have a gift for description, as well as a talent for conversation, many word pictures of the Tuscan scene can be developed as you go along. So that one way and another twenty pages have gone before the boy appears who makes the tale. Children in Huxley's stories are usually noisy nuisances, but here is a sensitive and sympathetic study of an infant prodigy.

There is a new dimension in this story, which opens with such fine water-colour sketches of the Tuscan landscape; man dominating nature to make civilisation possible. Set in that scene, we have the energies of the self-willed woman who wants the child and nothing can stop her getting him. She destroys him and a fine brain is lost which might have helped the race a little forward; and the elegy to that lost child is a description of Florence, where so many geniuses have made their contribution. The stories in this volume begin to follow the pattern of all Huxley's imaginative work; they begin to offer a commentary on life. This last story is touched with pity, as was the portrait of Uncle Spencer and, as in that portrait, there begin to be reverberations.

Two or Three Graces

'Two or Three Graces' is a very long story which is remarkable for its portrait of D. H. Lawrence. Three commercials make up the volume. 'Two or Three Graces' opens very slowly, and much more heavily than most of his stories. For thirty pages there is hardly a hint that we are going to have a vivid picture of the hectic cocktail party life of the twenties, brilliant sketches of the decade and a particularly fine sketch of one of its denunciatory prophets. Kingham, who is so like D. H. Lawrence, cries out in the opening scene, 'Everything that's easy and momentarily diverting and anaesthetic tempts—people, chatter, drink, fornication. Everything that's difficult and big, everything that needs thought and effort, repels.'

They are in Paris and next morning Kingham arrives in Wilkes's bedroom to make a scene. Wilkes is the narrator, not Huxley himself, but a music critic. Kingham loves a scene and towards the end of the story he will make a splendid one. Lawrence was always making these violent scenes and one extraordinary medical theory is that he kept himself alive on them. Rage released pituitrin, which stimulated his diseased body. Here, Kingham denigrates himself and then attacks Wilkes and the English middle classes: 'Your great defect is spiritual impotence. Your morality, your art —they're just impotence organised into systems. Your whole view of life—impotence again.' Very Lawrentian, and he then disappears for two years, when he comes back to make the story.

A bore interrupts them and we then have ten pages of another bore, Peddley, a solicitor. His wife, Grace, will make the tale. She will become a great success in fashionable artistic London, but to mark the contrast with her life as Peddley's wife, we have fifteen pages of a portrait of an essentially dull woman and her children, a picture of English domestic dullness. None of Huxley's stories begins so heavily and in forty-five pages the only lively writing is the opening sketch of Kingham.

The interest builds up when Wilkes almost unawares begins to bring Grace out. She loves to hear about the world of art and music she has never seen. Wilkes finds himself preparing her, grooming her to be ready to go into that world. As he is a music critic, he begins by taking her to concerts. She tries very hard but she will never understand music. The story still lacks action and Grace is so rustic, so countrified in her clothes, her make-up and her manner that we still wait for some character who will attract us to go on. It is a weakness of the tale that so much dullness must be accumulated to give contrast to the vivid scenes which will follow. But Huxley's virtuosity triumphs; the amused tolerance of the narrator carries us along.

At last, when almost a third of the long story is over, we meet Rodney Clegg, a fashionable painter. Clegg is the kind of social painter who gets along by creating bizarre fashions. He is also an accomplished philanderer and when Wilkes sees an affaire developing between Clegg and Grace, he sees with chagrin that unwittingly he has been playing the pander and has a pang of jealousy. Why had he never thought of making love to her himself? Clegg has been transforming Grace, who is suddenly smart and desirable. This is all good fun and the story begins to cheer up. We are taken to Clegg's parties and there is measured criticism of this phrenetic society; when a young man cries out that being modern is being promiscuous, Wilkes 'could not help wondering why he should call it modern. To me it rather seemed primeval—almost pre-human. Love, after all, is the new invention; promiscuous lust geologically old-fashioned.' Grace would not have listened to this. She was having an adventure, which nevertheless did not interfere with her family life. That remained correct, untouched.

Then Wilkes, perhaps stimulated by watching Grace, falls in love and marries Catherine. The faint echo of Thackeray which this sketch of the London 1920 Vanity Fair produces is intensified now, for Catherine Wilkes is like Laura Pendennis, a very levelheaded spectator of the phrenetic scene. Catherine and Grace become friends at once and that prepares us for the powerful half of the tale. Kingham returns. He still loves emotional scenes, still talks endlessly, still strips the pretences from social life.

Then he meets Grace, who has been having a bad time. Rodney Clegg is dropping her and she is more hurt than they had expected. She goes to greater pains to conceal it than they can watch comfortably. There is a mature compassion in their reactions to her distress which is a new maturity in the writer. Wilkes has tried to avoid a meeting between Grace and Kingham, but she happens to be there when Kingham comes back with him after a concert: 'All unconsciously, I was playing Pandarus for the second time.'

We have come to a sophisticated love story, very well told. Grace immediately sets her cap at Kingham. We are taken below the surface of this flippant attitude, to be reminded that Grace was fundamentally innocent. What in a sophisticated woman would have been naughtiness was in Grace a childish reaction to her pain. Of course it roused the puritan in Kingham. He accepted her at her face value, 'an aristocratically reckless hedonist in wanton search of amusement', to which he reacted half in contempt, half with amorous curiosity. He took Grace for a vampire. His moral indignation was increased because he thought of himself as her victim. He was always falling for vital young women and 'frank and unbridled vice had irresistible attractions for him'. Macabre humour has come into the tale and we echo back to a comment a little earlier that 'affection implies intimacy; and one cannot be intimate with another human being without discovering something to laugh at in his or her character'.

Huxley has now to develop a very painful love story and he makes every move clear with the clarity of fate. Grace began to tease Kingham amorously and he was very open to such an attack. Then she fell very seriously in love with him, which was fatal. Even a casual affaire with a man like Kingham would have been very different from her first trivial affaire, but when she fell in love, she was lost. Kingham gave himself to amorous experiences every so often and was accustomed to strong emotions. He enjoyed his orgy and when it was over he felt free to detach himself. After all, it was over. Grace conceived a love for him which was a longing for identity with him and, in one of these doomed brief sentences with which Huxley now occasionally ends his paragraphs: 'There was no such meeting here.'

It was some weeks before she gave herself to him. He assailed her like some Timon of Athens, talked of her 'devilish concupiscence', called her 'utterly ruthless and unscrupulous', all of which Grace loved, because it showed she was playing successfully the part she had chosen.

Then the eye of the narrator falls on Kingham: 'there are certain individuals who, by their proximity, raise a higher tide, and in a vastly greater number of souls, than the ordinary man or woman. Kingham was one of these exceptional beings... There was a glow, a vividness, a brilliance about the man.' Grace was playing with a greater fire than she knew. Kingham was a man who 'felt too easily and he was too fond of feeling'. He had persuaded himself in those few weeks that he had a violent passion for Grace and was suffering torments from her refusal. So he makes a highly-wrought scene in his rooms and when she will not submit when he demands it, he turns away and at last comes back to her, weeping. She gives in at once and realises that she loves him.

The reader is carried through the storms and stresses of the affaire stage by stage, at times hearing the creative laughter of the gods, at times in a turmoil of degradation. Kingham thrives on it. Grace becomes worn and abject. When Huxley judges very rightly that the reader has had enough of this tempestuous affaire, the narrator is packed off to Italy for a holiday, and the reader is taken away from the dark tempest to sunny descriptions and travel sketches. The return to the distressing theme is made through the husband, Peddley, who is at his holiday post at Modane, waiting for whom he may bore. Grace had left him and was living with Kingham.

At last the narrator is in Kingham's rooms again. No one is there, so he picks up a book and begins reading. It is Kingham's book of *abbreviated essays or expanded maxims*, and long quotations are given which is Huxley's neat way of deepening his study of his character. They are relevant to the affaire and explain its course and its inevitable end. The rest of the story is a study of Kingham's satiety, the break and the rescue of Grace from self-slaughter. It is easily managed. The narrator unwillingly overhears the final scene, which is as intensely dramatic as a scene in an Elizabethan play. Nowhere else in Huxley is there anything so heavy with disastrous emotion. The quarrel plays itself out and Kingham escapes. The narrator is able to come out of his concealment with some show of ordinary feeling and invite Grace to dinner when she is about to throw herself out of the window. The crisis dissolves in ordinary moments as they walk together in the London streets and at last arrive at his house. Catherine takes her over and Wilkes retires to his study to recover. What will happen to Grace? He plays his piano and finds the simple answer, *da capo*. She will go back to Peddley and the children, and then another affaire.

The remaining stories in the volume are commercials. In 'Half-Holiday' Peter Brett is a poor young man, lonely, he stammers

and he has wonderful day dreams about meeting beautiful and
attractive girls. One day his dream comes true. The anecdote is
competently dressed up over twenty odd pages.

'The Monocle' is another period sketch without even an anecdote to carry it along. Again there is a young man, Gregory, who
wears a monocle because he has an inferiority complex. With its
support he goes to a party. But he could not get used to his
monocle; it was not really his style. He was a midland grammar
school boy a generation before it was all the rage to be a midland
grammar school boy.

'Fairy Godmother' is a particularly horrid little tale. Mrs
Escobar is a very rich and selfish woman, who took in the orphaned
Ruth and Sue when her friend, their mother, died. Ruth married
a penniless young man but Sue did not escape, and they are on
their way to see Ruth, with presents for her little son. The afternoon is anything but a success. In the car on the way back, Mrs
Escobar talks about her gigolo who is coming to dinner and discovers that Sue is in love with him. Delighted that Sue is jealous
of her, Mrs Escobar's good humour is restored and Susan submits
to her affection. A very horrid, nasty little sketch.

Brief Candles

His last volume of short stories, 'Brief Candles', contains four very
good short stories, ending with his best and most original story
until twenty-five years later he published 'The Genius and the
Goddess'. The theme of 'Chawdron' is a relationship between an
old man and a young girl, and it is developed maliciously. 'You
can't write a good book without being malicious', we read at the
beginning of the story, in which the old man is a millionaire, like
some other Huxley non-heroes, and the girl is probably a fraud.
The story of their affaire has a frame which is old-fashioned and
reminds us of Conrad. The narrator and his friend Tilney are at
breakfast in his rooms. Tilney had ghosted the autobiography of
Chawdron, the millionaire, whose death is now reported in the
newspaper. Tilney gradually leads us into the Chawdron story.
There is a rich tradition in English storytelling of these carefully

worked-up frames. They make very interesting period reading. This is a good example, rather late, but unashamed and successful. When half the story is over, we leave the frame for the anecdote. We have had good literary talk, with Tilney's admission that Chawdron's autobiography was the best book he had ever written, and he could never prove it. Chawdron had destroyed the evidence.

It is not difficult to suppose that Tilney speaks for Huxley in this morning conversation. 'With ideas I'm at home. I've lived most of my life posthumously, if you see what I mean; in reflection and conversation after the fact.' Tilney has the malice which Huxley enjoyed in that decade, as in his description of Charlotte, the cellist who was 'a jolly little tarantula', who hooked Chawdron and went off to America to fulfil concert engagements and came back to find herself supplanted by Maggie Spindell. Everything about the story, name and all, is the Huxley who writes with gusto, his invention bubbling with his own enjoyment. In Tilney and the narrator he has created perfect vehicles for his own conversation. The story corruscates with good things and it is told in the intellectual way of the narrator offering comments on life and by that means unfolding the tale. We are told about the beginning of Chawdron's affaire with Maggie by means of a conversation on the nature of nemesis. Chawdron, like other Huxley millionaires, is all hog-wash, religiosity and sentimental mush. Maggie had an enormous capacity for auto-suggestion, she was undernourished for spiritual reasons, she was given to having headaches. She was not interested in money. 'What she wanted was his interest, was power over him, was self-assertion.' The headaches became a regular feature of her life. It bound Chawdron to her; it gave her the power her nature required. Later in life, Huxley was to spend volumes in analysing characters of this nature. It is intellectual comedy at its best, with the whole silly world of men's minds for subject. But it denigrates the race.

'The Rest Cure' does little to restore our pleasure in it. It is one of these stories about the English in Florence which our storytellers are compelled to write from time to time. Moira Tarwin suffers from nerves, which one glimpse of her husband explains, and she must live quietly in Florence. This is the pleasant penalty of being rich. She was brought up by her grandfather, a Harley Street specialist and was spoiled by him and his friends. She married to get away from these old men; that was five years ago now, and she is waiting for her 'cavaliere servente' to come to tea. Her husband is a research worker, cancer is his subject, and he is very seldom able to come out to Florence. So she is lonely and this young Italian has become useful.

The affaire pursues a normal course. He grows more and more tired of her and finds himself an attractive girl. He borrows money from her, and then one night she thinks he has stolen her purse. Her husband's words come back to her—he is a 'black-haired pimp from the slums of Naples'. It is unbearable. She shoots herself and the pay-off is the discovery of the purse by the servants jammed between bed and wall. A cheap little story, quite as nasty as Maugham's later 'Up in a Villa' on a similar theme. With the benefit of style, Huxley can get away with more than seems possible.

'The Claxtons' is written in the 'My love is a Theosophist and lives on Weeta Weeta' tradition and in a D. H. Lawrence manner; the affectionate accumulation of malicious detail. It is a family portrait, rather than a story but it is a portrait that develops in time and with delicate malice.

By contrast, the final story is sensitive and compassionate. The characters are sympathetic and it is time and the generations and not one another which makes things go awry. 'After the Fireworks' is one of the best stories Huxley wrote and he could hardly have made a more effective farewell to short story writing. It is another story of an older man and a fresh young girl falling in love, but this time they are both nice people; and it is the girl who falls so much in love first of all and he who resists, for he knows the outcome of such affaires. Miles is a well-known novelist and she has written him a fan letter. She is twenty-one and wants to know who and what she is and is sure that he is the only person who can tell her.

The story is original in the sense that the narrator is Huxley, with his own voice and thoughts. So many of the stories have been derivative, there have been so many echoes of other writers when they were good, and no resonance at all when they were pedestrian and commercial. But here is creation with his own mark upon it, intellectual, sensitive, interested, compassionate. Pamela keeps a diary in which she can endlessly analyse herself. We watch in action what we have been led to expect from the diary; that satisfactory trick in fiction which Huxley does not neglect. We observe her interest in fiction, in the characters in Miles' stories who experience life as she is doing, and we watch her speculating about getting past fiction to the reality which is Miles. We have quotations from his novels which are not very reassuring and at the end of Pamela's day we meet a character who will stay to the end, Guy Brown, a young man she met at dances and found pleasant.

She has an attractive and sensitive mind, this young woman, and we sympathise with her dilemma. She is ready to come to Miles and she is very aware that he is holding back, fending her off with sallies about old men and young girls, which she says is nonsense as you are only as old as you feel. The relationship is becoming domesticated and she is able to sit and do his mending for him while he goes on with his writing. When he is moody or wants to go home and write after lunch, she can always ring up Guy and go out for the evening. Then they have a quarrel and there is nothing like a quarrel to help a love affair. They make it up and are closer than ever before. In the next diary entry she gets tickets for the fireworks and that is where things will come to a point.

Three months later it is all over. They are up at Monte Cattini, so that Miles can take the waters. He has got jaundice after a chill caught when they were making love one night on the hillside. As he foresaw, amorousness has broken him, but Pamela has become even more beautiful, and childish uncertainty has given place to decision and repose. Though now, in this dolorous place, full of sick people as lavishly stressed as in a Rowlandson print, she wears a shut and sullen face. There is a backward glance at the excesses which have caused his illness. Miles, who has restrained himself for so long, gives way to a craving and uses his power over her against her will and to his own undoing. She realises by this time that Miles is right, she has never been in love with him. He has always been honest with her. She will leave him as soon as he is fit. That will only be a day or two and the ending is that she writes to Guy, asking if he is back again in Rome.

It is not so much a love story as an elegy for all love stories.

From the beginning the elegaic note is there, the sadness of the distance between the generations, the sadness of the middle-aged lover. The sadness that age can never teach youth; that there can be no progress because we must all begin at the beginning again. The sadness of the girl's disillusion. But at the end, an assured young woman arranging her next love affair. There is the familiar intellectual play and the extravagance of learning; but it is subservient now to real experience. Life is not, as in the first collection, very much something read about but something that has been lived with due measure of pleasure and pain. There is the malice that enlivens the narrative but best of all there is the prose technique that will reflect all these moods and adjust its pace to their needs.

There is a passing reference in this last story to a moment in Homer when Odysseus and his companions watch six of their number being devoured. That evening they prepared their meal expertly and only after enjoying it wept for their companions. The same incident is retold at the opening of the collection of essays called *Music at Night*. It is this very personal form that Huxley will use from now on for his shorter pieces.

His skill in short story writing is clearly comic. When he attempts the other kind he does not go beyond tenderness and the tenderness is about men in middle age. Passion is sometimes present but is not fully shown. The narrator in these tales instinctively avoids that. He is such a skilled talker that he can make a gawky anecdote amusing, and the bare bones that may seem so angular in these summaries are always clothed attractively. Short stories are usually balances between anecdote and character and their mood can come from either. Huxley can do either but his gift is for character sketching. He revels in it, whether he is feeling malicious or tender. The mere anecdotes are told rather metallically, the characters usually come alive and give their liveliness to the story. Huxley is not a natural storyteller. He is interested in people and in ideas, intellectual ideas about the nature of humanity and of life. He is serious. We usually find him pessimistic; but not in the stories. The moods range from exuberant fun to tenderness, but looking back on them all, we have enjoyed them for the gaiety and the brilliant talk. As seriousness became dominant, the form was no longer useful for the things he was impelled to say.

The Novels 2

Brave New World

'O brave new world
That has such people in't.'
SHAKESPEARE   *The Tempest*

BRAVE NEW WORLD is in great contrast with his earlier novels, which rely on characters, mood and atmosphere, qualities which are achieved by subtle and sensitive writing. *Brave New World*, a nightmare scientific future for Britain, requires the plain, quiet prose of scientific exposition. All the more because in this techni-coloured technological future our values are turned upside down and the narrator must make it easy for us to suspend disbelief. Affection and loyalty are unnecessary, beauty is a synthetic pro-duct, truth is arranged in a test tube, hope is supplied in a pill, which by its action annihilates identity. Huxley supposed his nightmare to be thousands of years away but later on, he wondered whether parts of it were not alarmingly near. He returned to his Utopia twice, in a Foreword in 1946 and in *Brave New World Revisited* in 1958. The skills involved in conditioning humanity continued to interest him; for his Utopia is a reaction to the growth of Mass Man, and the masses have grown more menacing year by year.

In an essay on 'Revolutions' he noted two phases: 'The indus-trials of last century were living at the time of the population's most rapid increase. There was an endless supply of slaves. They could afford to be extravagant... Wage-slaves were worked to

death at high speed; but there were always new ones coming in
to take their places, fairly begging the capitalists to work *them* to
death too.' While already in the twenties, Huxley says: 'In the
most fully industrialised countries the Proletariat is no longer
abject; it is prosperous, its way of life approximates to that of
the bourgeoisie. No longer the victims, it is actually, in some
places, coming to be the victimiser.' Just what Ortega was saying
then in Spain and Jaspers was saying in Germany.

As so often in the Huxley oeuvre, a subject much on his mind
appears in his fiction as well as in his essays. The rise of Mass
Man impelled him to science fiction and the result is still his most
popular novel. He uses a formula which Orwell adopted in *1984*,
horror supported by a strong sex theme. Huxley took his horrors
gaily; Orwell took them savagely. Both books are dismal develop-
ments of one of the Utopian traditions in English writing. The
other tradition is the optimistic idealism in More's *Utopia* (1516),
right through to Morris's *News from Nowhere* (1890), and Wells's
Modern Utopia (1905). The satirical tradition develops from
Swift's *Gulliver's Travels* (1726) to Butler's *Erewhon* (1872), and
the same vigorous, satirical inventiveness is seen in *Brave New
World* and *1984*. Each strain is critical and corrective.

In More, the best kind of human being, his Syphogrants,
Wells's *Samurai*, would lead the rest towards more agreeable
ways of living and there would be a steady evolution towards
heaven on earth. More's *Utopia*, like all classics, is contemporary.
We can still profit by listening to him. He is against the waste of
working hours in manufacturing unnecessary rubbish; he is all
for a kind of Christian communism to abate our island acquisitiveness; he notes that men are much better ruled by men of other
nations. These sixteenth-century suggestions would much improve
our prospects. Morris is romantic, less practical, which is odd in a
man who used his hands more than More ever did. *News from
Nowhere* takes us back to a dream Thames valley agricultural
heaven in which everyone is happily at work, doing what he likes
and therefore never idle, always diligent. From More to Morris
our Utopians are against our English idleness. The atmosphere of
Morris is the endearing atmosphere of the youth of the world,
when everyone was so sophisticated that society was gay and easy.
We are reminded that all our classical Utopias are agricultural
heavens in which there is no population problem but plenty of

room for everyone. Everyone is well clothed and well fed. Most important of all, it is taken for granted that everyone is sane. The mental diseases which are universal among the human species and which have always prevented our English communities from becoming a society, have all disappeared.

It is our modern preoccupation with social and political insanity which colours our modern Utopias, and makes *Brave New World* and *1984* so different even from the satirical Utopias which went before. It is ironic that when at last all men could be properly housed, clothed and fed, we are teetering on the edge of an almost universal destruction and conduct our affairs with apparently irremediable lunacy. It may be that our knowledge explosion with its shattering technical progress, has knocked us off balance and when we recover we shall succeed in imposing control. It may be that the natural balance in human affairs requires that great advances imply equally great dangers. When Huxley and Orwell wrote their Utopias, western man was struggling in the deepest trough of his despair. It seemed that the mental and spiritual life of mankind was so distorted that it could never recover. It was difficult in those decades to see any hope for the human race and their visions give typical pictures of our despair.

In *Brave New World* Huxley is facing particularly the fear of overpopulation, which since then has become a nightmare. In 'The Double Crisis', as essay published in *Themes and Variations* (1950) he says: 'The human race is passing through a time of crisis, and that crisis exists, so to speak, on two levels—an upper level of political and economic crisis and a lower level of demographic and ecological crisis.' He goes on to argue that the one affects the other and offers sensible solutions. It is a very living problem and has been so for a long time. Even in the twenties, the press of people on the earth was noticeable and it was apparent that they were forming a mass. What passes for education had made them so and as early as 1915 Wilfrid Trotter had demonstrated the necessity for new techniques of mass management in his *Conduct of the Herd in Peace and War*. The most eloquent analysis of the situation was offered by Ortega y Gasset in his *Revolt of the Masses* (1930). 'Europe', he says in his opening sentences, 'is suffering from the greatest crisis that can afflict peoples, nations and civilisation.' He was not thinking of the coming war in Spain or the still more dreadful conflict which was to unsettle the world. He was thinking of population. 'Towns are full of people, houses full of tenants, hotels full of guests, trains full of travellers, cafés full of customers, parks full of promenaders, consulting-rooms of famous doctors full of patients, theatres full of spectators, and beaches full of bathers. What previously was, in general, no problem, now begins to be an every day one, namely, to find room.'

Huxley and Orwell face the problem of ruling these masses. They look at what we have made of our English democracy and substitute for that insanity a satirical insanity much more odious. Orwell produced a sick man's nightmare of sadism based on his observations of European totalitarianisms. Huxley wrote out of his scientific background and mass-produced his population in the fashion long popular in science fiction, growing them in bottles and conditioning them from birth in all the ways proposed by psychologists. Both heredity and environment were absolutely determined. These bottle products were released from moral tensions because they were so conditioned that none of their actions had moral consequences. They could always escape from reality very easily by the use of the standard drug, soma, which was a great improvement on alcohol or anything else known because it produced no unpleasant reactions and was benignly addictive. The people were always in a state of euphoria because the human spirit had been prisoned and confined in a perfectly conditioned healthy cadaver. 'And that', put in the Director sententiously, 'that is the secret of happiness and virtue—liking what you've got to do. All conditioning aims at that: making people like their inescapable social destiny.'

The old trouble in human societies, that some are more equal than others, has been resolved. The population problem has been resolved. People are manufactured as they are needed, a few Alpha Plus specimens, hundreds of Epsilons. It is fascinating, because, as in all these satires, it is a twist of known data, with the creative spirit working at white heat pursuing every absurdity the original twist suggests. The normal is the extravagant and outrageous and once the reader has been conditioned to accept this inverted normalcy, opposition is introduced to make the tale. Accidents happen when the bottles are in production and that gives us two high intelligence characters who are misfits. A little alcohol accidently splashed into the bottle, perhaps. The story wants something more, so the Savage is introduced. He was born viviparously, out of a careless Beta Minus who had gone with an Alpha Plus male on a trip to the native reservation, one of the settlements of old type human beings still in existence. A pregnant Beta Minus could not possibly be brought back to England, so she stays to give birth to a son and supports him by prostitution. He is a young man when we meet him, with a strong individuality stimulated by reading Shakespeare; just the opposition the story requires, a romantic idealist in a controlled society.

The purpose of the book is to give us a full picture of a society scientifically manufactured and controlled and the story is a means to that end. If any reader flags, he will be sexually titillated. Orwell used the same device. Huxley is creating a country according to the prophet Ford, who developed mass production. 'Standard men and women in uniform batches.' Electric shocks when babies crawl towards pretty flowers or pretty pictures: 'saved from books and botany all their lives.' Erotic play in children encouraged; they will be young for all the sixty years of their lives and enormously potent, and in this will lie their natural happiness. The women will never conceive and everyone can and should be completely promiscuous. It would be unnatural and unsocial to go steady. There are no families and there is no mother love. What we call friendship develops only between the misfits. Average citizens lived under the influence of soma all their lives and therefore without individuality or integrity. In 1932 Huxley thought this was a remote nightmare but already in 1946 he confessed that his brave new world was coming quicker than he had expected.

The core of the book is the argument on happiness between the Controller and the Savage. They argue like a couple of Oxford dons on the name and nature of happiness in society. The Savage reveals a power in dialectic for which his past life, one would have thought, had hardly prepared him. Huxley is right. It would have been better if the Savage had had another background, something worth preferring. As it is, he has to choose between the squalor of the Reservation and the spiritless shallow happiness of the world according to Ford. He tried to find another alternative. He sought solitude and silence in a disused lighthouse on the south coast. Despite his continued study of Shakespeare he could not get away from thoughts of Lenina. Huxley later confessed in *Texts and Pretexts* a small slip there: 'I wanted this

c

person to be a platonic lover; but, reading through the plays, I realized to my dismay that platonic love is not a subject with which Shakespeare ever deals.' The Savage flagellates himself to subdue the flesh. He is observed. All the resources of mass communication go into operation and very soon hordes of the public descend upon him. Among them is Lenina, the fair temptress. The Savage makes the escape of the creature that is hurt too much; he kills himself.

It is the parable of the individual in the mass community. We live in the age of the mass. The politicians, the salesmen, the entertainers, all who batten on the mass exacerbate the instincts which sway human beings as a mass. The decent individual is carried along, still protesting but more than ever lost. In our timid totalitarianism the individual is bruised and frustrated by forces as impersonal as nature herself. In *Brave New World* and *1984* the implacable scrutiny of the state is directed on them all the time. The 'proles' are easily controlled; it is the individualistic party member who can cause trouble, the misfit Bernard and the pitiful Winston. With individuals so marked, dynamic progress becomes impossible and both these books present us with the static state. As such states have always crashed, Huxley and Orwell are at pains to explain how the rulers secured stability.

Stability in a community is based upon organic progress and in his 1946 Foreword Huxley would offer the Savage as a reasonable alternative to a totalitarian state according to the enlightened visions of nineteenth-century Europe. Anything else surrounds us with muddle. He concludes his suggested revision with something from a different world of thought; he introduces the idea of the 'intelligent pursuit of man's Final End, the unitive knowledge of the immanent Tao or Logos'. (We recall that *The Perennial Philosophy* was published in the same year.) This completely changes the totalitarian version of the Greatest Happiness principle back towards something as old as the Hindu caste system, which catered for the evolution of the individual until he was fit to become part of the Whole. A complete contrast to the grubby materialist totalitarianism towards which our masses are dragging us.

Twelve years later, in 1958, Huxley returned to his Utopian theme in *Brave New World Revisited*, not to enlarge upon the civilised alternative he suggested in 1946, but to express his alarm at the speed at which his prophecies in *Brave New World* were being fulfilled. He had thought that: 'The completely organized society, the scientific caste system, the abolition of free will by methodical conditioning, the servitude made acceptable by regular doses of chemically-induced happiness, the orthodoxies drummed in by nightly courses of sleep-teaching—these things were coming all right, but not in my time, not even in the time of my grand-children.' Our gruesome planet was radically different from the gruesome brave new world. 'Ours was a nightmare of too little order; theirs, in the seventh century A.F. of too much.' But now, in 1958: 'I feel a great deal less optimistic than I did when I was writing *Brave New World*.' He sees that: 'The nightmare of total organization has emerged from the safe, remote future and is now awaiting us, just around the next corner.' It follows inexorably from having so many people.

He agrees that 'for a long time to come we shall remain a viviparous species breeding at random' and it follows that control must be post-natal; but his book is about the very adequate control now available to rulers and tycoons. It has been found that the best way with men, as with animals, is to dangle rewards in front of them and to give enough to ensure that they go on reacting to the reward system. Men are proving easily corruptible and the very concept of freedom is fading. Free men are being drowned in the Mass, which has been produced by the machines and the chemists. This, says Huxley in 1958, is the urgent pro-blem of our age and all our thoughts about conquering space are irrelevant.

It has been noticed before that a study of Huxley's work is a study of the mood of intelligent Western Man over four remarkable decades. In these decades Western Man was nearly destroyed and almost completely overpowered by his own cleverness. The pre-vailing moods were anxiety and pessimism, moods which Huxley shared. There was a balancing mood of stoical optimism which he could not enjoy. The European philosophers and writers who shared this view, saw the great possibilities for good in the know-ledge explosion. They worked hard in the late forties, when the war was over, to pull things together again and the basis of their efforts had to be hope in the future. Their hopes have been ful-filled. The optimists are just as right as the pessimists. Western Man is now economically better off than any society has ever

been; and he is just as spiritually benighted. The knowledge
explosion presents him with unbelievable possibilities of advance;
and may lead him to self-destruction. But in the sixties, we
clambered out of immediate misery and anxiety and we began to
get our human affairs under control again. It is really no good
saying we are heading for universal destruction and social chaos.
Or that we are all going to starve. We have come back to the
feeling that humanity will go on existing as before in precarious
balance; and we know that if we put our minds to it we have the
means of feeding all the people in the world, and bringing all
men everywhere within reach of the material standards of Western
Man.

In the concluding chapter of *Brave New World Revisited* Huxley
asks what can be done, and his answers are all things which need
doing, if we are to achieve sane societies. He would pass laws to
prevent the imprisonment of men's minds. We protect ourselves
by law against adulterated food and dangerous drugs, he says, so
why not protect ourselves against 'the unscrupulous purveyors of
poisonous propaganda' and he names public officials, civil and
military, as well as politicians. Less directly, he mentions his old
enemies, the advertisers. He has little faith in his remedy: 'liberal
forces will merely serve to mask and adorn a profoundly illiberal
substance' and a little later: 'The underlying substance will be a
new kind of non-violent totalitarianism.' It is so easy to agree that
this is very much what we have arrived at; that we are, already,
what he foresees: 'The ruling oligarchy and its highly-trained
élite of soldiers, policemen, thought-manufacturers and mind-
manipulators will quietly run the show as they think fit.'

Huxley is hardly inspiring in this last word on the shape of
things to come. He goes through the problems in a hurried way
again, echoing sometimes the manner of H. G. Wells, who
preached his sermon so often he sometimes hurried his delivery.
Overpopulation comes first and today we are able to say, as he
was not, that the pill looks like working. We can also say that it
looks as if we shall one day be able to control sexing and then we
shall only have to persuade mothers to want boys and we shall
soon reduce our breeding stock and bring the population within
reasonable limits. He speaks of educating farmers, but the people
who want educating are those who prevent the farmers growing
all they could. The world could feed itself if it put its mind to it

in the way it puts its mind to wars and space enterprises. The seas could be farmed and many deserts reclaimed. When he comes to consider the vote and the over-organisation of our affairs, he falls back on general decentralisation and the old, old remedy, encourage the smallholder. Decentralisation would help: it would restore the possibility of prompt and sensible action; but it is no good encouraging the smallholder. He is too overworked to think, too tied to the earth, too exhausted after battling with the luxuriance and ferocity of nature to be free. We had much better depend on the machines to give us freedom. They work selflessly for others, and they now work so well that all men could be free, simply by following the morality of the machines. We need not be tied to them any longer; we have simply to abate our acquisitiveness and the machines will set us all free.

He denounces the 'modern metropolis, in which a fully human life of multiple personal relationships has become almost impossible' and exhorts us to 'leave the metropolis and revive the small country community'. Here he touches truth. Men do not have to be smallholders to live in the country and in the country we can enjoy the good life intelligently, enjoying our books and our music; yet always in touch with the earth which keeps us sane. Which is not an apology for commuting; that way madness lies. Our island has many areas more and more deserted, as the acquisitives clamber over one another round London, and these areas have or could easily have the services on which our reasonable comforts depend.

If our population gets out of hand, it could be exported. It is insane to let our doctors and scientists struggle to preserve the mass, when it could be exported to countries large enough for them to live on the earth and become sane individuals. If we accept Huxley's view that human society should be based on the 'conscious and intelligent pursuit of man's Final End', we shall accept that this is more easily done where silence and solitude are possible. Salvation, in the nature of things, is for the individual and the individual will go on trying to save himself. He will have a better chance if he is touched by good air and the earth. So we must be disappointed by the tepid stoicism of the closing words of *Brave New World Revisited*: 'Perhaps the forces that now menace freedom are too strong to be resisted for very long. It is still our duty to do whatever we can to resist them.'

It seems to be a weakness of English intellectual life to suppose that the best days are over. In the days of our knowledge explosion and our economic revolution it seems so evident that much more wonderful days will come, if we are sensible. This view is put eloquently by Erich Fromm in his *The Sane Society*, in which he quotes the whole of Huxley's 1946 Foreword along with passages from Schweitzer and Einstein. The Summary-Conclusion which ends the book echoes the ideas which Huxley puts forward. Fromm discusses the great blights which have taken away the individuality of man, the machines, the great cities, bureaucracy and so: 'Not having a sense of self except the one which conformity with the majority can give, he is insecure, anxious, depending on approval.' There are two kinds of men, he says; on the one hand those who have the capacity to love, individuality, integrity; and the majority whose mentality is Stone Age and who sway about in a mass of totemism and idol worship. When he turns to the two great political systems, communism and capitalism, he shows that they produce the same kind of men, and his summary would do for a description of Huxley's brave new world: 'Life has no meaning, there is no joy, no faith, no reality. Everybody is "happy"—except that he does not feel, does not reason, does not love.' Our danger, in a word, is robotism. Our hope, according to Fromm, lies in what he calls 'humanistic communitarianism'. Man must be restored to his supreme place in society and it is only man who prevents it. It is man who prevents in man the development of reason, goodwill and sanity. Man must become fully human, loving, understanding, capable of sympathy, creative, fulfilling himself.

All this (and *The Sane Society* was published in 1954) is true and good but it is hardly enough. It was difficult in that decade to hope sufficiently. Yet we find it among some European philosophers who lived through the anguish of the thirties and forties, and particularly among the French. Paul Valéry, in the early thirties, was seeing the knowledge explosion as a new wonder in a world that would become wonderfully new. The French intellectual has seen very clearly the chaos the knowledge explosion has caused, but he has retained his intellectual stability unimpaired.

It is this need for steadiness which has produced our contemporary Existentialists, our modern Stoics. So when we turn to

Gabriel Marcel, who faced the problem of the masses twenty years after Ortega, and look at the conclusions of his *Man Against Mass Society*, we find the better atmosphere of hope. He echoes Huxley and Fromm in assessing our present condition. He attributes our low spiritual level today to the growth in population which has produced the masses. This means that man must be defended against mass, not merely physically but mentally and spiritually. The greatest crime of western man in this century has been the mass crime, the destruction of man's own image. Marcel's first ethical commandment therefore is: 'I must not sin against the light.' The methods of Ford, developed in *Brave New World*, are all sins against the light. Marcel goes on to say that it is our duty to allow the light to have a passage through us. In the creatures of the *Brave New World* the light is blocked.

How does Marcel offer hope? The mind must seek its support from the highest expressions of human genius; and many of us turn to the quotations in Huxley's *Perennial Philosophy*. These have universal value and when we enjoy them the light shines through us. In this way the aristocracy of mind survives in the world, resisting the levelling down of the masses, resisting the impersonality of the machines and bureaucratic processes. Marcel maintains with religious intensity that there is a universal purpose in the world and it is love and truth, the virtues abandoned by the Controllers in *Brave New World*.

The individual, in his daily routine, must discover how he can best contribute to the universal purpose, so that he can bear witness for it against the lie, which is the mass. This serenity of purpose, which comes of simplicity achieved through much striving with complexities, was not easy for Huxley, though it would have been a just reward for all his striving. It is the surest defence against pessimism. It helps us to accept the miracle which is at the heart of the human story; that a few individuals go on appearing in every generation, however bad the times, and through them the light shines and they carry things forward.

Eyeless in Gaza

'Promise was that I
Should Israel from Philistian yoke deliver;
Ask for this great Deliverer now, and find him
Eyeless in Gaza at the mill with slaves,
Himself in bonds under Philistian yoke.'
       MILTON   *Samson Agonistes*

EYELESS IN GAZA is the most difficult of Huxley's novels to read and the most worth reading. It does not proceed straight through time, but begins in 1933, jumps to 1934, back to 1933 and then drops through time to 1902. It then hurries forward to 1926, but returns to 1902 and proceeds through fifty-four chapters to move about in time as fluently as Huxley's novels have always moved through space. There is a series of chapters beginning in 1912 and remaining in 1914. There are two in 1931. For the most part, the stories are in 1914, 1926–7, and 1933. The last series moves into 1934 and the final chapter, about the principal characters, Anthony Beavis and Helen Amberley, is in 1935. Every series is about Anthony, at his prep. school, at college, as a sociologist and finally as a middle-aged man who has come to terms with himself and knows how he must react to the totalitarian movements in Europe.

We have to get into his mind to watch this and Huxley uses his simple and favourite technique for admitting us. Anthony keeps a diary. It is as good as Huxley's own would be, fluent, relaxed, intimate, absolutely honest and therefore revealing and sympathetic. Huxley liked it so much that when he was making a selection of his writings for the Everyman Library, the only extract from his novels was forty pages of this diary. It is so much the centre of all the movement in the novel that we can describe

Eyeless in Gaza as the account of a human mind at every stage of development until it reached maturity; the story of a very high Intelligence Quotient for just over forty years. Running parallel to it all the time is the story of a beautiful and sensitive woman, from the childhood which Huxley always described with such sharp sensitivity to maturity achieved after much distress. Anthony and Helen are the most full and sympathetic portraits in the great gallery of Huxley's fiction. Once the reader has accommodated to being moved through time and space with the speed of thought, he discovers that meeting them in the hectic middle of their lives and then going back to their childhood, before following them towards tranquillity or the possibility of peace of mind, is a very sympathetic way of getting to know them.

Anthony was a little older than Huxley, went to the same school and university, had similar interests and faced the same social and political problems. The fascist-communist clash becomes a main theme. The problem of intelligent man in a mass society, which was the satirical theme of *Brave New World* is faced earnestly here. The spiritual problems which will appear so often in the later books are treated imaginatively here. As always in Huxley, there is a wide spectrum of human behaviour, and in Anthony we see Huxley's own struggle between the sensualist and the ascetic.

When Anthony discovered ascetic longings in himself, he found a Scots doctor who became his guru, a favourite figure in fiction at that time when political and social events were making spiritual stability difficult. Dr Miller was an exponent of active pacifism, he preached it and lived it steadily. He was a completely honest and integrated character without any touch of the crankiness we are apt to suspect in Huxley's own eager approach to these subjects.

There is another character of this kind, Mark Staithes, a friend of Anthony's from prep. school days. He is rich and adventurous, apparently a thoroughly competent businessman; but gradually we see him as a compassionate man who supports weak and helpless people who come his way. A model for businessmen. It is Mark who takes Anthony to America in the 1933 sequence, to help a friend mount a counter-revolution. It is a holiday abroad for the reader, like the holiday in India in *Point Counter Point*. Both derive from Huxley's own travels. Both introduce necessary characters, who could have been found without this long-

C*

distance travelling. In this instance, Anthony meets Dr Miller.
Brian Foxe is a more fully developed study. He is a tragic
example of youthful inadequacy. He was nearer than Mark to
Anthony at prep. school; gentle, stammering, highly strung, he
had a crushingly possessive mother. Mrs Foxe does good works
with slum children and is unwittingly cruel to her own son. When
Brian falls in love with the vicar's daughter, he is inhibited by his
mother's pretended encouragement, and by his upbringing, which
makes him react with guilt and shame to his budding sexual
desires. The girl is equally innocent, as Anthony discovers when
he kisses her for a bet. She needs to be kissed and interprets
Anthony's frolic as a serious bond between them. She must break
with Brian, and Brian kills himself, feeling that he has been
betrayed both by the girl and his friend. It is a shocking little
parable of innocence. It haunted Anthony, for he was much too
callow to be able to put things right; and as it haunted him
through all his days, the story is told at intervals until the dramatic
suicide comes only in chapter fifty-two, just before the peace of
mind which comes to Anthony when he resolves upon a fitting
atonement in the final chapter.

So many of the subsidiary characters and sequences in this
novel read like parables. The sequence about the twenties, for
example, displays the less amiable characteristics of that hectic
decade. It is the sequence in which Anthony is instructed in love-
making by the experienced Mary Amberley. In which her daughter
Helen defiantly tries a little shoplifting and is psychologically disturbed as a result for some time. In which Helen is seduced by
one of her mother's lovers, Gerry Watchett, who makes love to
Mary Amberley so that eventually he can persuade her to buy
dud shares. In which Helen makes love to Hugh Ledwidge, a
shy, impotent young scholar, whom we first meet being ragged
at prep. school. He so much wants to remain safely a bachelor
but he marries Helen to get her away from the squalid household
of her mother. That comes in chapter forty-five, so that evolution
of Helen's earlier life proceeds along with Anthony's.

The next series is in 1933 and by this time Anthony and Helen
are together. The book opens with them together, sunbathing
naked on an Italian roof. It is his forty-second birthday. The
rooftop scene proceeds for four chapters, intertwined with other
sequences, until horridly a dog is dropped from an aeroplane on

the roof beside them. They are splashed in its blood and once again Helen has a strong psychological reaction and leaves Anthony at once, leaves the resort, and goes to her mother's squalid flat in Paris. She tells him later that she vowed then that she would never live with him again. In reaction, she does an unforgivable thing. She makes Mark open and read to her a letter from Anthony. It is a love letter. Their brief affaire and its dénouement had shaken him into realising his love. Mark tells Anthony and the 1933 sequence slides into the narrative of their expedition to Central America, the meeting with Miller, and the beginning of the conversion of Anthony to active pacifism.

Helen meanwhile proceeds towards grace in her own way. She falls into an admiration for a young German Communist, Ekki Giesebrecht and becomes totally involved in his communism. When he is called to Switzerland by the comrades, she goes with him. He is betrayed, carried over the border into Germany and killed. She is totally disillusioned about the communists and is ready to be Anthony's support again. By their separate ways they have come to grace and we are allowed to believe that they will come together in peace and harmony.

Once the story is known, the reader is not only able to follow the various narrative threads but he can enjoy the echoes and cross-references and the consistent development in the characters. But if ever there was a novel to be enjoyed fully only at a second reading, it is *Eyeless in Gaza*. It requires all Huxley's gifts, style, wit, intellectual brilliance to keep us at it, until we are impelled to go on and find out what happens. A novelist usually contracts with his reader to give him his pleasure at a single reading. The second reading is normally a tribute to special quality. Huxley defies the convention here, for even the most intelligent and lively reader must be at a loss when he is hurtled to and fro through time and mood at the beginning of this novel, and he cannot see the time plan of the book at all until he has finished. Nor does Huxley offer any easy concessions at the beginning to hold the reader's attention. It may even be fair to say that it is written selfishly, the author enjoying his intensely involved fabrications and more concerned with his own amusement, with his intricate pattern of echoes and connections through time, than with providing comfortable reading for his audience.

The core of the problem which Huxley sets himself, is to bring before his reader all the decades of Anthony's life and the moods of each decade. Prep. school days at the beginning of the century, and the heavy Victorian reaction of his father to death. College days in the next decade, are reminiscent of college days in any decade; these open monasteries change so little. There is a special quality in the 1926 sequence, the atmosphere we already know so well from Huxley's previous novels. Mary Amberley becomes the dominant character, a woman going to the bad as unpleasantly as she can. Her story is the familiar progress of the sensualist through time, from lovers to drink and on to drugs. She grows poorer and poorer and lives in surroundings that become more and more squalid. The twenties, by the middle thirties, had a very unpleasant appearance.

Helen, by contrast, burgeons with the passage of time. She is impelled towards good as inevitably as her mother is impelled towards squalor and dirt; but she does not feel so. 'I am all dirt', she cries out to Anthony, and her life is a contrasting sequence of natural graceful enjoyment and service to her consorts; and a vivid consciousness of inadequacy and sin. In the last scene of all she is with Anthony again, gaily watching his reactions to her prattle about taking another young man, who seems very bed-worthy. But we sense that she is drawn to Anthony as she was drawn to Ekki, because he is daring to stand up to his political enemies and take every risk in supporting the right.

This novel essentially is a progress through the mental life of Anthony Beavis. Like Helen, his natural partner, he is bound by his nature to evolve towards virtue. In his case, it is active pacifism, and it may be that Huxley believed in the thirties that the only hope of Europe was for serious men to preach pacifism so effectively that war would be averted. We see from what happened to Miller and from what we are led to suppose would happen to Anthony, that he knew they must fail. The masses were being conditioned to destruction and they must prevail. Anthony's conversion to active pacifism is a mystical experience, rather than an intellectual decision. It brings a new dimension to this novel; balancing the increasing obsession with physical squalor there is an urge to find words to recreate mystical experiences.

The unending conflict between good and evil is focused by Mark in chapter fifty-one as Huxley leads up to the dénouement. He is disillusioned and quotes Rochester:

> *Then old age and experience, hand in hand,*
> *Lead him to death, and make him understand,*
> *After a search so painful and so long,*
> *That all his life he had been in the wrong.*
> *Huddled in dirt the reasoning engine lies,*
> *Who was so proud, so witty and so wise.*

Huxley quotes the same passage at the climax of *Texts and Pretexts*, when he is stating his conclusions. There, he comments first that: 'Reason emerges scatheless from Rochester's attack, which is directed in reality only against man's habit of reasoning on inadequate data.' In the novel Huxley is gentler with us; Dr Miller remarks that it is very hard to think correctly about something that is very complicated. In the anthology, Huxley's final comment on his quotation is that men 'have discovered experimentally that to live in a certain ritual rhythm, under certain ethical restraints, and as if certain metaphysical doctrines were true, is to live nobly, with style'. Anthony ends the discussion with a gesture: 'I think I shall go and make myself ridiculous with Miller.' He is consciously taking the first steps towards his particular asceticism, public interference by active pacifism. *Texts and Pretexts* and *Eyeless in Gaza* have come together for an important moment. Anthony's diary has an obscure reference to Prince's 'Abode of Love'; but the story is told fully and joyously in an essay called 'Justifications' in *The Olive Tree*. Just as the places in Central America in the novel will be found also in *Beyond the Mexique Bay*, as well as the original for Dr Miller. The traveller through Huxley's mind finds constant pleasure in these cross-references and cross-fertilisations.

The diary of Anthony Beavis is autobiography in the most interesting way, for it is a detailed report of the development of the author's own mind, idealised at the end which describes Anthony's heroic reaction to the situation in which he finds himself. It has in places a gently elegiac tone; remembrance of beauty lost and experiences gone for ever. But it moves towards an end of heroic resolve. It has its own style throughout, the style which is the mark of a fine mind, the gallantry of the perpetual human search for truth: 'how to combine belief that the world is to a great extent illusory, with the belief that it is none the less essential to improve the illusion'? That is the essence of our modern Stoicism. Even though it is all illusion, it is our personal

responsibility to develop increased awareness and control over
our nature and our actions. We must also see, if society is to
survive, that mass man evolves into individuals, so that he can
accept the responsibilities of awareness.

We find it all in *Ends and Means* and *The Perennial Philosophy*,
but in the novel there is a vibrant personal quality in this search
for truth. We watch Anthony evolving inwardly towards the
sustained meditation at the end. In the entry on 15 September,
we get the first sign that he is sufficiently disciplined to carry
through such a meditation. He writes of goodness as 'a whole
system of thoughts and sentiments. It is this whole system that I
hold, quite still, perceived simultaneously in its entirety—hold it
without words, without images, undiscursively as a simple, single
unity.' Entries on goodness and on meditation continue. Their
tenor is summed up simply in words he used in *The Perennial
Philosophy*. 'The end of human life is contemplation, or the
direct and intuitive awareness of God.'

In the final scene Anthony is alone. He goes to his rooms and
finds the letters in which he is threatened with personal violence,
if he speaks that night. He knows he must go, and that he must
not ask for police protection; but he goes through all the temptations to stay away. For he is afraid that he may not have the
courage to be non-violent, and go on accepting the blows. He
might get into a complete funk, as he did with the drunken young
Mexican, who pulled a gun on him. Why should he not retreat,
and quietly get on with studies, which were, after all, his true
work? Why not ring them up and tell them he was ill, and then
go to the south of France on doctor's orders?

Absurd temptations. He knew that he was committed to his
friends, and equally to his enemies. 'There was nothing he could
do but would affect them all.' For this is: 'Unity of mankind,
unity of all life, all being even.' Then he moves towards an
ecstatic state, as his thoughts begin to burn. This is the climax
of his thinking for over a year, and all the labour he put into
thought is now bearing fruit. Not the easy acceptance of a sacra-
ment, still less a drug-procured revelation, for there can be no
revelation except of what has been stored in the unconscious by
much labour. In this meditation, Anthony discovers what men
have been able to discover in all the records of thought and
contemplation, but which each man, if he wills, must discover

for himself as a burning experience. That evil separates, and good unites; that good must prevail if human life is to continue; that the function of evil is to make continuous prevailing possible; that the individual affects others for good or evil, and that the whole of life is a unity, in which the struggle goes on perpetually. With the goal always ahead: 'Unity beyond the turmoil of separateness and divisions. Goodness beyond the possibility of evil. But always the fact of separation persists, always evil remains the very condition of life and being. There must be no relaxation of the opening pressure. But even for the best of us, the consummation is still immeasurably remote.'

Such ideas give grace and stature to the human condition, and they were much canvassed by European philosophers after the war, when the first need was to recover the idea that Western Man could behave in civilised ways. The last three pages of this novel are more like the heightened peroration of a great argument, than the closing scene of an imaginative fiction. It was Huxley's answer to the attack he had made on the novel earlier in the book, that it was inadequate, because it did not deal with the whole truth of life. Here, then, at the end, in long sustained paragraphs of heightened prose, he essays to show the reader the solution to the central problem of Western Man. 'Frenzy of evil and separation. In peace there is unity. Unity with other lives. Unity with all being. For beneath all being, beneath the countless identical but separate patterns, beneath the attractions and repulsions, lies peace. The same peace that underlies the frenzy of the mind. Dark peace, immeasurably deep.'

The remainder of that long paragraph is devoted to visualising a mystical experience. Is it successful? We can use Anthony's words to Helen, 'it is a matter of choice'. Those who get most pleasure out of D. H. Lawrence's novels accept this sort of thing. Huxley is obviously accepting from Lawrence this extension of the function of the novel; it was necessary at the time in which they were writing. It was necessary to preach. Huxley never does it with such Lawrentian intensity again, but if we choose, we can acclaim this ending as a successfully imaginative statement of what he was teaching in his expository books. He was not to attempt these heights again until his last novel, when again, he tried to mirror the intensity of thought and passion which is required for transcendence.

After Many a Summer

'Man comes and tills the field and lies beneath,
And after many a summer dies the swan.
Me only cruel immortality
Consumes.'

TENNYSON Tithonus

THERE IS SOME TALK of tilling the fields; and a good deal about immortality, which becomes a science horror story at the end. The setting is a variation of the Peacock plan, people gathered together in a great house. There is conversation; but there is also seduction and murder. It is the mixture as before, with the oppositions more extreme than ever; the whole gamut from violence to contemplation. The great house is Californian concrete Gothic, and belongs to a millionaire who is so vulgar that the reader winces, whenever he opens his mouth. The love-making is between his mistress and his Levantine physician, who is researching on longevity, so that the millionaire can live for ever. There is a young technician, Pete, in the research laboratory, an idealist who will be a useful audience in the conversations, who is in love with the mistress and gets himself shot by the millionaire in a jealous rage. Material for a popular film script.

The conversation comes from the other characters, Propter and Jeremy Pordage. Propter is a school friend of the millionaire, a man of means who lives simply, and spends a good deal of his time rehabilitating small farmers who have lost their land. He is the author of a book Pordage likes very much, *Short Studies in the Counter Reformation*. He is the Good Man who appears regularly now in Huxley's novels. His passion is the *Ars Contemplativa*, and he is a practising contemplative. When the English scholar, Jeremy Pordage, comes along to catalogue the papers of an English family renowned for its longevity the two meet, and their talks provide us with the serious interest of the book.

These two have to be realised, and we may begin with Mr Propter, who is realised through his farmers. He had no illusions about them, these poor men out of Steinbeck's America. In a soliloquy at the beginning of chapter eight in Part One he said there was no hope for them, if only because they could not see that they were partly responsible for their own disasters. As he thought about a poor fellow from Kansas who was living in one of his huts, he saw that: 'His gravest offence had been to accept the world in which he found himself as normal, rational and right. Like all the others, he had allowed the advertisers to multiply his wants, he had learned to equate happiness with possessions, and prosperity with money to spend in a shop.' Huxley's old enemies the advertisers worrying Mr Propter too.

We proceed from the poor man from Kansas to St Peter Claver. That is easily managed by telling us that Propter had devoted a study to him. The saint had spent his days in the holds of slave ships, tending the sick, encouraging the weary and 'in the intervals had talked about their sins. *Their* sins!' It is a typical interpolation, part of Huxley's endless search for an understanding of the human spirit, a minor example of his preoccupation with the saintly life. He makes Propter reject the saint's way and prefer the Buddhist, the use of the intelligence and the devoted search for the 'more-than-personal consciousness'. As he says a little later: 'The experience of timeless good is worth all the trouble involved.' Mr Propter thinks again of the farmer from Kansas, and the optimism of the reformer overcomes him, and he feels that something could be made of the man.

Then he recollects that he had not come out to think of these things, but to experience himself for a moment that sense of existence outside his own personality which was his own way to mysticism. He quotes again to himself the mystics he had re-called at the opening of the chapter, Cardinal Berulle (whom we shall meet in *Grey Eminence*) and John Touler: 'A nothingness surrounded by God, indigent of God, capable of God and filled with God if man so desires. And what is God? A being with-drawn from creatures, a free power, a pure working.' The induc-tion of the state had only begun when he is interrupted by the approach of Pete and the Englishman, who thus, like the gentleman from Porlock, deprived us of something interesting. We have so few descriptions of mystical experience.

The Englishman had been realised at the beginning of the book. The gentle scholar was a favourite character with Huxley, one of the stock characters it always amused him to create again. Jeremy Pordage has come to stay with the millionaire, Jo Stoyte, while he catalogues the Hauberk papers, all twenty-seven crates of them. The interest to Jo is that the Hauberks lived a long time, and the last of the family will provide the science fiction at the end. That gives Jeremy one connection with the Levantine physician Dr Obispo. The other is pornography. The crates are full of rare examples and both Obispo and Jeremy are connoisseurs.

The third character in the conversations is another stock character, the idealist young man, Peter Boone, Dr Obispo's technician, who had fought on the government side in Spain and had there enjoyed a world in which all men were brothers. His part in the dialogue is to express that longing, and to be the foil to learned men. What follows immediately on their meeting, is a dialogue rather in the spirit of Lowes Dickinson. It opens with talk of longevity between Propter and the young man, who is asked how his experiments in prolonging the lives of dogs are going. It is a contrived echo, or foreshadowing of the dénouement, when longevity is associated with a growing back instead of growing up, growing back to the savagery of our animal ancestors. It is a macabre evolutionary joke, adumbrated here, and developed at the end of the book.

The talk naturally leads to a discussion of time. 'Time's a pretty bothersome thing', says Propter. The Englishman suspects the theme, nervous of where the argument may lead, but Propter assures him he will not talk of harps and wings but of psychological eternity, because that is fact, not dreams. It is fact to him because he has experienced it, and was about to do so again, when they arrived. 'The experience of timeless good', he tells them, 'is worth all the trouble it involved.' The interest of the discussion, however, lies not in eternity, but in time. Propter tells Pete that time is 'the medium in which evil propagates itself, the element in which evil lives and outside of which it dies'. He goes further, and says time itself is evil.

The discussion continues in chapter nine. Time and craving

are aspects of the same thing, and certainly craving or desire require time for their existence. Propter will not accept the existence of good in time, with the sole exception of acts which liberate us from craving and from personality. He is speaking of essences; essential evil depending on time and space and carnal existence, essential good being a property of the spirit, which is eternal and outside time.

The young man brings him back to social good by mentioning democracy, and asking whether that does not involve personality. Of course it does, but personality is a prison, and potential good helps you to escape. 'Actualized good lies outside prison, in time-lessness, in the state of pure, disinterested consciousness.' This touches on a difficulty inherent in the nature of human society. We cannot behave with complete honesty. We must be tactful, compassionate, and at times we must overlook and ignore. In our modern words, we must double-think and double-talk, or society would fragment. This may be compassionate or merely con-venient, but it is inescapable and prevents even the most sophisti-cated of us from being a pure working. Man in society must be a failure. The young man brings Propter back again to social things: is science good or bad? He gets the familiar answer; it can be either. The young man, still representing idealist youth, harks back to the camaraderie of the fighting in Spain and then to the question of what we do when threatened with fascism. Propter thinks there is a better answer than fighting back, but fails to take the clear stand of Anthony Beavis.

Most of us accept the limitations of the human condition in ourselves and in our societies. We must act with the others, not as a herd, but as a responsible society, and our best hope is to exist in peaceful conditions so that we can forget ourselves, in helping others. The nearest eternity for mortal man is forget-fulness, and the purest form of that is found in losing ourselves in helping others. That is the way man in society deals with the problem of effacing personality. The mystic, like Mr Propter, deals with it otherwise. He escapes out of time. He withdraws out of society and life in time. In ordinary social thinking this seems pure selfishness. But those who have considered the dilemma urgently, argue that the sum of things is added to for all of us by contemplatives. It seems the only possible apology in social ethics for withdrawing from social responsibility.

Huxley, through Propter, pursues a more astringent argument. He admits that reformers can temporarily palliate particular distresses, but he is unable to admit that they do more than deflect evil 'from old channels into slightly different channels'. More they cannot do because, 'the nature of things is such that, on the strictly human level of time and craving, you can't achieve anything but evil'. When Pete presses him to tell him what he can do in these conditions, Propter extends the argument from the individual and society to the further conditions of man; on the one hand, an animal, and on the other, a spirit. In the herd areas, it can be fruitful to be active, but as personalities and as social creatures we fuss and worry and destroy ourselves. Fortunately, we spend much of our time in a condition of 'harmless animality' and many of us have 'little flashes of illumination—momentary glimpses of the nature of the world'.

The dialogue has ended and its conclusion is adorned, according to the traditional dialogue form, with a few phrases of natural description. The reactions of Pete and the scholar are amusing. The young man becomes more than ever attached to Propter after his disquieting talk, because somehow he is 'self-effacing and yet more intensely *there*, more present, so to speak, radiating more life than anyone else'. This is exactly what happens. Anyone who has waited for a friend to return from a mystical experience of non-personality knows how intensely present he is when he returns. Jeremy's reactions come last, so that they end the chapter, bringing us back always to cosy animality. The scholar is annoyed by this effort to dig him out of his safe retreat, to expose him to reality, and loses himself in remembrance of his mistress and 'infinite squalor in a little room'.

The next two chapters discuss again our failures as social animals. As animals we can behave naturally, according to our condition, and a few of us occasionally realise our spiritual possibilities. The failure is in the area in between, in social relationships, and until we correct that, both the animal life and the spiritual life are thwarted. Propter subscribes to the traditional view that independent men form the best societies. He says he is a Jeffersonian democrat, he stands by the American constitution and if that is going to work, citizens must be self-supporting. They must be independent of big business and bureaucracy.

It seems plain that we have evolved beyond that fine possibility.

A few are born with this kind of independence and a few can achieve it; but even they find life simpler if they use the electric grid and the mass-produced car. We must come to terms with the monsters we have evolved in our unmanageable societies. We can take a hopeful view. We can come to terms with the monsters we have collectively made, the Behemoths and Leviathans he discusses so formidably in *Texts and Pretexts* and in *The Devils of Loudun*. We could not now do without them, and they do not often get out of control. There is much less worry and much less pain than when Huxley wrote this novel. We can do many things that make us more agreeable social animals. The catalogue of human advantage in the western world since Huxley wrote is a long one, thanks to the knowledge explosion. In the setting of our sophisticated societies, the fleeting moments of our existence can be adorned with very agreeable animal pleasures and spiritual experiences.

In this novel we are grateful to him for raising so many interesting questions. For his deft handling of his erotic material, which is tolerable because it is so scornfully sophisticated. For his outrageous joke about longevity, which accords so well with his erotic theme. Great skill goes into the management of this conflicting material, which demonstrates that in the human condition, animal and spiritual must learn to co-exist. Huxley had an itch to show extremes meeting, and in this novel he goes as far as he can possibly dare. It requires all his tact and virtuosity to succeed, but he does; and perhaps the most remarkable thing about his success is that he does it in such short space. Reading *After Many a Summer* is an agreeable way to meet the ideas which Huxley wished to advocate.

Time Must Have a Stop

'But thought's the slave of life, and life time's fool;
And time, that takes survey of all the world,
Must have a stop.'
        SHAKESPEARE *Henry IV*, *Part 1*

THE NOVEL HAS an interesting theme, it is a sermon for the times, but it begins with five chapters of dull muddle. In the sixth chapter we leave London behind and go to Florence, and at once everything is clear and amusing. After five chapters all we have is a middle-class English family, most of whom we hardly meet again, and the sad fact that Sebastian does not have a dinner jacket. Much will depend on that, but it hardly seems worth sixty pages of hard reading. Sebastian is a pretty boy of seventeen, whose mother is dead and whose father has practically given up a brilliant career at the Bar to work for international socialism against the fascists. An Italian anti-fascist is introduced and this contact will have serious consequences later on. Cousin Susan is introduced, so that Sebastian can talk about his adolescent dreams and erotic imaginings, and read to her his adolescent verses. It is hardly a satisfactory relationship. Mrs Ockham appears in the opening scene, then fades out till she comes to Florence, so she merely adds to the opening confusion. We meet Uncle Eustace, but Uncle Eustace in London is a dim, slightly ridiculous figure, very different from the splendid figure we shall meet in Florence. He is rich and self-indulgent and is always quarrelling with his brother John, Sebastian's father, who is a natural Puritan and distressingly efficient; 'everything, in short, that was tiresome, efficient, meritorious, healthful and social-minded'.

In chapter six, Huxley leaves it all behind, the prickly relationships in that middle-class family, the grubby little scene with a prostitute which depresses us still more. There was even a diary once again, Susan's diary, but that is the poorest one Huxley wrote. Then, in chapter six, everything is transformed. We are in Florence, with Uncle Eustace in his own sophisticated world, and now we shall meet Huxley's most wicked woman, and one of his very saintly men. Veronica Thwale and Bruno Rontini are real characters among a collection of vividly painted marionettes. They are the usual contrast between the sensual and the ascetic which Huxley was impelled to stress.

Yet the magic never works in this novel. The characters do not come alive and the old formulas do not really serve. It seems that the shadow of the war, which paralysed imaginative writing, was still upon him. He did so much better with the same serious themes in his anthology, *The Perennial Philosophy*. The clever talk in this novel about literature and life leaves us jaded and the quotation from Keats, 'the giant agony of the world', is echoed only in the epilogue. Even the powerful formula, the opposition of good and evil, hardly operates here, for Veronica and Bruno are in juxtaposition rather than opposition. Right through the vibrant middle of the book she has the stage and Bruno has one brief scene, then disappears for ten years into a fascist prison. He comes into his own in the epilogue, where almost everything of value in this novel is said, and Veronica is only the shadow of a shade.

While Veronica is on the stage she is believable in every detail. She was the daughter of a poor clergyman, and she married at eighteen a young solicitor who quickly died, leaving her the choice of continuing a life of good works with her father at fifty shillings a week, or being companion to Mrs Gamble, the old, blind, wealthy mother-in-law of Uncle Eustace. She chooses the easier life, and is looking out for a husband who will provide her with rich living for ever. She finds what she requires in a young American, de Vries, and to catch him acts superbly her part of the chaste virgin with serene, oval face.

At the same time, she seduces young Sebastian to satisfy her overwhelming concupiscence. That is not difficult, as she is exactly the imaginary mistress Sebastian had invented to tease cousin Susan. But though it is not difficult to debauch the boy, it will not be safe until she can somehow get him entirely in her power. When that happens, he will be too frightened to talk. She wants to go to bed with him and teach him the arts which will reduce them to being, 'Twin cannibals in bedlam' and at the same time be absolutely certain that no hint of it will interfere with the rest of her life. That is where the dinner jacket comes in. Eustace had promised Sebastian the jacket, and in their last talk had given him one of the Degas drawings he had bought that day. When Eustace dies of a heart attack that night, Sebastian realises he has lost the promised jacket. So he sells his drawing, not realising he has no proof that his uncle gave it him.

No proof seems to be needed until Mrs Ockham arrives as the beneficiary and brings with her a solicitor, a tedious fellow who has to be created to make an inventory and discover that Eustace had bought a couple of Degas drawings and one of them is missing. Sebastian panics and denies all knowledge of the drawing. He must get it back at all costs, so he turns to his uncle's old friend, Bruno Rontini, who is a bookseller. In Huxley, art dealers are bad, but booksellers are good. Sebastian gets his drawing back and promises Bruno to make a clean breast of it. But again he is thwarted, this time by the art dealer. The picture is returned, but the truth about what happened is concealed and an innocent child, a child of a servant in the house, has already been punished for it. Veronica sees what has happened and is able to blackmail Sebastian. She has him in her power and can do what she likes with him. Huxley uses his best energies to display the bestial side of her nature. It is as if he challenged himself again to do his best or worst in that direction. There is no woman in Huxley who is so eaten up with lust, so proficient in seeking satisfaction or so devilishly attractive.

At the other extreme is Bruno. Bruno is a saint. By the chance of his position in time and place, the late twenties, he works actively against Mussolini, then at the height of his power. His practical view of life is given us by his disciple, Carlo Malpighi: 'there's only one corner of the universe you can be certain of improving, and that's your own self... So you have to begin there, not outside, not on other people. That comes afterwards, when you've worked on your own corner. You've got to be good before you can do good—or at any rate do good without doing harm at the same time.'

That is what Bruno cares for when Sebastian goes to seek his help. He will try to get his drawing back but he knows that Sebastian must get out of his muddle of deceit for that to be of any use. So when he goes off to retrieve the drawing, he leaves Sebastian with the thought of the genealogy of sin, searching back for the causes of the offence.

There was an ironic twist for Bruno in the genealogy of Sebastian's sin. The boy was known to the fascist police as the son of a friend of a prominent Italian exiled liberal. Bruno was arrested for being in contact with the boy, and sent to prison for ten years. Malpighi makes certain that Sebastian knows what he has done. Tension is relieved, and the Florentine scene dispersed soon afterwards when Sebastian is recalled home by his father. We do not meet the characters again until 1944 in the long Epilogue, which is like the sustained finale in an orchestral work. Then the characters and themes return to be expressed in the mood appropriate to a finale.

It begins as the first movement began, with Sebastian and Susan. Now, she is happily married and a mother, and she is trying to marry Sebastian happily, for he has lost his young wife. Sebastian recognises in Susan and her family the pillars of society: 'It was thanks to their goodness that the system worked as smoothly as it did, and thanks to their limitations that the system was fundamentally insane.' For they had an 'absolutely sterling goodness, but limited by an impenetrable ignorance of the end and purpose of existence'. We are then given some extracts from the random notes, commentary, he has made during the past few months, and that leads Huxley, with skill now very familiar to us, to drop back through time for five years, and let us know about his characters. Sebastian is in the south of France and de Vries is there, and so is Veronica, still Sebastian's mistress, the 'irresistible, the dreaded and fascinating vehicle of an alienation more total than that he had known with anyone else'.

We have gathered by this time that Sebastian went to Oxford, is a playwright, and has lost a hand in the war. Then we meet Bruno again, now 'an old man, bent and horribly emaciated', but still 'the bright blue eyes were full of joy' and still he has the same compassionate understanding, for he knows that Sebastian is a 'predestined target' for the arrows which 'seem to have started flying'. Sebastian had taken the dying man to a little house in Vence, where, from the verandah, he could see the

Mediterranean and murmur his Leopardi, *E'l naufragar m'è dolce in questo mare*. Sebastian nursed him and when the end came buried him. In these last days Sebastian enjoyed 'a kind of participation in the knowledge of which that joy (of Bruno's) was the natural and inevitable expression—the knowledge of a timeless and infinite presence'. As opposed to the alienation Veronica bred in him, Bruno made him sure of 'an essential identity'. Some readers may find this a sentimental portrait of a good man, much less firm than the ironic certainty of the strokes which make Veronica. But it is a fine attempt and nothing in fiction is more difficult than to create a character whose essential virtue is goodness.

We return to the notes Sebastian has been making, very typical of the thoughts of an intellectual pessimist during the postwar chaos, very like Huxley, and very like the brilliant unco-ordinated utterances of H. G. Wells.

The essential wisdom of both these novelists could be distilled into the few pages that will contain the essential wisdom of any teacher. Huxley, in these pained reflections, writes as if Sebastian were plucking the arrows from his spiritual wounds, writes a little more coherently while he is offering a sermon on the text which is the title of the book. Like many sermons, it is in three parts, one to each of the clauses in the quotation from Hotspur's speech. The sermon stirs us when it comes to 'Time, that takes survey of all the world, must have a stop'.

'It is only by taking the fact of eternity into account, that we can deliver thought from its slavery to life. And it is only by deliberately paying our attention and our primary allegiance to eternity, that we can prevent time from turning our lives into a pointless or diabolic foolery.' The ending of the novel is optimistic in essence, for Sebastian's father comes in unexpectedly and we see a new relationship between the son and the aged, defeated parent. The son is behaving to the old man as Bruno would have behaved, with delicacy, understanding and compassion.

Will anyone describe the novel as a success? It is at any rate very much better than the inchoate opening would suggest. He makes a good pulpit for himself, and preaches a very good sermon. He had been reading oriental religious texts and some of the ideas in this novel come from *The Tibetan Book of the Dead*. When Bruno sees that his old friend Eustace is dying, he exerts spiritual pressure upon him so that the Clear Light streams through him. When, after his death, the spirit of Eustace floats around, the idea comes from the Tibetan text, but the effect is of a suburban séance. These Eastern ideas will be better managed in *Island*.

Ape and Essence

'But man, proud man,
Dressed in a little brief authority—
Most ignorant of what he's most assur'd.
His glassy essence—like an angry ape,
Plays such fantastic tricks before high heaven
As make the angels weep.'

SHAKESPEARE *Measure for Measure*

HUXLEY was always committed to the torments of his times, and the torment which has afflicted Western Man most, since Hiroshima, has been the bomb. So he set himself to show what could happen in California, if the bombs fell there. He used the speed and luridness of a film script as the best way of presenting the horror. For preface, he gives us a short story glimpse of an entirely worthless present world, the world of the film studios with the hinterland of desert, in which human beings scratch enough subsistence for them to be able to breed.

There is the brief story of the narrator's friend, Bob Briggs; within that, the story of William Tallis, who wrote the script, *Ape and Essence*. All of it written at a great pace, competently and without any charm. An arid sketch of people not worth the effort involved in atomising them. It is the prelude to greater horrors, pictured at film speed. All the values of our world are upside down, and the human race stripped of all its dignity. Explorers from New Zealand are landing on the coast of California about twenty miles due west of Los Angeles, and find a repulsively degraded human community. One New Zealander is captured by the natives, a Dr Poole, who is the sane observer of the Satanic scene. There must be love interest, even here, so he takes up with a girl called Loola. The story so far has Hollywood quality, but now we come to the indignities and the degradation. A group of natives are rifling graves, for they depend on cemeteries for fine cloth. Poole talks to the head of the gravediggers who presumes that if he comes from a country where they have engines, he can tell them how to build them. The reader recalls Huxley's remark in *Beyond the Mexique Bay*, that the loss of a few thousand technicians would mean the collapse of any modern western country. But Dr Poole is a botanist and he tells them that the only way he can help, is to show them how to grow better strains of cereals. They are about to bury him alive—such fun— but the head man saves him. If he can help grow more food he will be useful. One girl complains at being denied her fun— people look so screamingly funny when they are being buried alive.

There is more horror. We learn of the babies deformed by gamma rays. The mothers of deformed children are rounded up every year and when a child is beyond an accepted limit of deformity, the mother is shaved and whipped, and made to attend a religious ceremony where the child is destroyed.

As the ritual murders go on, Dr Poole is called before the Arch-Vicar, who shares his meal with him and conducts the discussion, which is the apology for their uncivilisation. 'Man pitting himself against Nature, the Ego against the Order of Things, Belial... against the Other One. For a hundred thousand years or so the battle's entirely indecisive. Then, three centuries ago, almost over-night, the tide starts to run uninterruptedly in one direction.'

It is an insane inversion of the discussion between Mond and the Save in *Brave New World*, and the Arch-Vicar enjoys himself at length. So, obviously, does Huxley. Never before had he arranged for himself such a mordant opportunity for pouring out his ideas. They are not new. He has said them all before, but he has never expressed them better.

He rages along, galloping one hobby horse after another against the horror background he has painted in with such cunning. In many of his novels, there is great music at the back of his mind. In this devil talk, with sanity inverted, it is not music but the insanity of western man in every age: 'Utopia lies just ahead and... it is your privilege and duty to rob, swindle, torture, enslave and murder all those who... obstruct the march to the

earthly paradise.' It is the demented inversion of the theme in
Ends and Means.

Beverly Hills is going down shouting: 'Are you aware, sir, that
from the second century onwards no orthodox Christian believed
that a man could be possessed by God? He could only be possessed
by the Devil.' The Devil is now in charge. The film dissolves and
re-forms in scenes of the annual bacchanalian orgy, dissolving
into a scene in which the New Zealand team sails away and then
dissolving back to the orgy. After that annual festival of lechery,
back to work and back to rigidly enforced chastity. Identity must
be forgotten for another year. Poole explains to the Arch-Vicar
the possibilities for food production, and the old bogey of over-
population appears. 'Worse malnutrition for more people. More
political unrest, resulting in more aggressive nationalism and
imperialism. And finally the Thing.' In fifty years, the Arch-
Vicar adds: 'the deformity will be double what it is at present.
And in a hundred years the triumph of Belial will be complete.'

We have had it all. But there is a reaction. Pessimism, lamenta-
tion and despair will not prevail. Poole had heard from the Arch-
Vicar of people up north who had escaped across a desert because
they could not deny themselves sexual desire, which is the basis
of identity. They were called simply Hots, and Loola is a natural
Hot. He arranges to attempt the journey with her. He needs great
courage to attempt it and he gets it from a volume of Shelley,
which he rescued from the fire. Shelley's verses represent the
knowledge of our own Essence, and the long quotations balance
the horror film sequences we have been through. Dr Poole has
found the poet who will prop his mind. And it is a poet, not a
mystic. We are back to the outlook in *Texts and Pretexts*.

Huxley had had some experience of film script writing, and he
knows how to provide a final sequence. The lovers are at the
grave of William Tallis, who wrote the script. We know that they
are going to be safe. It is not the real grave, but the one he wanted,
in the desert, with the lines from Adonais:

> *Thy hopes are gone before: from all things here*
> *They have departed, thou shouldst now depart!*

Loola thinks the poet must have been a very sad man, but Poole
asks her to listen to the next stanza, which he reads from the
volume he had rescued. Beauty and love have prevailed:

That Light whose smile kindles the Universe,
That Beauty in which all things work and move...
Burns bright or dim, as each are mirrors of
The fire for which all thirst, now beams on me,
Consuming the last clouds of cold mortality.

Absolutely relevant to Poole's situation; and effective. The book was written at a time when the restraints were off. It seems as natural as a mental illness after too much stress, that these diabolical words and images should stream into the making of this ugly parable; and encouraging beyond words that great verse should so effectively bring us back to reason.

The Genius and the Goddess

'Professionally, in relation to his chosen speciality, a man may be completely mature. Spiritually and sometimes even ethically, in relation to God and his neighbours, he may be hardly more than a foetus.'

The Perennial Philosophy

As a younger writer, Huxley had written many successful long-short stories; now, he adds a brilliant one. *The Genius and the Goddess* has all that the form requires; a good story line with the characters, setting and situation developed beyond the capacity of the short story proper. For most of the way, it is in direct descent from Chaucer; comic, with ironic misunderstandings and unadmitted embarrassments between the characters; the interest, as usual in the extended story, falling so much on a character that the story is only there to show the character responding to the situation; and, equally Chaucerian, there is a professional control of the verbal medium which reflects sensitively the changing moods.

In the presentation, Huxley uses the technique he had employed so successfully as a young writer; the story is set in a frame, and the frame is as carefully constructed as the picture. As so often in these frames, Huxley is the writer, sitting opposite the narrator, who is not the principal character but a very good one, as a narrator must be. The narrator, John Rivers, like Huxley, is in the sixties, a well-known physicist who tells this story of thirty years before. He is perfectly detached from his young self, and can tell it all without emotion. If there is bias, it is only that memory serves to makes him a more acute commentator than an outside spectator could have been. His intellectual capacity and background is as fine as Huxley's so we are, as usual, provided with excellent conversation.

The time is carefully chosen. It is Christmas Eve, a moment when old men look back, and we are reminded of the moment during various interruptions. The technique of the interruption at the approach of crisis in the tale, is used more than once, holding us in suspense without allowing us to feel a painful break, allowing time for extra energy to be accumulated for the crisis. Huxley tells us in *Literature and Science* that 'this systematic shifting of attention from one order of experience to another is a literary device of rather recent invention' and says it is a method for expressing 'the unshareableness of private experience. In a fictional narrative this is rendered by the juxtaposition of two parallel inwardnesses, or else of an inwardness and some simultaneous, but unconnected and irrelevant objectivity.' It is, in fact, part of the technique of the frame, and Chaucer used it.

The story is a strong one, two interlocking triangles within the frame. Rivers as a young man is invited by the genius, Henry Maartens, to join him as a research assistant. He accepts, and when he arrives he finds a domestic set-up which reminds him of the Marx brothers. The genius is perfectly incapable of coping with everyday life. Over against him is the goddess, Mrs Maartens, a Valkyrie, who is mother, wife, secretary, mistress and general protector of the genius. The children are Ruth, who is just beginning to grow up, and Timmy, a boy whose only function is to report the accident. In the background is Beulah, the Negro housekeeper, a rich comic character, who provides her own zany, perceptive comment on the action. Huxley is in no danger of attempting to show us a genius. He reports the idiosyncrasies, the deficiencies which are the outer man, the actions and thoughts which are all that are necessary for the story.

The central figure is the goddess, Katy, the Wagnerian blonde, who is the mature maternal woman who has all the instincts of the perfect mistress. When the time and the need comes, she takes young Rivers for her pleasure and gives him delirious satisfaction. She has a natural and complete understanding of how to complement the male in body, mind and spirit. She is the female principle incarnate, a goddess. Huxley had drawn women faithfully and skilfully all his life, old and young, dull and ravishing, insipid and witty, frigid and eager to love. He had a particular

D

gift for drawing girls in the freshness of their youth, trembling on the verge of knowledge. He brought them shimmeringly alive. But he had never before drawn a mature woman with the generous instincts for earthy encounter and maternal support for the male. When he draws a stripling girl in this story, it is with a difference. Ruth is a long-legged girl when he arrives, and comes to puberty during his stay. Her development is misshapen by the people and circumstances surrounding her. The poor child lives under the shadow of a goddess. She is more than usually sensitive, and her outlet is writing verse. She falls in love with a schoolboy and, when she is rejected, falls in love with Rivers, who does his best to manage this embarrassment. He fails because Ruth's mother completes this triangle as well as the other, in which she and Rivers cuckold Henry. Ruth is jealously aware.

It is not a sordid affaire, but a pagan fulfilment, arranged instinctively by Katy for the express purpose of saving Henry's life. Henry had the familiar habit of selfish old men. He fell desperately ill when his protecting female wanted to leave him for a while. Katy was called to her mother's bedside. When the mother was reported to be dying, Henry unaffectedly rejoiced, for Katy would soon be home, and would never have to go on that mission again. When a clever young doctor saved her, and Katy had to stay on, Henry fell sick. He became so ill that Katy had to be recalled. She could do nothing. Beulah explained it in the theological language appropriate to the situation; the virtue had gone out of her. It had all been used up at her mother's bedside.

When a telephone message comes one night that her mother has died, she is at the end of her tether, and with true pagan instinct goes in to young Rivers. She seduces the young intellectual so skilfully that he behaves like a man. Next morning, when Beulah sees her, she cries: 'Praise the Lord! We're going to have a miracle.' They had the miracle. Katy was once again in 'a state of animal grace through satisfied desire' and she transfers her new-found virtue to Henry, who at once begins to recover. (It must be plain why Chaucer was spoken of at the beginning.) Katy is now ready to be sensible. Henry is nearly better and the children are coming home. She tells Rivers: 'Things will have to go back to what they were before'; the natural cry of the satisfied female. Katy only once attempted to condone her conduct to

Rivers, and she did so scornfully: 'A sick genius and the poor woman whose job it's been to keep the genius alive and tolerably sane. His huge, crazy intellect against my instincts, his inhuman denial of life against the flow of life in me.'

There was another reaction to the situation, Ruth's. She suspected what had been going on, and what follows is a story within a story. Katy takes Rivers to prepare their country cottage for Henry, and they refuse to take Ruth. At siesta time they go to bed together, and afterwards Rivers looks at a poem Ruth had given him before they left. It is a ballad attacking the adulteress, and Huxley describes it in terms of the centuries of horror and insanity in the European mind. In his guilty mood after pleasure Rivers shows it to Katy, who has always affronted him by taking their carnal pleasures in moral ease. Against this attack by her daughter Katy has no defence. From now on the tragic dénouement approaches inevitably. Katy sees that she cannot prevent Ruth destroying them all by telling her father. The only way out is for Rivers to go away, but before he can do so they set out for the country holiday. There is a car accident. Timmy, who survives, is able to tell them that Katy and Ruth were quarrelling bitterly. They are killed and at that moment the reader realises that he has been listening to a threnody, sung by an old man on Christmas Eve. For throughout the narrative there is a murmuring mention of death. Two old men on Christmas Eve turning their thoughts to their latter end, celebrating the violent death of a perfect mistress who had been faithful in her own fashion.

In the opening sentence Rivers says that fiction makes too much sense and reality never makes sense. Fiction, unlike fact, has unity and style. When we have read to the last sentence we feel that this fiction has these things to perfection. It is another artistic impression of the fact that evil is inextricably intertwined with good, and sometimes one prevails, sometimes the other. It is one of the recurring themes in Huxley's work. The two women, mother and daughter, could only act according to their natures. Rivers came into their lives and destroyed them. Yet the final impression this novella leaves with us is not sad. The two old men who form the frame, ease the sharpness of the tale. They are old enough to accept Predestination, to discuss it in a gently civilised way. They provide the atmosphere of discursive brilliance in full flood. It is a quality enjoyed by the best essayists, enjoyed

by Montaigne and by Hazlitt. Huxley's intellectual brilliance gives
him something of that quality. So when he contrives a character
like John Rivers, who talks with the zest and impetuosity and
range of an essayist, we have the best that he can offer.

Island

'He's being sent to an island. That's to say, he's being sent to a place where he'll meet the most interesting set of men and women to be found anywhere in the world.'

Brave New World

'Indeed, good pictures of non-attached men and women are singularly rare in the world's literature.'

Ends and Means

IN *Eyeless in Gaza* in 1936, a Scots doctor talked about an ideal human society. In *Island*, in 1962, a Scots doctor had helped to found that ideal society. All his life, and increasingly as the years went on, Huxley was preoccupied with the idea that human beings could live much more fully, that the frontiers of experience could be pushed out very much farther than we believed. He lived and wrote through the decades of the knowledge explosion, which encouraged his belief; suddenly, there was very much more to know. 'Human beings are multiple amphibians, living simultaneously in half a dozen radically dissimilar universes—the molecular and the ethical, the physiological and the symbolic, the world of incommunicably subjective experiences and the public worlds of language and culture, of social organisations and the sciences.' Huxley goes on (in his 'Introduction' to his wife's book, *You are not the target*) to say that men and women are capable of being devils and lunatics, and, on the other hand, of being saints, heroes and geniuses. Not new; his biographies and many of his novels had been concerned to show the dual nature of man. He goes on to say that on the whole human beings prefer to behave decently, and asks how they are to do so in practice. 'What must multiple amphibians do in order to make the best, for themselves and for other multiple amphibians, of all this strangely assorted world?'

Then he says that for two or three years he has been trying to find answers to these questions 'plausible enough to take their place in a kind of Utopian and yet realistic phantasy about a society (alas, hypothetical) whose collective purpose is to help its members to actualize as many as possible of their desirable potentialities'. The research required was very considerable. He lists among many items, Greek history and translations from the Sanscrit and Chinese and Buddhist texts; scientific papers on such subjects as pharmacology, neuro-physiology, psychology and education; all the subjects, in fact, which he had been studying avidly for forty years and which have appeared throughout his writings. It was going to be a final summing up.

The island he gave himself was inhabited by a very civilised and apparently Bengali people, with an admixture of Scot of a Calvinistic strain. This genetic admixture produced a highly intelligent and sensitive people who could say all the things that Huxley wanted to say. His main theme is like a valedictory message: be more aware; seek to extend the frontiers of human knowledge. Get away from the belief in the eternal opposition of good and evil into the bright world, where evil is unnecessary and can be exorcised. For the rest, he went over old themes, giving them imaginative glow and colouring; civil government, self-government, over-population, education, hallucinatory drugs. His treatment of these familiar themes is persuasive, except perhaps in the case of education, which is confused with cranky oddnesses; and there is frequent confusedness in the book caused by distracting ideas on every subject that is suggested by the progress of the story. Finally, the theme of death comes in all through, and there is poignant preoccupation with death by cancer. Two of the women characters die of it and the progress of the disease is described without reticence, as if Huxley was outfacing the disease which he knew was killing him.

The island is called Pala, set in southern seas, and it has a geographical misfortune which turns out to be fatal. It is close to the mainland state of Rendang, which has a history of exploitation by every European trading nation, and has suffered everything from gin and missionaries to oil-men. It is ruled by a dictator, who, in the way of dictators, is seeking *lebensraum*. Pala

has been ruled benignly by Rajas for over a hundred years, and
the Rajas have been advised by the offspring of the Scots surgeon,
who was brought from Madras to operate on the Raja early in
last century. The happy relationship which developed between
the Raja and the Scot and their descendants produced the ideal
state to which we are introduced by Will Farnaby.

Will Farnaby had made a regular mess of his life, and in a
series of those backward glances which Huxley managed with
such virtuosity, we are given the more disgraceful of them. He is
a journalist and becomes the private agent of a tycoon, Lord
Aldehyde, interested in oil and copper as well as the Press. He
is told to see if he can get on to the forbidden island of Pala and
see if he can get the oil concession. Pala had cut itself off from
the exploiting commercial world, but Aldehyde knew the Dowager
Rani and knew that she wanted funds to promote her bogus
religion. He also knew that other oil companies were closing in
on Pala, which oozed oil at its southern end. One agent of these
rival companies was the dictator of Rendang, Colonel Dipa, who
was having a homosexual affaire with the young Raja of Pala,
who was about to become of age. He was corrupting the young
man with American ideas of material wealth, and at one point
in the story the boy is discovered reading the gorgeously techni-
coloured sales catalogue of an American mail-order firm. So the
state is being corrupted from within before Will Farnaby succeeds
in landing on it.

He does so in an acknowledged adaptation of the *Erewhon* opening. His boat is capsized in a storm, he is thrown ashore and
manages to climb the cliffs to safety. Not without damaging
himself when he falls down the cliff (after grasping a snake which
he took to be the branch of a tree). He is discovered (*cf. Erewhon*,
chapter six) in a nastily shaken and bruised condition by two
children, who cure him of his shivering by a simple analysis of
the fright the snake gave him, and send for the doctor who binds
up his scratches. He is taken to the Experimental Station, the
local Rothamsted, where Dr McPhail's daughter-in-law, Susila,
gives him more analysis, to encourage him to be in the mood to
allow his natural restorative instincts to come into play and effect
a self-cure. To give the *vis medicatrix naturae* a chance, as Dr
Robert put it. The very latest sensible medical techniques, in
strong contrast with, as Huxley is at pains to explain, the familiar

psycho-analyst who treats one part of a corner of the trouble.

Fortunately, the Palanese share the oriental pleasure in talking and displaying the joys of their civilisation, so very quickly, with Will Farnaby, we learn a great deal about Pala and its history. The book is given up to these descriptions for they, and not the Graham Greene-like story, are its purpose. The rest of the story is as tawdry as it is brief, and easily outlined. The oil companies are going to exploit Pala and the only question is which will get in first. Aldehyde's company has got Will Farnaby into a good position for negotiating, and Farnaby is given powers to offer the necessary bribes. The tale is managed to allow Farnaby to meet the Rani and the young Raja and their friend, the Ambassador from Rendang, Mr Bahu. Mr Bahu will double-cross his Leader (who is backing the oil-men who have the Rendang concession) for an appropriate sum, and he makes it quite clear that the sum is £20,000. Bahu is a smooth villain, 'the bony, emphatic mask of Savonarola positively twinkled with his Voltairean smile'; and what could be better than that? The Rani will give away anything to get enough money to finance her 'World-Wide Crusade of the Spirit', and the young Raja will do anything to get enough money to turn Pala into a Developed Country and be able to buy anything he wants from his mail-order catalogue. They succeed, of course. Pala has no army, no defences against oil-men. Bahu explains that it is inevitable. He agrees that it will destroy Pala, but happiness and freedom are impossible for three-quarters of the human race. Pala cannot remain different from the rest of the world. It isn't right that it should. It must become part of the American empire.

Farnaby, regenerated by his Palanese friends and in love with his fair analyst, will have nothing to do with it. So the mechanised forces of Rendang, led by the young Raja, invade. We are led to suppose that they shoot the doctor, who had been the young Raja's good angel, and probably the doctor's close associates. What happens to Farnaby and the girl we are not told. It is unimportant. Huxley has had the opportunity he wanted to give an imaginative glow to the ideas he most wished to canvass. Among them was the idea that death consisted in walking into the Clear Light.

There are too many ideas in the novel. He dissipates his energies. The book scintillates with suggestions so that when the

light is focused on the main ideas, there is not enough contrast.
Brief evaluations of western medicine and psychiatry are followed
quickly by a discussion of Trantrik Buddhism, which introduces
a long discussion on Maithuna, which is *coitus reservatus* and also
an aspect of the main theme, awareness. There is a mention of
'continuing revolution' which is interesting in the light of sub-
sequent events in China, and a comparison of Hitler and Stalin as
representing the Peter Pan type, the boys who fail to develop and
the muscle men who always overcome them. The population
problem is irresistible, but it is managed easily, and is not a
main theme as in *Brave New World*. Here it is associated with
DF and AI, deep-frozen sperm for artificial insemination. The
Palanese had a store of the sperm of outstanding males which
married couples could apply for. It gave variety to their family
and was rapidly improving the IQs of the population. 'We chew
grace' is an example of the triviality which loads the book. Instead
of saying grace, they chewed the first mouthfuls thoughtfully.
Thanatology is mentioned as a much-needed study but that also
relates to a main theme, cancer and the business of dying.

Death is called 'The Essential Horror' and chapter fourteen is
given up to it. First Will tells Susila how his Aunt Mary died of
cancer. The progress of the disease is described in masochistic
detail: 'a little piece of her body started to obey the second law
of thermodynamics.' Later in the chapter, after diversions which
reduced the intensity so that it could be accumulated again, we
are brought in with Will to witness the death of Lakshmi, wife
of Dr Robert. Her family was present to help her remain aware
as she went into the Clear Light. It is the most carefully developed
set scene in the novel and in making it, Huxley seems to be
exhorting himself. It is associated with two other main themes,
awareness and *Karuna* or compassion. At the beginning of the
novel, when Dr Robert visits his wife, she hears the bird outside
repeating *Karuna*. These talking birds were an idea of the old
Raja's. They would fly about the island, repeating the words and
phrases they had been taught, reminding anyone who hears
them: 'Attention', 'Here and now, boys', *Karuna*.

The word 'Attention' is the first and last in the book. It is the
most common call of the birds, a constant reminder that we should
be aware, concentrating on the present, more capable of absorbing
the life around us. It is the most urgent desire of this dying

D*

novelist, the desire which invited him to take all the risks associated with the drugs which raise our awareness for a time. That we must put away the past in order to concentrate on the present, to increase our awareness, is an adaptation of a Buddhist idea, which was a recognition of the dangers of living in the past. Old people especially have to remember that dwelling on past sorrows and errors is dangerous and quite useless.

Will Farnaby is introduced to the idea of concentrating on the present, right at the beginning, when the child tells him that he can't be here and now until he has forgotten his fright with the snake. A little later, when Dr Robert is dressing his cuts, he asks the doctor, 'Attention to what?' and is told, 'Attention to attention'. When he tries that, the pain is not so bad. Huxley is saying there that attention involves choice, thought-control, but does not seem to know that he has said so. There is so much that is present at any moment of our awareness, and if we want sensible help in choosing what we admit to our thoughts, we can get it from Huxley's so greatly admired William Law.

Attention will bring awareness of the order described in the old Raja's *Notes on What's What*. It is Huxley's device for giving his ideas the concentration of expository prose. There are so many echoes of European mystics in these Notes, as well as Oriental thinkers, that we may marvel a little at the range of the old Raja's reading. We may also rejoice in his mastery of our difficult English language, for some of the best writing in *Island* is in these Notes in chapter five. We learn in them that the present has all we require, if only we are able to see that it is part of eternity. There follows an attack on the Manichee attitude we commonly accept. Huxley holds that the conflict between good and evil frustrates our realisation of Good Being. 'Conflicts and frustrations—the theme of all history and all biography. "I show you sorrow", said the Buddha realistically. But he also showed the ending of sorrow—self-knowledge, total acceptance, the blessed experience of Not-Two.'

A little later, the Notes explain the necessity for awareness: 'Good Being is knowing who in fact we are; and in order to know who in fact we are, we must first know, moment by moment, who we think we are, and what this bad habit of thought compels us to feel and do. A moment of clear and complete knowledge of what we think we are, but in fact are not, puts a stop, for the moment, to the Manichean charade.' Then the positive side, the hope in awareness: 'Good Being is in the knowledge of who in fact one is in relation to *all* experiences; so be aware— aware in every context, at all times and whatever, creditable or discreditable, pleasant or unpleasant, you may be doing or suffering. This is the only genuine yoga, the only spiritual exercise worth practising.'

This is the antithesis of the trend in our modern mass communities, where everything encourages diminished awareness, not seeing the people in the streets or in eating places, avoiding any frank assessment of the work to which circumstances have condemned us, keeping thoughts of suffering and death out of our minds, wandering contentedly through existence because we have learned to be unaware. Unawareness is the protection of industrial man. Unawareness holds industrial communities together.

To make tolerance possible, we resort to double-think, compassionately putting out of mind much that is said and done to us. Orwell never developed this healing quality in double-think and Huxley will not accept it. The old Raja notes: 'Dualism... Without it there can hardly be good literature. With it, there most certainly can be no good life.' In another place, Huxley accepts that children must be Manichean dualists, but would have his adults so mature that the saving grace of double-think would be unnecessary. The note on the novel is interesting: how would any novel get on without the Manichean tension of good and evil, the light and the dark?

Huxley takes his discussion of awareness further. Our western philosophy, he says, is talk. 'Western philosophers, even the best of them—they're nothing more than good talkers.' They do not mould our lives. While in the East 'philosophy is pragmatic and operational'. For example, *Tat tvam asi* means 'Thou art that' and 'anyone who's willing to perform the necessary operations can test the validity of *tat tvam asi* for himself. The operations are called yoga, or dhyana, or Zen.' As these themes unfold we can well believe that two years of hard study lay behind this novel.

That our western philosophers are talkers, is repeated later when Dr Robert says that in the West we are all Platonists: 'You worship the word and abhor matter!' He is for concrete materialism, but that 'is only the raw stuff of a fully human life. It's through awareness, complete and constant awareness, that we transform it into concrete spirituality.' He relates it to the problem of power. Who are so thirsty for power? The Peter Pans and the Muscle People. Each of these delinquencies can be treated, Huxley says, and lead to eventual wisdom and compassion.

The sooner we start the better. But is Huxley quite fair to our philosophers? Surely our moralists, as distinct from our metaphysicians, are just as practical as the orientals, and doesn't Huxley quote some of them, notably William Law, very well in his *Perennial Philosophy*? In the context of the novel, these recommendations of the old Raja are an integral part of Palanese culture. As it is in any traditional religious society. It gives them order and structure. Because we seem to have lost these qualities in our industrial communities, Huxley feels compelled in creating his ideal state to restore them. It is the art of living and 'it is to be judged by what all the members of the community, the ordinary as well as the extraordinary, can and do experience in every contingency, and at each successive intersection of time with eternity'.

This is the freedom of the mind and the spirit, which our knowledge explosion has encouraged humanity to dream of again, it is the emancipation which the Existentialists preach, liberation by enlightenment, which with them is an awakening to total individual responsibility. The idea is inherent in *Island*, and this makes it a complete antithesis to *Brave New World*, where responsibility had completely vanished and awareness was regularly numbed by the soma drug. In *Island*, the *moksha*-medicine produces increased awareness. 'A century of research on the *moksha*-medicine', says the old Raja in his Notes, 'has clearly shown that quite ordinary people are perfectly capable of having visionary or even fully liberating experiences.' Dr Robert calls it 'the reality-revealer, the truth-and-beauty pill'.

We are given two examples of its use. First, before the service in the Shiva temple in chapter ten, in which Huxley expresses the longing of young people for enlightenment, now so evident among us. As Will watched, he saw 'the dawning illuminations of delight, recognition, understanding, the signs of worshipping wonder that quivered on the brinks of ecstasy or terror'. Huxley is at pains to repeat his theme of universality, expressed by the old Raja as 'Nothing short of everything will do'. In the sacred dance in the temple: 'Nataraja dances in all the worlds at once—in the worlds of physics and chemistry, in the world of ordinary, all-too-human experience, in the world finally of Suchness, of Mind, of the Clear Light.'

In the second example, Will is at last invited to try it for himself. We are given an imaginative reconstruction of Huxley's own experiences, which he described with careful scientific coolness in *Doors of Perception* and *Heaven and Hell*. Here, his purpose is not clinical but imaginative. It is the imaginative writer, challenged to describe what we usually say is indescribable. The pace of the prose increases, the temperature heightens. We are completely involved, as we fail to be in the Shiva temple. 'Ultimately and essentially there was only a luminous bliss, only a knowledgeless understanding, only union with unity in a limitless, undifferentiated awareness.' It carries us back to the original unity of the universe, before the Manichean duality, and it is the 'fruit of the ignorance of good and evil'.

Then Huxley turns to a musical analogy, as so often before. He takes the fourth Brandenburg and makes that the background for Will's mystical experience, the structure on which his experience develops. For Will now the music 'had been reborn as an unowned awareness' and now it 'had an intensity of beauty, a depth of intrinsic meaning, incomparably greater than anything he had ever found in the same music when it was his private property'. In his own actual experience, Huxley had tried Gesualdo's madrigals and Alban Berg's *Lyric Suite*. It was appropriate, in the heightened imaginative description of Will's experiences, that Huxley should rely on the more massive structures of the Brandenburg. Similarly, in the next stage, when he turns from hearing to sight and opens his eyes, in *Doors of Perception* he sees a chair and finds himself on the brink of panic. In the controlled imaginative reconstruction, Will expresses 'a kind of metaphysical terror' but his 'fear was allayed' while 'the wonder only increased'.

The comparison of personal experience and imaginative reconstruction of it can be pursued. In each, he speaks of jewellery and landscape. When we come to the crisis in Will's experience, when, after the music, he falls into an abyss of silence and infinite suffering and cannot even cry out, we find such an experience

adumbrated in *Heaven and Hell*, especially in Appendices six and
eight, especially in the extraordinary quotations from Thomas
Carlyle. But in Will's experience, the contact with infinite suffering
is immediately replaced by contact with the compassionate hands
of Susila, who brings him back from the abyss to the most delicate
and sympathetic love scene that Huxley ever wrote. Nothing is
made of it. No conclusion is reached and none is required. It is
the sustaining love of two mature people who have just recovered
from almost infinite suffering.

The brief, harsh ending destroys the idyll as quickly as the fall
of a guillotine blade. American imperialism breaks in. We are
led to suppose that Dr Robert and probably his assistant Vijaya
are shot. The ideal state was shattered in an hour by the totali-
tarians. What happened to Will and Susila we are left to guess.
Pala had no defence; that was known and accepted by her rulers.
Their only bulwark was their mental and spiritual training.
Whether any of them could survive with their integrity unimpaired we are left to conjecture. It is perfectly legitimate to
leave us to do so. A more valid criticism perhaps is that Pala
apparently had no administrative services at all, and this criticism
would apply equally to the brave new world. Neither Dr Robert
nor Mustapha Mond seemed to feel the need for a civil service.
A heavenly state, no doubt, yet in everything but the ideal states
of literature somebody has to look after things. The ignorance of
imaginative writers of administrative machinery is extraordinary
and most unfortunate. They could do so much to urge reform of
the utterly otiose. But writers know that the rule in fables is that
anything is allowed, even such a great gap in social machinery,
provided we believe in it, and while we read we believe in this
heavenly island, just as we believed in the hell that England had
become in *Brave New World*.

The novel has never been greatly liked. It may be that the
reader has to prepare for it in the same way as the author. For
those who have prepared for it by studying all the Huxley texts
which led up to it, the novel is a very adequate reward for much
study.

Texts and Pretexts

THE BEST ANTHOLOGIES are those we make for ourselves, and *Texts and Pretexts* is made of pieces which Huxley had chosen for his own use. The selection of English verse is as refreshing as the French, and the commentary is a development in the concept of the anthology. It makes it a viable organism, a developing argument, and it brings up the quotations in the same way as a skilful setting improves a precious stone. Fourteen years later, he published another anthology as a prop to our minds in very difficult times. *The Perennial Philosophy* is a commentary but this time the quotations are organic to the argument, quotations which strengthen this textbook for those who want to arrive at the true end of human existence. The second anthology is complementary to the first. His anthology on the art of living in this world was followed by one on the art of achieving the next.

In the Introduction to *Texts and Pretexts* he indicates his principles of choice. He says that science advances so fast that educated people spend their time keeping up, and 'seldom have time to read any author who thinks and feels and writes with style'. To be informed, one must read many 'merely instructive books'. To be cultivated, 'one must read slowly and with a lingering appreciation' the books written by men 'who lived and thought and felt with style'. Whether or not our poets are our legislators, they are certainly the aristocrats of our language, and in 1932, Huxley was providing for the Other Culture.

There is no more illuminating passage in all Huxley's writings about himself than the loosely connected paragraphs of this Introduction. One of them illuminates also the feeling of the decade in which it was written. He says it would have been better to write the whole argument himself, verse and commentary. If he had had the gifts of Dante, he would have done so; but 'Would even Dante's abilities suffice to inform our vast and swiftly changing chaos, to build it up into a harmonious composition, to impose a style?' This is the challenge of the knowledge explosion, and our poets have not yet succeeded in meeting it.

In another paragraph he speculates about our contemporary Ideal Man and says: 'Nobody, I suspect, will know (how to define him) until such time as a major poet appears upon the scene with the unmistakeable revelation.' He reminds us that the Ideal Man of the eighteenth century was the Rationalist, of the seventeenth, the Christian Stoic, and so on. But which of us will describe successfully our own? In the state of flux which a knowledge explosion brings, it is difficult to have a metaphysic. Huxley says elsewhere that we cannot live without one so, like him, we must await a poetic revelation, and use anthologies like his until it comes.

The anthologies are complementary, and we do not go far in *Texts and Pretexts* before we find a foreshadowing of the later collection, that concern for knowing about ourselves and all creation. 'It is only exceptionally, when we are free from distractions, in the silence and darkness of the night, or of night's psychological equivalent, that we become aware of our own souls and, along with them, of what seems the soul of the world.' This parallelism with the subject matter of the later book goes on for some time, until he comes to the great commonplace about happiness in the section on 'Country Ecstasies'. 'For all of us, the most intolerably dreary and deadening life is that which we live in ourselves. Happiness is to "become portion of that around me"—portion of the *essence* of that around me, Keats would qualify. We are happy only when the self achieves union with the not-self.' Happiness is being lost in something other.

Soon after that, in the section 'Man and Nature' we come to an analysis which begins a cumulating argument of great intensity. It begins quietly enough, with another allusion to our need of the poet, the artist: 'He discovers, in the dark, chaotic mass, veins of hitherto unsuspected treasure—new meanings and values. He opens our eyes for us, and we follow in a kind of gold-rush.' Nature, behind this artistic activity, does not change, but the artists see to it that what we see in Nature is constantly changing. He quotes seventeenth-century poets, those high-spirited gentlemen who talked in their natural voices about absolute values, and we feel the sense of flux coming through his argument, of everything being relative. Then he brings us back: 'We are not free to create imaginatively a world other than that in which we find ourselves. That world is given.' There is 'a thing in itself outside and independent of our consciousness, a thing which is unchangeably what it is'. He has just been quoting Blake, who wants things to be different: 'If the doors of perception were cleansed, everything would appear to man as it is, infinite.' Giving possibility of choice and change. We believe Blake, Huxley says, when we read him, because he is 'a great and most persuasive artist' and his gnomic utterances will turn the strongest head. But in the morning the cold light of reason prevails, as it must for all those who seek to open the doors of perception by whatever means. They will only find in themselves what is already there.

What we find outside ourselves can be terrifying, as he demonstrates in his next sections, beginning with the familiar passage from Wordsworth's *Prelude* when the boy took his boat out on the lake. Nature, Huxley comments, 'sometimes reveals herself unequivocally as the most terrifying and malignantly alien of deities'. He goes on to quote Leigh Hunt's sonnets on fish: 'The fish is for us an emblem of that beautiful, terrifying and incomprehensible universe in which... we have our precarious being.' In the next section he voices the just man's complaint against the universe: 'There can be no humanity except in an inhuman world, no virtue except against a background of Behemoth and Leviathan.' It is an Existential conception of the terrifying nature of the universe, those appearances through which poets can glimpse unchanging Reality. Good depends for its existence on evil.

After terror, calm. After the storm, the healing sunlight. Huxley turns to the earthly paradise, which is young people making love. Then a delirious description of Piero di Cosimo's *Mars and Venus*, and the mood turns again, 'the earthly paradise is always on the further side. Self-hindered, I cannot enter and make

myself at home.' And a few pages later, 'the earthly paradise
turns rancid and becomes strangely repulsive'. This is the chastity
of mind which marked the Edwardian Ideal Man. It is a quality
which has been treasured for a long time and is well expressed in
George Herbert's, 'I struck the board once, No more', a quotation
which ends the long section of sensuous delights. At the end of
his anthology of love poetry, Huxley returns to his original idea:
'Living is an art; and, to practise it well, men need, not only
acquired skill, but also a native tact and taste.' It is better to be
fastidious. Life must be conducted with style: 'My lines and life
are free.'

When he comes to quotation and comment on old age, he does
so from a great distance, from early middle age. He is horrified
by the 'insentient apathy and indifference' of old age, whereas
those who have arrived at that blissful state, find its indifference
one of its greatest charms and rather like the 'holy indifference'
which Huxley later praised so much. In the end, he finds a
defence against age which satisfies him. It is the defence which
the Existentialists and other philosophers in Europe propose and
it is quite simply, love. And this Huxley well describes as 'an
infinitely difficult art'.

He turns to public concerns. He has witty quotations on
England; George Herbert on Sloth (the English disease); Coleridge
on Committees; excellent pieces from Clough and Brome on
Money. He wonders, since money plays an enormous part in all
our lives, why it appears so little in literature. But if we look
about, the Edwardians were full of it; and we do not do so badly
today.

There is an interlude on literary techniques, a subject on which
Huxley expressed himself frequently, and always with fastidious
delicacy. Then, having recovered from the feverish excitements
which had culminated in the terrible quotations on The Worst
Side with absolutely no comment, he returns to subjects very
near the preoccupations of the later anthology. After discussing
the area of thought and experience which is beyond expression,
he has a section called 'God' and again there is no comment at
all. What need had he for comment when Blake expressed so
well what he thought himself? 'What are the treasures of Heaven
which we are to lay up for ourselves, are they other than Mental
Studies and Performances? What are all the Gifts of the Gospel,

are they not all Mental Gifts?' And again: 'to labour in Knowledge
is to build up Jerusalem'. Why is Blake so little known? Huxley
relies on him in this anthology as on no one else; and this is a
good example of how Huxley quoted differently from the run of
anthologists.

A section on 'Distractions' (a subject which will appear in
another connotation in the later anthology) gives him an opportunity of quoting another writer who fascinated him, Maine de
Biran, whose *Journal Intime* provided him with the theme for an
essay very much later. Maine de Biran takes the sensible scientific
view. Our moods depend upon our bodies and if they are in good
condition, we can be happy. Maine de Biran was sophisticated
and amusing, and what he says in this quotation, goes well with
the dialogue in *Brave New World* between Mond and the Savage,
published in the same year as *Texts and Pretexts*.

In the rest of the anthology darkness prevails until a pale Stoic
light breaks through at the end. He begins the section *amor fati*
by saying that 'man's intelligence... makes him behave more
stupidly than the beasts', simply because he is not intelligent
enough. Pascal is brought in again to say that we become exempt
from all the passions by being sick and Kierkegaard is introduced
to say that 'the difficulty is to become sick enough to be healed
by Christianity'. Most Englishmen fight their way out of despair
but Huxley plumbs the depths as gallantly as a Frenchman.
Under 'Misery' he offers: 'The daily dreariness mutes and muffles
the life within us till we feel ourselves hideously diminished, less
than human.' Under 'Escape' he offers a sentence like a blow:
'The world in which our bodies are condemned to live is really
too squalid, too vulgar, too malignant to be borne.' Then he
produces the escape. It is into the higher life, but there is still a
chilling reminder: 'There can be no higher living that is not
based solidly on an income.'

We are coming to the climax, the old Stoic formula for escaping
the vulgarity which is human bondage. 'Living is a process of
creation. Every life is a work of art and every spirit has its own
distinguishing style, good or, more often, alas, indifferent or
downright bad.' After that, we have the last statement on religion
in his Pyrrhonic phase, the last rejection of traditional western
religion before he found his own: 'Religion, it seems to me, can
survive only as a commonly accepted system of make-believe.'

Men accept it 'simply because they have discovered experimentally that to live in a certain ritual rhythm, under certain ethical restraints, and as if certain metaphysical doctrines were true, is to live nobly, with style'. This is the humanist voice we hear in *Do What You Will*.

The Travel Books

HUXLEY wrote three travel books. *Along the Road* describes reactions to his own European civilisation; *Jesting Pilate* offers lively and Pyrrhonic comments about a journey round the world and lingers in India; *Beyond the Mexique Bay* reflects the exuberant wildness and energy of Central America, and a later development of the writer's mind. They all satisfy the challenge of travel writing. The descriptions make the places interesting; and the comments reflect an interesting and attractive observer. Travel writing is an extension of the essay and depends very much on the way it is written; on style, which is a portrait of the writer. That is one reason why our best travel writing is about Arabia; the hot sand developed English characters.

Huxley's first two books were written in the twenties, when he was still the Pyrrhonic aesthete, an intelligence brimming over with comments and comparisons; a precocious virtuoso in managing our difficult language. The travel books connect with the imaginative writing; a professional conserves his material. *Along the Road* connects with short stories and *Those Barren Leaves;* *Jesting Pilate* with the curious diversion in *Point Counter Point*, discovering young Quarles and his wife in India and bringing them home; in *Beyond the Mexique Bay* there is a Scots doctor who appears in *Eyeless in Gaza* and *Island*—the aesthete by that time had become absorbed in the wearisome condition of humanity.

Along the Road

He opens *Along the Road* with the question, 'Why not stay at home?' He asks, because he has noticed that so many tourists are unhappy. One met them in those days, unhappy even in Italy, forcing themselves to travel because home seemed so good afterwards. Now, Italy is an Ortega nightmare of Mass Man in great human packages, American, German, Briton; while in those days Italy still seemed full of Italians. It was the Italy of Norman Douglas and D. H. Lawrence, as well as of Huxley, who writes well enough to quicken comparison with them. He has the learning and classical balance of the one, and something of the lyrical quality of the other. The seven introductory pieces of the first part are an aesthete's guide to tourism. They cover everything from the excellent advice that we should stay at home, like Emmanuel Kant, to lists of the books we should take with us.

The first part has the carefree mood of the traveller. He has detached himself from responsibility. He can look at the follies of men without worrying about them. He is out to enjoy everything that comes his way. He watches people and refuses to meet them, for that would mean getting involved. He concludes: 'With me, travelling is frankly a vice. The temptation to indulge in it is one which I find almost as hard to resist as the temptation to read promiscuously, omnivorously and without purpose.' There are various themes, amusingly developed, and his prose modulates and varies in pace to reflect them.

If the first part is virtuosity and fancy, the second is virtuosity of prose description. These quickly brushed descriptions of places remind us that this was the year of *Those Barren Leaves*. We cannot but notice that in Italy he is on his own ground, describing places which warm him because he understands them, while the cities of the Indian plain are alien and leave him cold. If the second part is a display of mastery of contemporary prose techniques, the third is of even greater interest, for it is an expression of Huxley's aesthetic philosophy. The basis of his values is expressed in a phrase on Piero della Francesca 'the man who painted it was genuinely noble as well as talented'. We see in these words Huxley's own values and his dislike of fashionable ones. His own are those he sees in Piero: 'I am attracted to his

character by his intellectual power; by his capacity for unaffectedly making the grand and noble gesture; by his pride in
whatever is splendid in humanity.' Genuineness, he says 'always
triumphs in the long run', even against the great charlatans,
touched with genius like Wagner and Bernini.

Tribute must be paid to admirable pieces on Brueghel and
Alberti in this part, and an outstanding treatment of Brunelleschi.
We have a fine tradition of art criticism in the nineteenth century
and the essay on Breughel proceeds to extend it. Consider: 'The
crowds who move about the white streets of Bethlehem have their
being in an absolute winter, and those ferocious troopers looting
and innocent-hunting in the midst of a Christmas card landscape
are a part of the very army of winter, and the innocents they kill
are the young green shoots of the earth.'

We are still very much in the nineteenth-century tradition, in
these essays. Huxley is the cultivated intellectual who appreciates
sensitively and has learned from many predecessors how to write
about painting and architecture. It is only in the last section that
he comes into the twentieth century, with its knowledge explosion
and its scientific and economic revolution. This final part opens
with the best bit of travel writing in the book, Huxley telling a
story against himself, how he was cheated by an innkeeper in a
remote valley of the Apennines. Again, we hear his forerunners
in his sentences. He opens as Hazlitt might have opened, he
grouses with a chuckle as Scots travellers did, Toby Smollett or
Norman Douglas. Then suddenly he remembers something. The
name of the little village in which he was stranded had an oddly
familiar sound—it was mentioned in Faraday's *Journal* for 1814.
For pages he discusses Faraday, his associates and successors. It
is a magnificent tribute, and its magnificence lies in its simplicity.
Faraday's *Journal* has no mention of Florence but gives two
pages to this hamlet of Pietramala, where he and Sir Humphry
Davy bottled specimens of natural gas. 'Faraday paid little attention to the works of man, however beautiful. It was the works of
God that interested him. There is a magnificent consistency
about him. All that he writes in his journal or letters is perfectly
in character. He is always the natural philosopher. To discover
truth is his sole aim and interest. His purpose is unalterably fixed.'
It is fine compliment, all the more telling for its simplicity. It goes
on for pages, gathering pace as the thought quickens ebulliently.

Faraday was always happy in his work, for he was able to do what he wanted to do. He was probing for truth, and he was able to 'contemplate the world *sub specie aeterni*, as a limited whole'. That was the mystical feeling and Faraday had it 'not perhaps in its most exquisite form, but had it genuinely'.

The reader is ready by this time for the break-through to the personal, but when it comes there is a sense of thrill. The direct address is so warm and quick. 'If I could be born again and choose what I should be in my next existence, I should desire to be a man of science—not accidentally but by nature, inevitably a man of science.' Even if he could be another Shakespeare: 'I should still choose to be Faraday.' What excellent reasons he produces. The artist must always begin at the beginning, while the scientist begins where his predecessor left off. The artist deals with emotion, 'and I personally would rather be subdued to intellectual contemplation than to emotion, would rather use my soul professionally for knowing than for feeling'. It is soon over, this twelve-page digression into science and the brief, passionate personal statement.

The next piece, 'Work and Leisure' develops themes which will be the basis of Huxley's scientific fable, *Brave New World*. Leisure, it would seem, is the ultimate fate of Western Man. Henri Poincaré and Bernard Shaw, Huxley says, thought that man would probably use his leisure to contemplate the laws of nature. H. G. Wells showed them, in *Men Like Gods*, conducting experiments in science and lovemaking. Huxley gets nearer likelihood by observing what the rich do. They play and make love, often by the Mediterranean, which is very like the developing habits of Mass Man. Tolstoy's ideas are introduced; leisure is an opportunity for work. But, says Huxley, 'Leisure is only profitable to those who desire, even without compulsion, to do mental work.' That leaves out most people and many of our people enjoy their leisure busily doing things for themselves and their friends. The average countryman is never idle. Huxley develops his dismal belief: 'intellectual development ceases almost in childhood; they go through life with the intellectual capacities of boys or girls of fifteen.' He says it cools our enthusiasm for education. He looks forward to leisure for all by the end of the century, and reminds himself that the nature of the race cannot be changed in that time. So leisure is likely to be bread and circuses and *The News of the World*. He ends his collection with essays on popular music and the theatre, food for his natural pessimism.

The essay has become a neglected form. The rush of progress has made it too expensive to print what essayists have to say, and we regret it even more than the loss of the short story. For it cheers us to listen to an amusing man of great intelligence, especially when he talks about himself. Huxley satisfies this desire in this collection more than anywhere else. He is talking about the great things in his own civilisation and we shall see in the next collection that when he wanders in alien lands among peoples whose civilisations are remote, he loses something of his tone.

Jesting Pilate

Jesting Pilate is written on a different plan, selected journal entries, rather than essays. What he has been looking at gives him an idea and he writes it down. Many of the ideas are for descriptions or it would be a book of maxims rather than a travel book. It is the plan Somerset Maugham used successfully in *On a Chinese Screen*. The opening pieces describe Bombay, and his thoughts reflect our imperial thoughts in the twenties. We had lost our nerve. We lacked the confidence to govern. So Huxley told the Indian how he could get rid of us. The Indian already knew and twenty years later events helped him. A very few thousand English people who had spent their lives fighting famine and flood, disease and ignorance, were withdrawn so that English traders could multiply. Huxley found India depressing 'as no country I have ever known'.

This reminds us that, in the hundred and fifty odd pages of this journey across India and into the mountains of Kashmir, there is very little about the Hindu and Buddhist philosophy and religion which fascinated Huxley so much in later life. It was in the Beverly Hills and not the Himalayas that he meditated on *karma* and *ahimsa* and *brahmacharya;* fate and compassion and chastity of the spirit. His life would have been different, if he had stayed in India among true ascetics. But that is asking a man to be quite other. Huxley was still the young western intellectual so he remained the cultivated tourist, skimming over the surface, occasionally touched to reflection. He explains his attitude simply later in the book, when he is in Malaya. 'One is all for religion until one visits a really religious country. There, one is all for drains, machinery and the minimum wage.' He was a twentieth-century western man strongly enough by the time he got to Calcutta: 'To one who believes that man is here on earth to adventure, to know, to try all things, to advance (if only for the fun of advancing, of not standing still) towards some quite unattainable goal of perfection, the Indian scheme of existence will seem unsatisfactory in the extreme.' It was not very long before he discovered that a not quite unattainable goal was central to the Hindu scheme of things.

For his fine descriptions of the Indian and Burmese scene we must be grateful. Our century and a half of occupation produced so few that are worth remembering. Hickey, Bishop Heber, a few glimpses of Macaulay's journal, Richard Burton, Kipling and, in our own time, E. M. Forster and Orwell. It is these last we recall as Huxley sails down the Hoogly and notices the sky. Both Forster and Orwell were eloquent about the sky which dominated life in the land of torturing heat and torrential rain: 'Above the flat plain of the delta the sky is enormous and peopled with majestic clouds. After these months lived under a perpetual flawless blue, the spectacle of clouds is a delight and a refreshment.' But as he looks back for the last time towards the great land mass of the Gangetic plain, it is the suffering and the desolation he remembers 'The mountains of unnecessary labour, of inevitable hardship and superfluous suffering, are piled up, patiently, higher and ever higher.'

He sailed to Rangoon and saw the Shwe Dagon pagoda, which was being repaired when Kipling saw it forty years earlier. He sailed up the Irrawady, as Captain Marryat had done a hundred years before; but Marryat had spent his time seeing great blocks of teak cut to stoke the boilers of his early naval steamboat. Two or three years after Huxley, Maugham sailed up the river to begin his lonely walk to Thailand. An eastern river is a fine subject for description, and all these writers show their skill. Huxley depends on description from now on. In India, he had been touched into reflection. India is the source of so much of our thinking. From now on, he remains on the surface, the gifted writer of descriptions.

In the second part he goes to Malaya; where he talks agreeably without having very much to say. In the third part he touches China and races through Japan. His reactions are significant; the vitality and energy of the Chinese, the unreality of Japan. He ends the brief part with a meditation on our civilisation as he crosses the Pacific, a meditation which at one point compresses into a sentence the essence of our anxiety about Mass Man: 'The modern civilisation of the West, which is the creation of perhaps a hundred men of genius, assisted by a few thousand intelligent and industrious disciples, exists for the millions, whose minds are indistinguishable in quality from those of the average human of the palaeolithic age.'

In the last section, he is back in London, assessing the value of his journey. When Maugham finished his long walk east through the Burmese hills, he was content to quote the words of an American he met; who had concluded that the heart of man is in the right place but the sooner he does something about his head the better. Huxley discovered that two old truths now had an apocalyptic quality for him. 'It takes all sorts to make a world' and 'the established spiritual values are fundamentally correct and should be maintained'. He spells it out: 'All men, whatever their beliefs, their habits, their way of life, have a sense of values. And the values everywhere and in all kinds of society are the same. Goodness, beauty, wisdom and knowledge, with the human possessors of these qualities, the human creators of things and thoughts endowed with them, have always and everywhere been honoured.'

Beyond the Mexique Bay

> Oh let our Voice his Praise exalt,
> Till it arrive at Heavens Vault:
> From thence (perhaps) rebounding, may
> Eccho beyond the Mexique Bay.
> Thus sung they, in the English boat,
> An holy and a chearful Note.
>   ANDREW MARVELL   Bermudas.

But Huxley was not cheerful. He began his journey in a winter cruising vessel, full of people with 'the imitation youthfulness of

middle age'; and he was living in the thirties, the most cheerless
decade in the century, heavy with doom. His reflections echo the
stoic severity of *Ends and Means*. He offers two main themes and
the first is a local one; the melancholy of hot countries. 'It was
six years since I had been in a hot country, and I had forgotten
how unspeakably melancholy the tropics can be, how hopeless,
somehow, and how completely resigned to hopelessness.' An echo
of his reactions after weeks on the Gangetic plain. Subjective,
perhaps, for he retains his melancholy when he gets to Mexico,
and we recall the dainty gaiety of Lawrence's *Mornings in Mexico*.
Most probably it was the decade. Lawrence was writing in the
gay, irresponsible twenties, when we did not have to think about
politics; Huxley was in the thirties, when politics were engulfing
the Western Mind. That is Huxley's second theme, the echo
from Central America to Europe: 'Central America, being just
Europe in miniature and with the lid off, is the ideal laboratory
in which to study the behaviour of the Great Powers.' If we want
to understand European politics, he says, we should read the
history of Central America.

The book is written on the same plan as *Jesting Pilate*, travel
notes inspired by new places and a different people. But, as in
Jesting Pilate, he has made some preparation for his journey. He
has read up the history of Central America and how it broke
away from Spain. He has read the suggested solutions for its
problems, by Chase and others. The nature of a people is decided
by the weather, and visitors from temperate climates who provide
solutions for tropical countries have not endured the weather,
which for generations has afflicted the natives. Huxley does not
fall into that error, and he saw that life for tropical neoliths is a
series of fiestas, with a minimum of consciousness in between.

In a sense, the book is a discussion of Mass Man. On the one
hand, the Central Americans, their lives managed on a balance
of prohibitions and orgies: 'the orgy-system of the Central
Americans, simple and unpretentious as it was, seems to have
been quite sufficient for their needs.' And on the other, the 'New
Stupid' as he calls them, the Mass Man produced by European
industrialisation, 'hungering for certainty, yet unable to find it
in the traditional myths of their rationalisation'. That early argument is echoed much later in the book, like so many others, when
he states that: 'A primitive is forced to be whole—a complete

man, trained in all the skills of the community, able to fend for
himself in all circumstances; if he is not whole, he perishes.'
While in the countries we are apt to call civilised, men are dependent on one another: 'All civilization, and especially industrial
civilization, tends to turn human beings into the mere embodi-
ments of particular social functions. The community gains in
efficiency, but the individual is maimed.'

This interdependence in our sophisticated societies has become
our problem. If primitive man withheld his labour, he hurt himself. If Mass Man withholds his labour, the whole mass suffers.
Mass passions are one of the main themes of the book. Naturally,
in the thirties, he approached the subject through race. And he
approached race from a discussion about the reasons for one
artistic tradition being different from another. Earlier or later, a
discussion of aesthetics would not have led inevitably to race and
so to race passions. He begins with the wars of Central America:
'none of them has had an origin which could possibly be interpreted as economic... They have not been wars of interest,
but of "political principle"—in other words, wars of pure
passion.'

Then he returns to Europe, where it all depends on the rulers.
They can rouse the people or condition them to peace. 'Rulers
who wished to do so could rid the world of its collective insanity
within a generation.' But in the thirties: 'War is the common
denominator of all the existing systems of scientific conditioning.'
He turns to the passions of Mass Man: 'hatred, vanity and the
nameless urge which men satisfy in the act of associating with
other men in large unanimous droves.' He analyses hatred and
points out, that it is 'more dangerous than lust, because it is a
passion less closely dependent on the body'. Lust abates after
satisfaction, but 'hate is a spiritual passion, which no merely
physiological process can assuage. Hate, therefore, has what lust
entirely lacks—persistence and continuity. Vanity comes next, the
vice that used to be encouraged by school history books. Hate
and vanity are complementary. 'Delusions of greatness are always
accompanied by persecution mania.'

What then must we do? He suggests a World Psychological
Conference, at which propaganda experts should decide upon the
emotional cultures to be permitted and encouraged in each state,
and the appropriate mythologies and philosophies to accompany

these emotional cultures. It has to be quoted to be believed. He comes in the end to the solution we all come to; the cultivation of individual excellence. If there are enough individuals they will leaven the mass and preserve it from complete self-destruction.

It is profitable, in considering a major oeuvre like Huxley's, to note the stage of growth of main themes. He was to become magnetically attracted to the study of human cruelty until, looking through his eyes, we can see human history as the record of the fiendish cruelty of man to man. He says here that Guatemala in 1840 seems to have been startlingly like Germany in 1933. All of us in the thirties became aware of the cruel possibilities in our nature, and became appalled.

The last part of the book is a troubled analysis of the opposition in the nature of things. There was a great deal of ugliness in Victorian England, he says—there are glimpses in the book of some northern industrial towns which are harrowing—so Marx fled from it into the future and Morris fled into Nowhere. Americans today, he says, fly to Mexico and Central America in the hope of finding primitive simplicity. Then reformers arrive among them, and write books on how to help the primitive. They recommend hygiene, for example, and what does that do but increase the population and villages become towns which become cities which become a series of suburbs and you end up with suburbans instead of primitives. Huxley is not for that; primitive man is whole and suburban man is a maimed creature, entirely dependent on his fellows surrounded by ugliness. 'Whenever men have the means to be vulgar they generally succumb.' The horrifying meditation on Mass Man goes on; we may not have evolved adequate orgies for him but we pour out trash to amuse him. War, we reflect as we read, has not solved the problem, nor has the knowledge explosion nor the economic explosion.

There was an argument then, as there is now, that education would dispel vulgarity: 'I doubt whether education can restore us to complete emotional and artistic health. The psychological, social and economic forces, now making towards vulgarisation, are too strong to be resisted by a handful of school teachers (themselves, incidentally, more or less seriously infected by the disease they are supposed to cure).' Then another of his unreal suggestions, this time from Morris; it would help to stimulate the production of handicrafts. Craftsmen are contented, fulfilled, and if we had enough craftsmen they would stabilise society.

He does not press it; he knows that we are faced with vulgarity: 'Vulgarity is the price we must pay for prosperity, education and self-consciousness.' He comes to the only possible conclusion for a man of his training and his nature, and as we read on in his books we see that he lives more and more in the light of it: 'Perhaps the wisest thing to do is to abandon them to their incredible vulgarity and ineptitude, and to concentrate all available resources on the training of a minority, that shall be capable of appreciating the higher activities of the spirit. *Il faut cultiver notre oasis.*' It is the decision of every intelligent man who looks at the ineducable mass and it is worth going to Central America with Huxley to listen to him at this stage on his way.

The descriptions which make up most of this book are like all descriptions; they describe the writer. It is concerned about human beings, concerned about truth; and when it comes to the atmosphere of the places he is describing, ready to be pessimistic. The prose is vivid, mellifluous without losing pace and at times rising to a lyrical quality. He is so much further on than in the earlier travel books, and this touch of poignance in his contemplation of the human scene marks it. He senses the sorrow at the heart of all matter, as in this passage on time: 'Indeed, any possible conception of time must be depressing. For any possible conception of time entails the recognition and intimate realisation of the flux of perpetual perishing; and to be made aware of the flux—the flux in relation to one's own being; worse, as a treacherous and destructive element of that being—is intolerable. Regular, one, undifferentiated, time goes sliding on beneath and through all life, beneath and through its various pains and pleasures, its boredoms and enlightenments and seemingly timeless ecstasies—always the same mysterious dark lapse into nothing.' On the Gangetic plain he had seen the eternal suffering of the human primitive; in Central America he saw in him the naked emptiness of life.

Proper Studies

'The proper study of mankind is man.
Placed on this isthmus of a middle state,
A being darkly wise, and rudely great:
With too much knowledge for the sceptic side,
With too much weakness for the stoic's pride,
He hangs between.'

POPE   *An Essay on Man*

THE BOOKS which provide us with the story of the growth
of Huxley's beliefs were written during all the decades of his
creative writing and not, as with so many imaginative writers,
when his creative faculty was failing. So we can trace the development of his credo from his earliest reactions to Mass Man in
Proper Studies to the much less rigid and more mellowed views
on politics and society in *Ends and Means* and on to the enlightenment of *The Perennial Philosophy*. It was a withdrawal from
concern about Mass Man to an immoderate thirst to explore the
frontiers of mental and spiritual experience. In the next decade,
the Appendix to *The Devils of Loudun* and *Brave New World
Revisited* demonstrated that he had not given up his concern for
humanity, far from it; but he had decided that the private
explorations merited his attention more. We can call it the oriental
side of his development. The oriental social structure had encouraged the few who could achieve greater awareness until they
were apparently able to extend the frontiers of experience. In the
West, Huxley says, we made our decision in the Renaissance
knowledge explosion to pursue our intellectual discoveries into
technology. We would improve the human lot in the material
world. Men would be more healthy and good health assists
spiritual progress. We would arrive at the same end as the orientals
but by our own means. Our Christian background made us concerned about every man. We must bring him forward, give him

an equal chance; which means that many people at the front are not as far ahead as they could be.

What Mass Man does with his equal chance we see all around us; and in *Proper Studies* we find Huxley's first reactions to the mass society in which he found himself. Anyone could see in the twenties that we were heading for mob rule, and mob rule ends in disarray and squalor. We have a social instinct for good order, and it is most strongly developed in the higher orders of intelligence. In Europe at that time, the reaction of intelligent people to the growth of Mass Man was on the one hand that of the liberal intelligence, such as Ortega y Gasset and Karl Jaspers, and on the other, the dominating intelligence, such as the philosopher of the Fascists, Vilfredo Pareto. In *Proper Studies* Huxley acknowledges his debt to Pareto and his essays show the debt. The idea of the rule of the élite appealed at that time very much to young men in a hurry. It still appeals; but the ugly twist given to Pareto's suggestion by the Fascists no longer disturbs us.

No one, says Huxley, can live without a metaphysic. It is not easy to evolve one in the turbulence of a knowledge explosion. In practice, we go to the philosophers and hope that they will prop our minds. We are fortunate that we are enjoying an age of fine translations so it is easy to fall back, as we have always done in this island, on the best that is being written in Western Europe. When we go to our philosophers, those who have concerned themselves with discovering a world view, we find that in general they discuss two trends. On the one hand, there is Mass Man; and out of our knowledge explosion has come a technology which can provide adequately for him. He can be pampered and controlled even if it comes to the extreme *Brave New World* situation. We are coming to a time when Mass Man can expect to live without anxiety or burdensome labour. He can be born without pangs, and die in a state of euphoria. His range of sensations and emotions can be circumscribed, so that his days can pass in an equable dream. He can escape from himself.

On the other hand, for those who want to extract all they can from life, there has not been such a surgence for centuries. We have become aware of the unconscious mind; at the other extreme to transcendence, we have discovered the unconscious, which can have such unrealised power over our conscious existence. In the field of transcendence, our translators have helped us again,

E

for we can all read now the oriental texts which describe the
secular methods of increasing the mind's awareness, pushing back
the frontiers of spiritual experience. When we read the oriental
texts, we realise that this is an aspect of man's capability which
has been thoroughly explored. We shall do well to get as far as
Hindu and Buddhist ascetics have succeeded in going for over
two thousand years. Nor are there any short cuts. If we resort to
drug taking to increase awareness, we can only discover as much
as we have developed in ourselves. So the knowledge explosion
has not given us anything new in this field beyond mapping the
world of the unconscious and giving impetus to our desire to
increase our field of awareness.

In *Proper Studies*, Huxley deals with both trends. The book is
made up of a series of eleven essays, independent but connected
so that they develop his ideas on the common man and how he
can be helped; and later on, his ideas on the nature and extent
of religious experience, which are to become the main themes of
Ends and Means and *The Perennial Philosophy*. In *Proper Studies*
he turns from his imaginative portrait of the decade to the bleak
intellectual and spiritual realities behind the forced gaiety of the
twenties.

By 1927, when *Proper Studies* was published, the shape of
things to come was not yet apparent; though we had Fascism to
show us what Mass Man was doing with political democracy. In
'A Note on Ideals' Huxley says: 'The rise of Fascism and of its
equivalents beyond the frontiers of Italy is an eloquent comment
on the ideal of political democracy.' Fascism and Nazism were
allowed to grow because they seemed too absurd to be taken
seriously. We had underestimated Mass Man. We were not ready
to listen to voices like Ortega's, foretelling a wilderness where
there had been civilised Europe. So in the fullness of time, Europe
became a wilderness, which could be miraculously restored by the
impulse of the knowledge explosion.

'The Idea of Equality'

The opening essay is concerned with Mass Man. Huxley has
said in his Introduction that he has 'tried to give an account of
what is', a full look at the worst, as it were, an exercise which
requires the highest intelligence. He proposes to begin, he says,
with individual studies of human nature, and on these he can

speculate about desirable institutions. 'Our democratic social institutions have been evolved in order to fit the entirely fabulous human nature of the eighteenth-century philosophers.' So, in the Introduction; and in this first essay he quotes Locke as saying 'with the calm assurance of one who knows he is saying something that cannot be contradicted' that man is by nature free, equal and independent. Where did this notion come from? Christianity spoke of brotherhood but not of equality. It comes, he says, from Aristotle, who was quite sensible in his *Politics*, for he was a slave owner; so he says that some are born to be masters, others to be slaves. It was in his *Metaphysics* he went wrong. It was a fundamental tenet of his metaphysical position that 'specific qualities are the same in every member of a species'. Essentially, human beings are rational animals, and that is the quality which distinguishes them. Leaping to the seventeenth century, Huxley reminds us that Descartes, who was not in the least interested in politics and 'concerned only with physical science and the theory of knowledge', agreed with Aristotle. At the beginning of his *Discourse on Method* he says: 'I am disposed to believe that (reason) is to be found complete in each individual.' This is just what eighteenth-century middle-class Frenchmen wanted to believe because they wanted a share in government. 'All men are equally reasonable. It follows that all men have an equal capacity, and therefore an equal right to govern.' And so we come to the doctrine of 'one man one vote' which we have discovered to our perpetual embarrassment has made good government impossible in Britain. We know perfectly well now, that most of our island citizens are barely capable of voting for a parish council but, as Huxley says, 'a metaphysic is difficult to kill', especially when it is in the interest of those who have secured power.

He concludes his essay with a list of conclusions which follow from the false assumption of the equality of man: that there should be universal suffrage; that the opinion of the majority is best; and one to which we are now abjectly committing ourselves —'that education should be universal, and the same for all citizens'. He then traces the story of the development of democracy from an eighteenth-century middle-class propaganda argument to its present status as a religion of the masses, which results in the almost universal pretence that Mass Man is fit to choose his leaders.

'Varieties of Intelligence'

Huxley's essay was written when we were beginning to investigate the kinds of intelligence, and learning how to measure them. We are apt to pretend that there is more of it about than there is. Man has an animal sense which tells him what he can do and whom he can trust. This was sufficient to sustain him in the simple relationships of village societies. When he took to living in towns, it was less easy to see who was cheating him, and he developed his animal cunning until he evolved the elaborate system of cheating, which is as much the true basis of British life as the sterling honesty which is its counterpart. Using them together in a system of double-think, we have emerged as a typical example of an acquisitive society.

Huxley's approach to the subject is scientific: 'I shall deal abstractly with the intelligence considered in itself.' He accepts Jung's classification into introvert and extrovert. 'The members of either type regard one another with incomprehension and distrust.' He is for peaceful co-existence so he discusses later how the two kinds can learn to live together. 'Men have to live together before they think; and to one who would live efficiently, peace of mind is of vastly greater consequence than logical consistency.'

It is a subject which has been studied intensely since Huxley wrote his essay, and everything he says has been absorbed into the common store. He moved on rapidly himself, for example by replacing Jung's classification with Sheldon's three types, as we shall see in *Ends and Means*. What remains interesting are the personal remarks throughout this long piece, which brings him into the family of Hazlitt and Montaigne. 'I have a great dislike of practical activity. I am interested in the external world, but only intellectually, not practically. My ambition and my pleasure are to understand, not to act; and when action becomes necessary, I grudge the time I must devote to doing things in a world I desire only intellectually to comprehend.' Languages are like lawns; it takes hundreds of years to bring them to this order of perfection. Huxley's normal tone in this first volume of essays, is well-mannered, straightforward and easy. The pace is equable, suitable to expository work; and he attracts us as an essayist should, because he is an interesting person, with sensible reactions to a difficult world. Society is in flux; a civilisation appears to be destroying itself, but is in fact becoming explosively something new, with almost limitless possibilities of social evolution.

'Education'

We have discovered a great many things about the intelligence, but we cannot congratulate ourselves that we have discovered how to develop adequate intelligence quotients in the island mass. We all know the ends of education, to develop good citizens and efficient workers. We all subscribe to the enlightened view that every intelligence should have every chance of developing its potential, for the greater happiness of its possessor. On the other hand, we suspect our governments as much as we suspected the Church when it was in charge of education. They cannot want us to be politically intelligent or we should sweep them all away. And is it really compassionate to develop the intelligence of the human animal doomed to live in one of our modern cities? For him, surely the later Huxley prescription of work fitted to his capacity, the soma drug and pneumatic bliss, is a kinder fate.

Here, however, Huxley is not interested in being kind, he pursues enlightenment. Which leads him to the same conclusion: 'The most we can hope to do is to train every individual to realise all his potentialities and become completely himself.' Which does not take us very often very far. We do well in our infant schools: 'The aim of them all is to teach the child to teach himself.' We still do well, though we should begin earlier to give the child with backward parents a more equal chance. After the infant stage, Huxley says, the trouble begins. Of course it does. Children are developing their differences. So education should develop the needs and interests which all children have in common and 'knowledge may be used to enrich ordinary experience, to test prejudices and conventions of conduct'.. The sadness of our society is that education must combat what is learned in the home and in the street.

Then comes the natural exhortation during a knowledge explosion; about using to the utmost the good brains available. 'The need is urgent. If we go on as we are doing now, we shall not merely fail to profit by the immense accumulation of knowledge which a few eccentric historical researchers and men of science have piled up; we shall carry our civilization headlong to disaster.' As we have done, and our anguish is not so much that we can all literally die together, but that we all live together in cities as we do. This is not a human way of life; it is rodent.

Throughout this essay Huxley is agreeably orthodox. He states the weaknesses of mass education with his familiar incisive skill. He becomes absorbed, as so often, in the latest panacea, which was then the Dalton Plan. He enjoys again the essayist's right to talk about himself: 'I have the kind of mind to which an academic training is thoroughly acceptable. Congenitally an intellectual, with a taste for ideas and an aversion from practical activities, I was always at home among the academic shades.' He has sound views on the lecture system at the universities: 'Lectures are as much an anachronism as bad drains or tallow candles; it is high time they were got rid of.' He advises Oxford and Cambridge: 'Students who are merely clubmen, snobs and athletes should be excluded.' He foresees the argument about the Two Cultures: 'ever higher and higher degrees of specialization will be required from individual men and women. The problem of reconciling the claims of the man and the citizen will become increasingly acute.'

'Political Democracy'

In the essay on 'Varieties of Intelligence' he said that western politics and morals were rudimentary compared with western science. Very few people are interested in politics and politicians are very careful to keep that interest on an emotional rather than an intellectual level. This may explain why any interest there is in political affairs concerns itself with national, rather than local government. Men are interested in the politics of their trade or profession, and the French have recently demonstrated that working men choose small group leaders sensibly. Beyond that, the trouble is that only dedicated people take an interest and they are often fanatical. When it comes to choosing members of parliament, he points out that proportional representation would lead to instability, and that democracy leads to demagogues, who are talented swindlers. There is another weakness in democracy; it is no good in a crisis, and a 'system of government which requires to be abolished every time a danger presents itself can hardly be described as a perfect system'. We echo that sadly now, when our technological advance seems to put us permanently off balance.

What alternatives are there? 'There is, after all, intelligence.'

And: 'I should be in favour of any system which secured intelligent men with a talent for governing to do the ruling.' Pareto again, all of us again, involving the kind of men who would never offer themselves to Mass Man for election. A section on aristocracy follows, and as he defines aristocracy, it would seem to offer exactly the kind of man we should like as ruler: 'A state that is aristocratic in the etymological sense of the term—a state, that is to say, which is ruled by the best of its citizens—must be socially much more democratic than any state we know of at present... True aristocracy can only exist where there are no hereditary advantages other than those of talent, and where the rich cannot claim to rule on the mere ground that they are rich.' He claims that aristocracy takes into account the unchanging realities of human nature and, that it is familiar to us in commerce and industry; and that the professions are genuinely aristocratic institutions. This is E. M. Forster's democracy of the aristocrats of the intelligence. Our administrators 'are definitely aristocratic' and certainly those of us who have watched them at work would applaud them if we could feel that they knew what they were doing.

The logic of Huxley's argument now drives him along: 'I have met members of parliament who, whatever their wealth or their powers of tub-thumping might have been, would quite certainly have been unable to enter even the lower grades of the civil services.' So let us provide them with a fitness test. This would automatically purge parliament 'of many of its worst incompetents and charlatans'. To make sure, he proposes 'a fairly stiff intelligence test for voters'. These, he assures us 'are political principles which ordinary common sense must approve'. Mass Man prevents such good sense, which is unfortunate for him as he may bring upon himself total rule.

'The Essence of Religion'

We shall watch Huxley becoming more and more concerned with mysticism, which is awareness of man's spiritual potentiality. Here, he is chopping logic with Professor Whitehead, who said, 'Religion is what the individual does with his own solitude' and Dean Inge, who comments that Whitehead's words 'emphasize the difference between the mere practice of religion and its *real* essence'. Having set about these statements with relish, Huxley admits that 'such religious life as I have is purely solitary' and gives it as his opinion that 'humanly speaking those who prefer solitary religion are superior people'.

He discusses the development of the religious faculty. It is like any other mental break-through. Like music, for instance. Once the new technical break-through is made, it is very soon perfected and we have Beethoven's symphonies and nothing greater ever appears. So with religious experience. Extraordinarily gifted individuals make the first step. Their technique is imitated and elaborated, and very soon achievement comes 'which may remain almost indefinitely unequalled'. The techniques of solitary religion have long been practised and never been surpassed. Mentally, we are likely to stay much the same for the next few thousand years, which means there will be few solitaries and many whose religion is sociability. He might have noted that the ratio of solitaries is higher in Eastern religions than in Middle Eastern religions. That will come later, when he has studied translations of the great oriental texts. Then he will develop the difference between the religion of Mass Man, and the solitary efforts of the contemplative to make contact with essential existence.

'A Note on Dogma'

He expresses it well in the next essay: 'The typical mystic has the sensation of being absorbed into God.' Again he is discussing Whitehead, and concludes that 'the beautiful simplicity of Professor Whitehead's theology is the chief argument against its validity'. It is a short essay, which demonstrates that the ideas which he will develop in *Ends and Means* and *The Perennial Philosophy* are already in his mind. He develops a distinction between the contrasting philosophies of transcendence and pantheism which he will abandon in later essays. They are 'the rationalization of two different intuitions'. Wordsworth had an awareness of being part of nature and reconciled himself to life by realising his place in the creation. That was his intuition. All men have the same sensations but they can have different intuitions and for an example of the intuitions of a mystic Huxley quotes St Teresa's account of the stages of ascent to God. Professor Whitehead is wrong, because he treats religion as he treats science, as if there were one truth to be discovered and formulated. But 'the intuitions which different human beings have had about the nature of God are irreconcilably different'. Every exploration of ultimate reality is solitary and may be unique.

'The Substitutes for Religion'

He turns from the solitary to Mass Man, who in the West has lost his priests. What has he got instead? The nature of man, he has already decided, remains unaltered. His needs are the same. So he discusses the genuine satisfactions of the religious needs of man, so that afterwards he can usefully discuss the surrogates. He catalogues the 'principal states of mind and action recognized as religious', a sense of awe, propitiatory ritual, asceticism, consolation and the doctrine of 'future compensatory states', absoluteness. Priests have a double function, 'mediators between man and the surrounding mystery' and confessors, advisors, spiritual doctors. None of the surrogates compensate for the whole range of religion, and man's religious desires are only imperfectly satisfied. This accounts for much of the restlessness of our times.

'Personality and the Discontinuity of Mind'

The essay is a discussion of Man's part in building his own personality. 'Man's part, not Nature's.' Our personality 'which is ours when we are worthy of ourselves' (he has been quoting Wordsworth), is a product of our efforts and the efforts of those around us. Our parents and teachers begin the work; and we inherit characteristics. All this we know; as we know that the mind works discontinuously because the body is perpetually changing its material. We are different men hungry and sated; on a May morning and in the dead of winter. The mind itself works intermittently; emotions come and go, and the unconscious balances the processes of conscious thought. There are very few unified personalities; and most of us wonder how anger can be controlled and jealous, suspicious thoughts kept away. Our aim is to train our minds to direct us worthily, whatever people say or do and whatever happens. Our chances of success are small.

The essay then develops to show the social framework of the twenties, within which the personality was to be developed. The point of life was no longer religious, but social success. 'A man imposes himself on society by doing well at his work.' That usually means being acquisitive and selfish; except in professional conditions, when men set out to work for others. At the end, he

E*

examines how the young in the twenties are facing life. This is
the material out of which Huxley was making his first novels.
Young people 'know that reason, will, intuition and covetousness
are the only valuable elements of the mind... They copulate
with the casual promiscuousness of dogs; they make use of every
violent emotion-producing sensation for its own sake, because it
gives a momentary thrill.' They are out for a good time and are
determined to accept no responsibility for their actions. In other
words, there were some young people then like some young
people now. Those of us who were young then may not recognise
ourselves in this indictment, and we seem to remember that more
discipline was possible then. Every generation gives the same
poor impression; and has the same fine potentiality. Every
generation of the young is the glory and the riddle of its world.

'A Note on Ideals'

This sermon may be expected to follow the last. The best
ideals are possible, that is, they do not contradict the facts of
human nature. But they are unrealisable, so the incentive to
pursue them never fails. Huxley is determined to be critical; we
are following ideals which are too easily realisable and when we
realise them we become cynical. Our ideals have degenerated; the
idea of Christian service has become American business efficiency
and so we come to that remarkable figure, Mr Glen Buck of
Chicago, who gave it as his opinion that 'almost the finest achievement of mankind is the very tangible thing that we call American
business'. Mr Buck's ideals are pondered and analysed at some
length; Huxley finds them something new in the history of Man.
It leads him to the conclusion that 'One thing alone is absolutely
certain of the future: that our Western societies will not long
persist in their present state. Mad ideals and a lunatic philosophy
of life are not the best guarantees of survival.' They persist.

'A Note on Eugenics'

He takes a text from Leopardi: 'The human race is divided
into two parts: some use oppressive power, others suffer it. Since
neither law nor any force, nor progress of philosophy or civilization, can prevent any man born or yet to be born from belonging
to one or other party it remains for him who can choose to
hoose. ' Nothing is more discouraging to the reformer than the
c

dogged determination of his fellowmen to refuse to accept any
sort of responsibility whatsoever. Eugenics could change that,
and it must be changed if man is to break through to a better life.
In *Island* man and wife chose the sperm of good men whom they
admired. Here, 'they will learn to breed babies in bottles', which
takes us as far as *Brave New World*.

We were very hopeful about eugenics in the twenties, so
Huxley is gloomy. If we bred out Mass Man we should have a
society of superior malcontents, for there certainly would not be
enough suitable work to go round. 'States function as smoothly
as they do, because the greater part of the population is not very
intelligent, dreads responsibility, and desires nothing better than
to be told what to do.' Orwell's beloved proles; the apology for
Mass Man.

'Comfort'

The essays have been serious. They do not acquire the force
of a connected argument, but a thread of connection runs through
them, and this increases their impact. Their greatest interest is
that they adumbrate the themes he will pursue in *Ends and Means*
and *The Perennial Philosophy*. Everything in the later books is
here in embryo. And here too are the ideas which will dominate
his fiction. But the last essay enjoys a different mood, like the
little comedy after a serious play. In this essay on our quite
modern weakness for comfort, he exploits the gifts which enter-
tained us so much in *Crome Yellow*. He is gay and mischievous;
and innocently so. His prose dances along. He happens on a
nonsense and develops it for all he is worth. It is clowning in the
best sense. He pauses to think and races off in another cascade of
agreeable nonsense. And back of it all is a good deal of good sense
and truth. The preacher has relaxed. We have come back to the
creative artist.

Ends and Means

'Wisdom denotes the pursuing of the best ends by the best means.'
FRANCIS HUTCHESON *Inquiry into the Original of our Ideas of Beauty and Virtue (1725)*

HUXLEY had the great advantage, first completely evident in *Ends and Means*, of relating all his mature work, imaginative and expository, to a conception of ultimate reality. Once he had a firm hold of that, he never lost it and his idea of it grew stronger and more firm.

His approach is patrician. In his opening pages he subscribes to the brahminical view of non-attachment. He is trying to find a word 'that will adequately describe the ideal man of the free philosophers, the mystics, the founders of religion'. He decides that 'non-attached' is perhaps the best. He is non-attached to his bodily lusts, his desire for power, his possessions, to anger and hatred, 'to his exclusive loves'. He is non-attached to wealth, fame, social position and even to science, art, speculation, philanthropy. And he is non-attached for a very positive purpose, so that he can properly exercise charity, courage and intelligence. In the Buddhist hierarchy of sins, and Huxley's philosophy of non-attachment is more Buddhist than Hindu, stupidity 'is a main root of all the other vices'. Non-attachment of this order 'imposes upon those who would practise it the adoption of an intensely positive attitude towards the world'.

He is patrician, so he does not actually say that his thinking is in strong reaction to the appearance of Mass Man in western industrial communities. But his revulsion is inherent in his approach to our social problems. European reformers have been

explicit, while in England it is one of our pretences that all men
are equally able to take part in social and political life. From
Ortega to Marcel and Jaspers, European reformers have firmly
stated the obvious, that the principal hindrance to the sane
development of our European societies, is the appearance among
us of Mass Man. Mass Man is moving, says Jaspers in 1949, in
his *Origin and Goal of History*, and this is a 'monstrous peril':
'Whereas the events of all former history had little effect on the
substance of humanity, this substance itself seems now to be in
flux, to be threatened at its core.' He writes of 'the inconceivable
horrors of abysmal mass existence' and describes the mass as
'devoid of specific character and cultural heritage, without founda-
tions and empty. It is the object of propaganda, destitute of
responsibility, and lives at the lowest level of consciousness.'
Jaspers, like the others, describes the worst in order to examine
how it can be changed, evolved into healthy, personal, social and
mental existence. So he writes: 'The question is, to what extent
is the individual and his intimate world... giving birth to the
new beginnings which may ultimately lead to the recovery of
humanity out of the mass.'

Twelve years earlier, in *Ends and Means*, Huxley was on the
same search, and he described the intimate world of the individual
in his three closing chapters. In the first of them, on religious
practices, he says something about Mass Man which brings him
near the views of Jaspers and the others. He says that most of the
founders of great religions 'have divided human beings into a
minority of individuals, capable of making the effort required to
"attain enlightenment", and a great majority incapable of making
such efforts'. For the masses, ritual has its uses, but the few will
remember that the Buddha listed ritualism among the 'ten
Fetters that bind men to illusion' and prevents them attaining
enlightenment. What enlightenment means to Huxley, he defines
in a phrase which illuminates his whole approach to life. Men
will attain enlightenment, he says, if they develop themselves to
the limits of human capacity.

Ends and Means, like *Proper Studies*, is about man in society,
and the solitary, seeking ultimate reality, is only discussed in
contrast. Only when he comes to *The Perennial Philosophy* is he
mainly concerned with the solitude and silence of the ascetic,
who withdraws completely from society in 'holy indifference' and

affects the world of men by his remote and non-attached sanctity. At this stage, he is considering religion as a system of education by which human beings are trained to develop their personalities and society for the better; and to heighten consciousness to 'establish more adequate relations between themselves and the universe of which they are parts'. He discusses the methods of worship; physiological, emotional and meditative. They can all be helpful. The physiological lulls superficial consciousness so that the worshipper may concentrate. The emotional can produce results with great rapidity. While 'the function of meditation is to help man to put forth a special quality of will'. Following and imitating a personal divinity gives worshippers strength to change themselves and the world around them; but that does not lead to the ultimate relation with God: 'the mystical union of the soul with the integrating principle of all being.' That only comes when the idea of a personal God is transcended as he describes in the next chapter on Beliefs.

In this chapter, which is the most important in the book for anyone wishing to understand Huxley's credo, he deals at some length with mystical experience. To the best mystics, ultimate reality does not appear as a personal God: 'It appears as a spiritual reality so far beyond particular form or personality that nothing can be predicated of it.' As usual in this exposition, he repeats what is important a little later in expanded form. He says that Christian mystics begin their career by becoming aware of supernatural personalities; they have been brought up to believe in a personal God. Later, they find that their awareness of a personality fades. The loss of the idea of personality can be so painful that he describes it as the dark night of the soul, in which it feels lonely and abandoned. 'St John of the Cross considers that all true mystics must necessarily pass through this terrible dark night.'

The purpose in stressing the absence of personality in ultimate reality then becomes clear. It 'testifies to the existence of a spiritual unity underlying the diversity of separate consciousness'. This brings us full circle to the opening arguments of the chapter about the unity in diversity, in the physical world. So there is unity in both worlds, but he refuses to presume any relation between them. Instead, he defines what is necessary if we wish to realise our unity with all being; man, nature and God. The primary virtues are necessary, love, compassion, 'and understanding or intelligence'. Once again he is insisting on the Buddhist criteria, which include intelligence. He concludes the chapter on Belief by reminding us that evil separates and goodness makes for unity.

His final chapter is on Ethics, and it opens with the restatement of this important proposition: 'Good is that which makes for unity, Evil is that which makes for separateness.' He does not take us deeply into the relationship between good and evil. That would not suit his purpose, which is to relate social problems to a theory of the ultimate nature of reality. Today, he says, we have no axioms, no universally accepted postulates, so our discussions of political, economic, educational problems are incomplete and can even be misleading. We must have a frame of reference to be able to discuss these things usefully.

The argument of the chapter in relation to ends and means is about good and evil on three planes; the body and its sensations, the emotions, the intellect. On the plane of the body, sickness is a sin. This belief has a long history, from *Erewhon* back to oriental contemplatives who emphasise the need of bodily health for spiritual union with ultimate reality. 'Awareness is the condition of any moral behaviour superior to that of animals' and awareness is helped by sound physical condition. On the plane of the emotions, he distinguishes the animal anger, fear and envy, and the specifically human emotions of pride, vanity, ambition, avarice. He has useful things to say about ambition: 'There can be no improvement in our world until people come to be convinced that the ambitious power-seeker is as disgusting as the glutton or the miser.' Huxley stresses, as elsewhere, a particular danger of the lusts for power and possessions. They are insatiable. Unlike the physical appetites, which end in satiety and fatigue, the craving for power is spiritual and is therefore 'unremittingly separative and evil'.

The discussion of the intelligence in relation to good and evil is the most interesting. Intelligence, he thinks, is one of the major virtues. 'Without intelligence, charity and the minor virtues can achieve very little.' It is used for coping with the external world and 'the phenomena of the inner world', the world of the non-self and the self. Very few of us are skilled in coping with both. The intelligence helps us in understanding ultimate reality, because it helps us to be more aware, more self-conscious and 'self-transcendence is through self-consciousness'. We must remember that persons are interdependent parts of a greater whole and we must succeed in becoming persons before we can transcend personality. 'This super-personal level is reached only during the mystical experience.' The most rare state of all is one which is 'rarely attained, but described by the greatest mystical writers of East and West, in which it is possible for a man to have a double consciousness—to be both a full-grown person, having a complete knowledge of, and control over, his sensations, emotions and thoughts, and also, at the same time, a more than personal being, in continuous intuitive relation with the impersonal principle of reality'. Those of us who have met such men in the East will realise how difficult it is to describe their faculty and how well Huxley succeeds.

Every discussion of ethics is likely to feature the weakness which interests the writer most. Huxley's discussion spends many pages on sex. It is all familiar and need not detain us here. Like everything else, sex can be good or bad. Excess is bad and abstinence can be abused. Gandhi was never tired of telling us that chastity was necessary for *brahmacharya*, but chastity can be used by Leaders because it makes it easier for them to induce hysterical frenzies. Sex is always a popular subject for discussion, but probably anger, which William Law dwells on, is a greater disrupter of social felicity.

At the end of the chapter there is a useful warning against the Puritan weakness for dwelling on past sins. The mystics say that it can 'result only in preoccupation with the self they are so anxious to transcend'. Obsession with our own sins is apt to lead to obsession with the sins of others. The better way is to make ourselves aware of our sins and stop sinning. A weakness of old age is to regret the sins we failed to commit, or to spend time regretting sins committed against those long dead. 'What we think determines what we are and do.'

That comes from the closing arguments of the book. It is impossible to live without an ethical code; and through that 'all the activities of individuals and societies are related to their fundamental beliefs about the nature of the world'. We are brought full circle to the earlier discussions by the statement on the last page that 'a discussion of political, economic or educational problems, containing no reference to fundamental beliefs, is incomplete and misleading'. We discover at college that all discussions very quickly lead back to God.

To live, as we do, in a knowledge explosion, is both inspiring and terrifying. The world of men has become so small that the stress upon us is very great. We know that all human communities lag behind the knowledge that has recently become available and our closeness to one another has made us sensitively aware that some lag more than others. Huxley begins his discussion of these problems with a chapter on the branch of preventive ethics which involves economic and political reform. The main source of evil is a lust for power. It can be overcome. Later on, he suggests how. Here, he sensibly reminds us that successful reform comes by stages, because it deals with that conservative organ, the human brain. 'The more violence, the less revolution' he quotes in the next chapter. It is on Social Reform and Violence, and it is a discussion of ends and means. Pressing forward zealously to Utopia, reformers are apt to countenance any means to reach their ends. The politicians who lead Mass Man are so divorced from the long powerful processes of natural evolution, that they honestly believe that violent reforms can succeed. The only reforms which work are those for which a majority in any society are ready. To most human beings, change is acutely distressing, so we should never attempt unnecessary changes or any great ones. That is the only way to reduce the dangers of violence to a minimum. The difficulty is in reconciling that with the advances to which our knowledge explosion attracts us.

The next chapter, 'The Planned Society' is very dated and we have lived and thought our way through all that Huxley says. We have had decades of planning since he wrote. It comes alive at the end when he reminds us that all reform must be by stages, or it will go wrong. We run the risk of planning ourselves into hell. Unawareness and stupidity are the deadly sins of planning; the selfish planning of nations for themselves threatens international chaos; twentieth-century political thinking is incredibly primitive; international relations are usually conducted with subhuman morality. In a note at the end he says that it is manifest folly for Britain to try to continue as a first-class power; and that was said before the trial of war. Much of our present misery stems from our inability to learn that. When shall we accept that in the realm of honourable values, first-class powers are not

distinguished? Powers should conduct themselves like people. If
they behave well and interfere with others as little as possible, and
only to be considerate, they will be doing all they can to promote
peace and harmony and progress.

In a brief chapter on the nature of the modern state he gets no
further than: there are few rulers and many ruled; the patience
of the common man is 'the most important fact in history'; habit
and inertia are extremely powerful. If we are to be delivered from
too much power and too much obedience we must have economic
reform. Deliverance must be far away, for he tells us that to get
economic reform 'we must change our machinery of government,
our methods of public administration and industrial organization,
our system of education and our metaphysical and ethical beliefs'.
Which could undoubtedly give us a brave new world; or something worse than we have now.

When he turns to centralisation and decentralisation his general
thesis is relevant today. We must decentralise to get nearer
responsible self-government. What he is really saying is that it
would be better if we were all more sensible about politics and
better equipped to take our share in government. The poet Auden
was saying the same thing at the same time, but recognising our
limitations. Most of us, he said, can choose parish councillors
but it is a little hard to expect us to do more. D. H. Lawrence,
who was hardly for democracy, thought that 'the working man
is fit to elect governors or overseers for his immediate circumstances but nothing more'.[1]

The suggestion is developed in the chapter on 'Decentralization
and Self-Government'. Huxley advocates group activities because
the mental life of a group is superior to that of a crowd or an
individual. He speaks of Mass Man. The crowd 'turns naturally
to the descending road, the road that leads down from personality
to the darkness of sub-human emotionalism and panic and
animality'. With an obvious shudder, he writes: 'To be a member
of a crowd is an experience closely akin to alcoholic intoxication.'
He quote's Lenin's contemptuous remark that wage slaves can't
be bothered with politics and adds on his own account that only
a few can think about large-scale politics. So we must concentrate
on groupings, and he quotes French experiments in organising
the largest industries into self-governing groups of never more

[1] Bertrand Russell: *Autobiography*, Vol. II, p. 21.

than thirty members. The French have consistently made more efforts to break up the lumpen masses than other industrial nations. The group helps to dispel apathy, and achieve responsible and active freedom. In his 1946 Foreword to *Brave New World*, he says: 'Only a large-scale popular movement towards decentralization and self-help can arrest the present tendency toward statism.' It is worth noting that when Erich Fromm quotes this Foreword in his *Sane Society* he puts this sentence in italics.

He discusses next, one of the major sadnesses of our evolving life which has since been much exacerbated by television. It is the decline of community sense. Even in the country, the telephone has made it unnecessary to see people and the motor car has made it easy to seek our pleasures outside our own community. In cities, we all know loneliness and carefully guard our anonymity. Life becomes so artificial that another danger has developed: 'The massacre of a few thousands of engineers, administrators and doctors would be sufficient to reduce any of the great metropolitan centres to a state of plague-ridden, starving chaos.' When he was writing, any hope for decentralisation was vain. The nations were preparing for war, which meant centralised effort, so that people could march united to madness and destruction.

The long chapter on War that follows is partly a revised reprint of articles which he contributed to *An Encyclopaedia of Pacifism* in 1937. It is a valuable summary of the nature and causes of war, but makes no positive contribution to our search for a sensible and peaceful world. At the very end of the chapter he asks for the impossible: 'Love and awareness—these are the primary, essential virtues.' For individuals these virtues are possible, but for nations they seem very far away. We can aim at more knowledge; and tolerance. To know is to be compassionate. And that leads us straight into the tenth chapter: 'Individual Work for Reform.' Throughout this chapter we hear echoes from *Eyeless in Gaza*. None from *Brave New World* where international problems did not exist. He says there is no need to preach peace to the peoples of the world; they desire it ardently. He quotes *The Imitation*: 'All men desire peace, but few desire those things that make for peace.' What can the individual do? It required the sort of courage that Anthony Beavis was given to say at that time that the solitary individual can undertake to sift ideas and build theoretical systems of good government, or become a propagandist, a disseminator. The masses and not the pacifists were marching then and the masses every so often are seized with a longing to march to their own destruction. Anger consumes the rational desire for peace.

Huxley was looking beyond the approaching years of European commotion to a period of sanity which could be produced by individuals and groups of men dedicated to achieving sane societies. He reminds us that groups must share unlimited responsibility, because that provides 'a liberal education in responsibility, loyalty and consideration'. This is like slipping back to the Middle Ages, which is absurd, for we must live in 'the hated world of the machines'. When we look forward, we must say that what the machines have made they must make wholesome. The men who work with the machines must become aware that the machines work very hard all the time for others. This is the difficult thing. Obviously: 'Unless peace can be firmly established and the prevailing obsession with money and power profoundly modified, there is no hope of any desirable change being made.' We may look about us and wonder how we can hope. Huxley hoped. He goes on advocating non-violent interference with the drift of society, of society at any time, and just then of society in imminent danger of war. He recognises that 'organized labour cannot be counted upon to work for peace'. Mass Man will hypnotically follow his leaders and if reform is to be achieved it will be in that part of society which produces leaders. He ends with a list of problems which must be solved if human societies are to be reformed. It is a list that would be relevant at any time in any industrial civilisation. Man has always been an imperfect social animal. He begins in the next chapter with Inequality.

This is one of the most interesting chapters in the book. He begins dogmatically by saying that we need 'intelligent co-operation between all members of a society' and that can only be expected when people inhabit the same world. Rich and poor inhabit different worlds, so abolish both their worlds and let everybody be comfortably off. He even mentions the limits of income, between £600 and £5,000 a year; multiply by four for present values and this is affluence for all. He goes on to psychological inequality, which is a still more intractable problem. He replaces the four humours and Jung's classification with Dr

Sheldon's somatotonic, viscerotonic and cerebrotonic, a classification he is to use for the rest of his life. The gulf between these types can be great, but they can meet, 'in the common world of action'. He would build bridges between the types. He would have reformers remove 'existing obstacles to free and frequent contact between individuals' and insists that 'new opportunities for contact' be created. He would even have people change jobs to increase their opportunities for personal relationships.

A man can be carried away by an idea and it is difficult to suppose that Huxley seriously meant a life of perpetual contacts and exchanges. In a sensible world we all get on with our work and have sensible relations with the people we have to meet and work with. Those of us who have managed things in town and country will agree that the countryman works with us more naturally than his town cousin. He does not make barriers. When it comes to leisure, Huxley allows that birds of a feather fly together. He also admits that a man 'has experience only of his relations with limited groups of similar or dissimilar individuals'. The word 'Society' is a meaningless abstraction, he says; and most would agree that few human communities deserve the title. Men co-operate in groups. They behave sensibly in small groups, and when they choose group leaders, they usually do so with good sense.

He is ahead of his time in suggesting that there should be fitness tests for managers and politicians. We are beginning to see that it is absurd to allow anyone to set up in business and employ men without having to demonstrate that he is fit to do so. But the idea that a legislator should satisfy us that he can do something more than talk and wear a label seems to remain repugnant to us. Huxley pays a fine compliment to the great professional bodies: 'A self-governing union of professional men, who have accepted certain rules, assumed certain responsibilities for one another, and can focus the whole force of their organized public opinion, in withering disapproval, upon any delinquent member of the society—such an organization is one of the most powerfully educative social devices ever invented.' That is magnificent, and it is just. We realised their power for sustaining professional excellence when zealous, but partially educated socialists came to power after the war and started interfering with health and relevant matters. The professional organisations combined to resist legislation which would endanger professional standards of work and conduct. That the legislation was passed and that standards were seriously damaged we all know, and that we have very inferior services we all regret, but the damage would have been very much greater and over a greater area if professional defence had not been organised. It was an important victory for professional standards over mob leaders.

Democracy has come to mean mob rule. Good government and Mass Man are the most unequal things in our society; they are irreconcilable; no bridges can be built between them. But it would help us all if our politicians would form a professional body which would require standards of fitness and conduct from its members. The safeguard against the Mass is the intelligence, firmly grouped against devaluation.

Huxley then proceeds to education. It was always a favourite subject with him. His writings have more outbursts on educational inadequacies than on any other subject. And certainly if we ever pursue the right ends by the right means, it will be because we have at last become an educated people. Unfortunately, teachers more than any other professional people are bedevilled by political and other well-meaning interference. Teachers are born, not made, and how those who are born to this most honourable work can bear to pursue it under present conditions is most difficult to understand. They are denied their proper place, which should be one of high honour; for their work is the essential basis of a good society. They are underpaid and they are overworked. It is unlikely that the strongest and best equipped teachers can function efficiently for more than three hours a day. Not if they are really teaching children who are educable. What passes for education in our over-lavishly equipped schools for inferior intelligences is only passing the time as quietly as possible until the end of the day.

The picture improves if we recognise the new literacy. Humane education is for the few in any community. For the rest, who cannot use textbooks, there is a world of literacy in drawings and plans and practical work. This world is often closed to the higher intelligences and, as they have supplied the curricula hitherto, it has been neglected. In this world, the common man is king and he provides the technologists who keep our cities going and all the communications between them. Our knowledge explosion has brought him into his own. We can move towards a healthy community by giving these studies space and status.

Every liberal intelligence will expatiate on education and most will sufflaminate. We all have our theories and few of us can teach. But Huxley is practical. He is concerned with ends and means, with the honest and intelligent conduct of human communities. It is something we must achieve because our communications have narrowed our great world into a struggling crowd. He knows that good social conditions are necessary for education; as we put it, just as much is learned in the street as in the classroom. He lays down that moral training is for freedom, justice and peace. When he comes to doing away with corporal punishment and tests and exams he simply notes that it was Lenin who tried that first and very soon there was a sharp reaction. The Russians very badly needed the best from all the brains available, so back came the discipline that healthy children respect and which healthy parents support, and back came the tests.

For adult social life, the chief purpose of education will be to develop the critical intelligence. It has to be developed against the politicians, the bureaucrats and the advertisers. Huxley, ever since his early copywriting days, was eloquent about the advertisers. He has brought us back to the Buddhists again. Intelligence or awareness is a basic social virtue as well as a primary need for the individual. Every child can be trained to capacity to use the intelligence he has and intelligence can be evolved. It will be as slow as any other evolution in nature, and any mistakes we make, Huxley reminds us, may mean progress lost for a whole generation.

All that Huxley says in this book is now generally known. But very little of it has been done; human prejudice and inertia have seen to that. So *Ends and Means* is still very well worth our attention, because he writes so well that he is always stimulating. He wrote it in response to the knowledge explosion and its balancing horror, the emergence of Mass Man. It remains relevant. Its eloquence and eagerness will help us to make the ideas in it effective.

The Perennial Philosophy

IN THE FOREWORD to *Brave New World* which he added in 1946 Huxley says: 'To-day I feel no wish to demonstrate that sanity is impossible. On the contrary, though I remain no less sadly certain than in the past that sanity is a rather rare phenomenon, I am convinced that it can be achieved and would rather like to see more of it. For having said so in several recent books and, above all, for having compiled an anthology of what the sane have said about sanity and all the means by which it can be achieved, I have been told by an eminent academic critic that I am a sad symptom of the failure of an intellectual class in time of crisis.' This reference to *The Perennial Philosophy* gives us the spirit of Huxley's explorations of ultimate Reality. It is not the pursuit of something exotic, it is the pursuit of sanity, of balance based upon an understanding of man's essential nature. For the perennial philosophy is 'the metaphysic that recognizes a divine Reality substantial to the world of things and lives and minds'. It is the Reality which is the foundation of existence, the value which does not change.

Right at the beginning of the book Huxley suggests that this is an area of possible contact with the essence of things which we never realise, because we do not try. We have spiritual faculties which are unexercised and unbreathed. 'In the ordinary circumstances of average sensual life', he says in the introduction, 'these potentialities of the mind remain latent and unmanifested. If we would realise them, we must fulfil certain conditions and obey certain rules, which experience has shown empirically to be valid.' A little later he says: 'this insight into the nature of things and the origin of good and evil is not confined exclusively to the saint, but is recognised obscurely by every human being.' If we would recognise them clearly we must be pure in heart and poor in spirit—by which he means we must have humility. Only those who have rid themselves of pride, greed, vanity and cruelty can come to the unitive knowledge of God.

This is the language of sermons and many chapters of this book, especially the later ones, give us all the pleasures of an eloquent sermon, denouncing, explaining, exhorting. They depend greatly on quotations, so much so that it is appropriate to describe the book as an anthology with commentary rather than as a commentary supported by texts. Many of his quotations come from the East, which is the home of the perennial philosophy and in recent decades we have become greatly indebted to scholars and learned presses for translations, sometimes first translations, of important texts in Hindu, Buddhist and Taoist thought. This opening up of a whole world of religious thought has become part of our knowledge explosion. We are equally indebted to translators of our contemporary European texts and for translating again the European classics. It enables Huxley to give us translations of Eckhart and Fenélon on the one hand and of *The Tibetan Book of the Dead* and Chiang Tzu on the other which read easily and vividly. We can realise how much good contemporary translations help by looking at the standard eighteenth-century translation of Jacob Boehme or even a nineteenth-century rendering of *The Cloud of Unknowing*.

Huxley's wide reading and the exertions of many translators give us a book which attracts us to the study of the true end of man, the unitive knowledge of God. It is the longest and the most important of the volumes in which Huxley attracts his readers to the usually unexplored possibilities in every human being, in which he expresses his dedication to greater awareness, to the exercise of every intellectual and spiritual potentiality in his being. While central Europeans were courageously uncovering the dark places of the unconscious, others, and Huxley joined them, were responding to the knowledge explosion by exploring the frontiers of mental and spiritual experience and seeking to extend them.

The date of *The Perennial Philosophy* shows that this search was Huxley's contribution to the rehabilitation of Western Man after the convulsions of the 1939 war. He knew, as all serious men knew, that western man needed propping up, needed steadying, if he was to recover. Earlier in his life Huxley might have turned to music and poetry, and recommended them as he did in *Texts and Pretexts;* but by now he had turned from the arts to pure mental and spiritual experience. We have seen the bias developing from vestigial indications in *Music at Night* and *Texts and Pretexts* to people in *Beyond the Mexique* and *Grey Eminence* and to fictional characters in *Eyeless in Gaza.* So, when the war brought an urgent need to repair the damage done to the spirit of western man (and his knowledge explosion had equally unsettled him), it was natural for Huxley to devote his great powers of reading and interpreting and all his inherited powers of preaching to the best that had been thought and said on the realities of our existence. He does it so well that anyone attracted to these questions will find it his most exciting book.

It is an invitation rather than a handbook. The only sure and safe way to explore the further potentialities of our consciousness is with a guru, a teacher. Without personal guidance it is difficult to begin, and easy to fail. An oriental ascetic would probably find the book inadequate. The Beverly Hills do not provide the same ambience as the Himalayas; western society is not unequivocally based on Reality as are the secular religious societies of the further East. Huxley remains too much concerned with man in society; many of the warmest paragraphs in the commentary are about the failings in our societies. He is, like most westerners, incapable of that 'holy indifference' to which he often refers. In the East, ascetics leave mundane things to God and pursue their own perfection so that they can become part of God. In the East, all men and all living things are moving towards that final end. In the West, we instinctively cling to identity, to individuality. That involves responsibility, which extends to those around us. The virtues we cherish most, courage, hope, altruism, love, are sensed by us in relation to others. Those who pursue the unitive knowledge of God within an oriental ambience go beyond these social virtues because they are becoming part of God. *Island,* Huxley's final imaginative contribution to these questions, shows how far he can go. He remains concerned about the good life in

society. Even death in that novel is a social occasion, because the
dying are being translated into the Clear Light and must be
encouraged on their way. In his own final moments, as we read
about them in the Memorial Volume, he was concerned for those
around him and not for himself; compassion and not transcendence.

The nearest western man gets to the idea of becoming part of
God is in the expression of the mystics and Huxley quotes Meister
Eckhart: 'I have maintained ere this and I still maintain that I
already possess all that is granted to me in eternity.' And Boehme,
when he was asked where the soul goes when the body dies,
replied: 'There is no necessity for it to go anywhere.' They do
not relinquish individuality, they enjoy the awareness of the
mystic, and it is to this increased awareness that Huxley is
inviting us. Awareness not of self but of the immanent spirit of
the universe. It is described as the Clear Light in the *Tibetan
Book of the Dead*. It is known as the Divine Ground to the
Buddhist. 'In Chinese philosophy it is the Tao as it manifests
itself on the level of living bodies.'

The reader who tackles *The Perennial Philosophy* for the first
time may find the first four chapters difficult unless he is acquainted
with the vocabulary and ideas of mysticism. It would be a pity if
this discouraged him, for after that the book becomes as easy to
read as it is rewarding. The opening chapters have so many un-
familiar words and ideas that it is like tackling a new science; and
that is precisely what the reader is doing. Huxley has a good deal
to say about this difficulty in the course of his book, it is his
favourite preoccupation, words and writing; and here it is the old
difficulty of the mystics, to find words for the inexpressible. To
use language which was constructed to deal with material things
for existences in the spirit. The ordinary reader will find things
much more easy when he comes to chapter five, on Charity, and
moves on familiar ground. All will be well at a second reading,
as so often, but the first reading of the opening chapters is apt to
be, much mystification ameliorated by splendid passages which
we can focus. Like this one, which is a good example of Huxley's
concern about society when he is discussing Transcendence. He
has just quoted a parable by that wonderfully commonsensical
Chinese philosopher, Chuang Tzu:

In this delicately comic parable Chaos is Nature in the state of
wu-wei—non-assertion or equilibrium. Shu and Hu are the living
images of those busy persons who thought they would improve
on Nature by turning dry prairies into wheat fields, and produced
deserts; who proudly proclaimed the Conquest of the Air, and
then discovered that they had defeated civilization; who chopped
down vast forests to provide the newsprint demanded by that
universal literacy which was to make the world safe for intelligence
and democracy, and got wholesale erosion, pulp magazines and
the organs of Fascist, Communist, capitalist and nationalist propaganda. In brief, Shu and Hu are devotees of the apocalyptic
religion of Inevitable Progress, and their creed is that the Kingdom
of Heaven is outside you, and in the future.

He continues to the end of the chapter on the theme of Inevitable
Progress, which he describes as 'the hope and faith (in the teeth
of all human experience) that one can get something for nothing'.

As we go through the book we can make for ourselves an
anthology of Huxleyan *dicta* on contemporary societies and world
affairs, those public evils against which he was continuously
tilting. In these vigorous pages we do not live entirely on the
frontiers of spiritual experience. The background must be prepared is what he implies, so that western man can seek the unitive
knowledge of God. There are more good things about exploiting
our natural resources, and then he turns to power: 'Of all social,
moral and spiritual problems that of power is the most chronically
urgent and most difficult of solution.' Then he develops the idea,
which is implicit in *Grey Eminence*, that the special danger of this
vice is that it grows with age. Physical vices often decline with
age, our vices leave us if we do not leave them, but mental vices
become more absorbing. He develops the power theme by saying
that 'no community that values liberty can afford to give its rulers
long terms of office'. This we know and would like to know how
to avoid it. Huxley reminds us of the Carthusians who elect their
abbots for a single year. That removes one possible abuse of
power, but the question is a morose one and many of us will
agree with Paul Valéry that no human being can be expected to
control a modern state efficiently. Our English democracy worked
when the State had little to do and when the rulers were elected
from a large effective middle class which could control them.
What we have now does not provide a sane and healthy back-

ground against which the individual can pursue the unitive knowledge of God.

We have strayed and the analysis of our complaint begins in chapter eight: 'And almost suddenly, within the last quarter of a century, there has been consummated what Sheldon calls a "somatotonic revolution", directed against all that is characteristically cerebrotonic in the theory and practice of traditional Christian culture.' (Sheldon had refined Jung's distinction of introverts and extroverts into endomorphs, mesomorphs and ectomorphs. The first two were extroverts, the one loving company, the other power, and the third was the introvert who had a passion for privacy.) It was Sheldon's mesomorphs, the muscle men, who were in control of the western world when Huxley was writing. They were a culmination of western man's decision in the late Renaissance to develop his mind at the expense of his spirit. The mesomorphs, with their somatotonic temperament, aggressiveness and love of power, used our new knowledge explosion to smash Europe again.

As a result, western man is still struggling to control his own technological virtuosity. At the end of the seventeenth chapter, Huxley says that this virtuosity has brought us into a world of wrong relationships, in which we do not recognise that we are all organically related to God, Nature and our fellow men.

> The results of these wrong relationships are manifest on the social level as wars, revolutions, exploitation and disorder; on the natural level, as waste and exhaustion of irreplaceable resources; on the biological level, as degenerative diseases and the deterioration of racial stocks; on the moral level, as an overweening bumptiousness; and on the spiritual level, as blindness to divine Reality and complete ignorance of the reason and purpose of human existence.

Very true and very well expressed. But if we want to seek divine Reality and a healthy social ambience is necessary for the search, we shall wait a long time. We must remind ourselves that in this world of good and evil sane and healthy societies have usually been spiritually dead. For a symbol of oriental transcendence we can take the devotee on the banks of the Ganges at Benares so rapt in contemplation that he is unaware of the seething mass of neolithic superstitious worshippers around him. In Huxley's writings, our symbol will be Anthony Beavis, on Christmas Day,

1934, noting in his journal that there is for him a fundamental
problem in the art of contemplation, finding suitable psychological exercises which will carry him away from mundane things.
He knows that there are exercises to suit every need.

> There is a great work to be done here. Collecting and collating
> information from all these sources. Consulting books and, more
> important, people who have actually practised what is in the books,
> have had experience of teaching novices. In time, it might be
> possible to establish a complete and definitive *Ars Contemplativa*.

The result of that note was *The Perennial Philosophy* ten years
later; and note how the necessity for a guru, a teacher, is stressed.
Anthony Beavis was living then against a background which was
anything but sane; but he lived like the rest of us under the
rules of time and could not wait.

Huxley admits in chapter ten that one of the most difficult
things is to cultivate 'holy indifference' to 'the temporal success
or failure of the cause to which one has devoted one's best
energies'. He offers a prop from Chuang Tzu: 'By a man without
passions I mean one who does not permit good or evil to disturb
his inward economy, but rather falls in with what happens and does
not add to the sum of his mortality.' Another difficulty is distractions—one of the great subjects in *Grey Eminence*. It is not
easy to concentrate. In a long passage in the chapter on Spiritual
Exercises he discusses the difficulty. We must never 'use violent
efforts of the surface will against the distractions which rise in
the mind'. Benet of Canfield gave the reason for this: 'The more
a man operates, the more he is and exists. And the more he is and
exists, the less of God is and exists within him.' Huxley's suggested
remedy is practical and simple. 'The distractions now appear in
the foreground of consciousness; we take notice of their presence,
then, lightly and gently, without any straining of the will, we
shift the focus of attention to Reality.' The whole discussion is
conducted with notable serenity and culminates in a long, magnificent quotation from Ashvaghosha's *The Awakening of Faith*. We
can leave it with the sensible recommendation of Fenélon:

> I would have you hold fast to this simple rule: seek nothing dis-
> sipating, but bear quietly with whatever God sends without your
> seeking it, whether of dissipation or interruption. It is a great
> delusion to seek God afar off in matters perhaps quite unattain-

able, ignoring that He is beside us in our daily annoyances, so long as we bear humbly and bravely all those which arise from the manifold imperfections of our neighbours and ourselves.

When western man follows the perennial philosophy, his most painful stage is giving up his individuality. 'Direct knowledge of the Ground cannot be had except by union, and union can be achieved only by the annihilation of the self-regarding ego, which is the barrier separating the "thou" from the "that" '. The perennial philosophy is not aware of separateness as an acute problem because we are all on the way to the unitive knowledge of God. Western man is aware of this separateness, and his pain is expressed in the forty-fourth chapter of *The Cloud of Unknowing*, the pain of aloneness, of separateness from God. It is the stage between giving up the individuality and being aware of being part of the divine Ground. Once we are aware of the unitive knowledge of God, all is well: 'For the individual who achieves unity within his own organism and unity with the divine Ground, there is an end of suffering. The goal of creation is the return of all sentient beings out of separateness and that infatuating urge-to-separateness which results in suffering, through unitive knowledge, into the wholeness of eternal Reality.' The subject is endless because it is the eternal subject, but one more of Huxley's illuminating sentences must suffice to convey an impression of the nature of the perennial philosophy: 'The completely spiritualized mind-body is a Tathagata, who doesn't go anywhere when he dies, for the good reason that he is already, actually and consciously, where everyone has always potentially been without knowing.'

Science, Liberty and Peace

THIS BRIEF ESSAY is part of the agonised debate among scientists after the atom bombs had dropped. How could they make sure that their part of the knowledge explosion would never be used for the destruction of mankind? In his imaginative work, Huxley dealt with the problem as horrifically as he knew how in *Ape and Essence*. Here, in the spirit of rational argument and exhortation, he begins by quoting Tolstoy, who had written, just fifty years before: 'If the arrangement of society is bad (as ours is), and a small number of people have power over the majority and oppress it, every victory over Nature will inevitably serve only to increase that power and that oppression. This is what is actually happening.' The Tolstoyan theme of working in contact with the earth, of decentralising to save mankind from disaster, is developed throughout the essay. The argument is based firmly on what he had written in *The Perennial Philosophy*. As soon as he had worked into his subject, he echoes the Perennial theme. Human beings have basic physical and psychological needs; food, clothing, shelter, and the chance to develop their mental capacity. 'And beyond these primary psychological needs lies man's spiritual need—the need, in theological language, to achieve his Final End, which is the unitive knowledge of ultimate Reality, the realisation that Atman and Brahman are one, that the body is a temple of the Holy Ghost, that Tao or the Logos is at once transcendent and immanent.' Towards the end of the essay, he returns to this transcendent theme. His argument is that man has been used for applied science and not applied science for man. He regrets that it had not been used for the 'benefit of the individual men and women, considered as personalities, each one of which is capable, given suitable material and social conditions, of a moral and spiritual development amounting, in some cases, to a total transfiguration'. He is carried away. We have heard him argue before that it is not by material things that man will move forward towards his Final End.

Here, immediately, he comes down to earth smartly and introduces another persistent problem which scientists discussed with the overtones of moral obligation: 'How are all men, women and children to get enough to eat?' The population explosion was foreseen and it was then thought that it was impossible to grow enough food. Huxley suggested that the best solution was to encourage farmers everywhere, so that every region could become self-supporting. If we relied on the great granaries of the world, we should be open to political pressure from super-states and in time of war food could not be transported. Our view now, is that the earth can support its huge populations but man cannot be trusted to distribute it fairly. We are a race of cheats and acquisitives and we must mend our manners if all men, women and children are to get enough to eat. It is not only England that suffers from middle-mania, those traders who sometimes never see what they are dealing in but live by adding to the price. Huxley states the moral problem broadly: 'Recent history makes it abundantly clear that nations, as at present constituted, are quite unfit to have commercial dealings with one another.'

Naturally, the Tolstoyan theme comes in again. If men grew their own food, there would be less cheating. It is when men are not concerned with crops, but with each other that the cheating develops. The nation of smallholders idea is older than Tolstoy, and seems to go as far back as civilisation. Those of us who have tried smallholding believe in it with obvious reservations. Physical labour becomes numbing long before we have grown enough and we find that we have neither the energy nor the leisure to take part in social and political affairs. The poet R. S. Thomas put it neatly: 'I am the farmer, stripped of love and thought and grace by the land's hardness.' The sensible smallholding formula was adopted by Machiavelli, who hired men to do the work and got

F

on with his reading and writing. Tolstoy followed that sensible formula and enjoyed all the advantages of living on the earth without the pains of excessive labour. But now, the arrangement of our society is so bad that a smallholding will not pay for labour. It remains an excellent retreat from the follies of Mass Man and his rulers, but it can only be enjoyed by those who enjoy living simply and quietly and have enough money to carry the losses.

Let us return with Huxley to his main theme, the problems of the applied scientists. They 'have equipped the political bosses who control the various national states with unprecedentally efficient instruments of coercion', and he means everything from tanks and tear gas to television. By doing so, applied science 'has contributed directly to the centralization of power in the hands of the few'. There is another aspect of the battle between the few and the many which we have seen a great deal of since Huxley wrote. The few are determined to keep things going and to progress despite the many. Mass Man has become more and more intransigent under the leadership of his demagogues. So the applied scientists, with their endless inventiveness make machines so that the community is served by reliable machines rather than Mass Man. The problem becomes moral at once; the machines get under the control of the politicians or the tycoons and there is far less progress than there should be. We are back with Tolstoy's statement again.

Huxley reminds us that technology is not only changing the pattern of our physical lives, it is profoundly affecting our mental climate. He brings us to a more cheerful area of the discussion. He reminds us that 'science is genuinely progressive. Achievement in the fields of research and technology is cumulative; each generation begins at the point where its predecessor left off.' As he pointed out long before, in *Along the Road*, every artist begins where we all begin with the art of living, at the beginning. In Samuel Butler's phrase, life is playing the solo part in a concerto while we are learning the instrument. Our trouble is that the scientists, and those who must control their achievements, are not doing any better than the artists. The doctrine of inevitable progress, says Huxley, is based 'upon the wishful dream that one can get something for nothing'. The Greeks, he said, knew better —and they had to cope with the first European knowledge explosion. They knew that Hubris is followed by Nemesis. We 'believe that we can be insolent with impunity'. We are on our way to the Golden Age, the scientists say, and one result of that belief is that it is reasonable for our governments to saddle us and succeeding generations with 'any amount of war and slavery, of suffering and moral evil' so that the golden age can come. We go back again to Tolstoy, the scientific victories over nature serve only to increase the power for oppression of our governments and tycoons. Huxley goes back to the perennial philosophy, which holds that man's final end is not in any Utopian future but in 'the eternal timeless Now'.

Huxley might have turned at that point to the distinction Karl Mannheim drew between ideologies and Utopias; ideologies being fictions meant to veil the true nature of society, and Utopias the dreams that inspire men and governments to collective action to change their societies. The scientists were making their take-over bid for control of our western societies so that they could achieve their Utopia. That had led to the debate on the two cultures, which Huxley takes part in elsewhere. Here, he concentrates on his declared theme; peace. When men invent weapons, they eventually use them, he says. The cloud of the atomic bomb was spreading after the war and it darkened all our lives for over a decade. We seem to have acquired the wisdom or the folly to forget it. We may do well to recall what Huxley says: 'The collective mentality of nations... is that of a delinquent boy of fourteen, at once cunning and childish, malevolent and silly, maniacally egotistical, touchy and acquisitive, and at the same time ludicrously boastful and vain.' Words can be a great comfort to those of us who have to bear our rulers silently, especially when they express our fears: 'the juvenile delinquent in some Ministry of Foreign Affairs will call up his colleague at the Ministry of National Defence and bang! the war to make the world yet safer for delinquency will have begun.' That was in 1947 and the writhing of these horrors is more demented now; gas, fission, bacteria, our applied scientists are busy with them all, working in a world of horror science fiction.

Huxley throws out one suggestion after another which would help to bring us back to sanity. He introduces one by saying that the only things so far given away without consideration of costs and profits have been armaments. Making them has kept people

at work and so kept great nations economically viable. He suggests
that we give away other things. This has been done and has been
useful, but we have found that it is not the answer to political
insanity. Some of his suggestions recapture the hysteria of the
time: little windmills would supply electricity for smallholdings;
Russian mirrors for solar power would give us independence
from petroleum.

In the end he comes to the question which has hung over the
essay all the time: will scientists permit themselves to be used by
politicians and militarists, or will they work exclusively for peace
and human development? He suggests an oath for scientists
similar to the Hippocratic oath: 'I pledge myself that I will use
my knowledge for the good of humanity and against the destructive forces of the world...' We know what has happened. The
scientists born of our knowledge explosion are no different from
other men. We have our Pugwash conferences, and we have
our Defence laboratories. If the men in them felt it necessary to
defend themselves, they might quote verses to remind us that,
in the wearisome condition of humanity 'If Nature did not take
delight in blood, She would have made more easie ways to good.'

The problem of liberty and peace has been increased by Mass
Man. If liberty is taken from him we can have peace; but our
liberty goes too. Mass Man chooses the leaders we get and the
hope of the western world is, as Ortega said in 1930 and as so
many intelligent Europeans have repeated since, that the European
community will unite so that there will be enough men of intelligence and probity to combine against Mass Man and those who
lead him. This is the best hope of the applied scientists in solving
their problems of social ethics.

The Biographies

Grey Eminence

HUXLEY USED biography as he used every literary form; it was amusing technically, and convenient for something he had to say. It enabled him to go further than he could go in fiction. In biography he could reconstruct the lives of exceptional individuals, who 'represent the wildest improbabilities, such as only life can make actual... truth is so much stranger, richer and more interesting than fiction'. These exceptional individuals were carefully chosen to give him a chance to discuss again the possibilities in human beings of evil and good, of sin and transcendence; and in the human race, the unalterable obsession with cruelty and depravity.

His first subject, Father Joseph, offered a particularly good example of the heights and depths to which the human being can go. As Father Joseph was *eminence grise* to Richelieu, we have a biographical study of Richelieu for good measure; and when Huxley wrote another biography he gave us not only the pitiful story of Urbain Grandier but also a study of Surin for counterpart and contrast. In each biography a good deal of attention is given to the background. In the first, the Thirty Years War, which illustrated the capacity for hideous cruelty in the European; in the second, the plotting to destroy Grandier again illustrated the human capacity for cruelty. In each, there is a study of a group of nuns. In the first, the Calvarians, very much in the background; in the second, the Ursulines of Loudun, very much in the foreground. Evil is better material for narrative than good.

Each biography provides the easy reading which conceals a great deal of study and thought. Huxley writes with his usual lucidity and grace and with that indefinable quality which gives his prose life. He treats his sources with respect and uses them with accuracy but occasionally, as in the opening of *Grey Eminence*, he permits himself to indulge in creative reconstruction. It is a short story of a familiar kind. A poor friar is making his way on foot to Rome. As he walks he meditates. It is pure George Moore. It was also an indication of the purpose of the book. His meditations on humility and love were distracted by thoughts of high political gossip and intrigue. Twenty-five years previously Father Benet of Canfield in Essex had taught him how to pray and still these distractions intruded. His meditation as he walked was on the love of God, but God had called him to play a part in the world of great events and concentration on divine themes was difficult. Here, as he is introduced to the reader, Father Joseph develops his meditation on love to a meditation on self-annihilation in the love of God: 'Die on the cross of mortification, die in the continuous and voluntary self-naughting of passive and active annihilation.' Distractions intervened again. He found himself thinking about the Pope's fears of a closer union between Austria and Spain and his anger with the French for ousting a papal garrison. It was from Father Benet, the Appendix tells us, that Father Joseph 'learned the technique of "active annihilation", by means of which he hoped to be able to disinfect his politics'.

This is the stuff of the opening and the closing of the book. Huxley always had the skill to conceal much matter in a deceivingly musical narrative prose. All we notice in the first pages is a threadbare friar walking steadily, thinking of things both human and divine and arriving at last at the Milvian bridge, where soldiers challenge him and, suspecting his foreign accent, take him to the guard room. The officer is vaguely insolent. He demands to see Father Joseph's papers. They are produced and the officer opens the packet. Astonishment and alarm! The first paper is a letter sealed with the royal arms of France and addressed to the Pope. The officer springs to his feet and pours out apologies. In the dramatic tradition, the Reverend Father does not spare his victim but humbly murmurs that the other papers are a letter from the Cardinal Nephew, one to the French Ambassador and a passport signed by His Eminence the Cardinal Minister. Complete discomfiture of the officer, who calls out the guard to line the way across the bridge into Rome as the friar hurries forward with bowed head.

This is the only elaborate imaginative reconstruction in the book. We have other glimpses of Father Joseph in which the man stands before us clearly, but they are historical, not fictional. Huxley, with conscious intent, was bringing his creative faculty to the service of biography. It was a much more serious purpose than this clever short story technique. 'The most complex events with which we have to deal are events of human history', he says, putting their complexity even higher than those we deal with in science. We try to interpret historical events for our own use, and that is beyond 'the capacity of the human mind in its present state of development'. So we over-simplify, which is fatal. Our interpretations become valueless. Everything is connected with everything else, and it is beyond us to see all the causes and connexions. 'This friar, for example, whom we have just left on the Milvian bridge—he seems, heaven knows, sufficiently remote from our contemporary preoccupations', but the book demonstrates that his life work led not only to the protracted horrors of the Thirty Years War but to our European wars in this century. 'He was one of the forgers of one of the most important links in the chain of our disastrous destiny; and at the same time he was one of those to whom it has been given to know how the forging of such links can be avoided.' That was the irresistible attraction of Father Joseph. Here was the riddle of a great and dual personality. Father Joseph was concerned to know God, as Huxley was. At the same time, he became more and more deeply involved in court intrigues and the international diplomacy which was so disastrous for the people of Europe. Huxley could not hope to find a better subject for exploiting his perennial interest in the extremes of conduct which appear in one individual.

The art of biography involves many skills. The prose which describes the childhood and youth of the subject is very different from the prose suitable to the description and analysis of the great events of history in which the subject is involved. As Huxley tells us about this child of a noble family he picks out the incident in which the child foresees the man; the child in tears as he describes the Passion. It provides him with the narrative trick of rousing our curiosity: this child was to become the man who taught his nuns to meditate on Calvary, while in public life he was doing everything he could to prolong the agonies of the Thirty Years War. That a man could do both at the same time is the riddle Huxley sets himself to solve. 'It is the business of the biographer', he says a little later, 'to discover why and in the name of what religious principle this potential John of the Cross preferred to become the right-hand man of Cardinal Richelieu.'

The young nobleman, known as Baron de Maffliers during his brief time at court, became a Capuchin. The order frequently attracted young noblemen by the severity of its rule, its evangelical poverty, and its natural contact with the poorest people. The Orwell syndrome, as we should call it now. For Huxley, the using of Capuchins in public life was the abuse of a spiritual force, a 'harnessing by evil of the power generated for goodness' and he considered it 'one of the principal and most tragic themes of human history'. This is the tone of the biography; a voice expressing tragic despair at the self-destructive instincts of the human race.

The life story is continued in the fourth chapter. There has been a long digression into mysticism which we shall return to, one of these digressions skilfully placed to keep the narrative from running away with the reader. It could clearly become too tense with the danger of coarsening into melodrama. So digressions modulate the main theme. We are led into them in the most natural way, they hold our interest and we may be forgiven for supposing that they were sometimes of greater interest to the writer than his theme. Father Joseph's early life as a Capuchin was exclusively religious. His reading was about mysticism and he began seeing visions, particularly associated with the crucifixion. He began teaching the techniques of mysticism to his pupils at Meudon and as the district was morally as well as socially disorganised by the religious wars, he began an evangelical mission round his district. He had a great success, and when he was transferred to Bourges his sermons were equally successful. He was invited by the prioress of what Huxley calls a country club nunnery of aristocratic ladies, to discuss the founding of a congregation of pure contemplatives among the nuns. He enlisted the help of a young priest who had a great reputation for ability and reforming zeal, Richelieu. 'Another link in the chain

of Father Joseph's destiny had been forged.' It was years before
the independent order was formed, but when the Congregation
of Our Lady of Calvary was at last founded Father Joseph assisted
the order for the rest of his life. However concerned he was in
the cares of state, he would break away to teach the nuns. At the
end, he was using them for his political purposes, using them as
a praying machine, using them to make his policies prevail; for
example, telling the King of their revelations, which neatly
supported the ideas which Father Joseph wished to impress upon
his royal listener. At that time, his reputation was of firmness,
mildness and humility. He saw visions, received revelations and
once at least, during a sermon, he passed into ecstasy and dropped
unconscious in the pulpit. One saintly priest at least was critical:
de Condren held that these revelations were aberrations of faith,
mere distractions that spoiled the simplicity which was the right
relation to God. At the end, as we shall see, de Condren was
again critical and declared himself incapable of preaching the
funeral sermon of a priest who had worked with Richelieu.

Father Joseph's first incursion into political life could not have
been more simple or meritorious. He was able to stop a civil war.
Marie de Medici, with her Italian favourites, was ruling France
as badly as if she had been a French king. The nobles rose against
her. Father Joseph, as Provincial of Touraine, saw their leader,
Condé, and then went to the Queen Mother and her army at
Tours. 'Father Joseph could play the diplomatic game with
twice the usual number of trump cards.' He was a nobleman and
could talk to nobles as an equal; he was one of themselves. He
was a friar, with a reputation for asceticism and revelation, and
so embodied the power of the Church. At Tours he was successful; and he also met Richelieu again. As politicians, they agreed
that a strong France was necessary, so the powers of nobles and
Huguenots must be curbed. On foreign policy, they disagreed,
Father Joseph wanting Catholic countries to unite against Pro-
testant, while Richelieu wanted to strengthen France at the
expense of Spain and Austria. After the Treaty of Loudun,
which stopped the civil war, Father Joseph was never able to
give his life exclusively to missionary work and mysticism. He
had proved himself too good at the diplomatic game.

As time went on, he became a person of consequence within
the Church. He went to Rome, stayed there for eight months and

F*

came away with all he wanted. One of the things he wanted was
the Pope's backing for a crusade against the Turks, which he
hoped would prevent a European war. The idea came to nothing;
the Pope's support was contingent upon Father Joseph securing
the agreement of Spain and Austria. Huxley's comments on the
idea are astringent. 'Father Joseph's zeal for a crusade was too
burning hot to be extinguished by anything short of a sea of
other people's blood.' When the blood has been spilled, what
then, he asks: 'liquidate the people who don't agree with you,
and you will have Utopia.' Then another comment on the nature
of politics: 'The results of any plan of action are always unknown
and unknowable; the plan must be pursued for its own sake, as
an end in itself. This is the bald truth about politics.' Social
organisation is so complex that results are unforeseeable. The
reactions of the human mind, individual and massed, are unforeseeable. It is here that history becomes even more complicated than science; the data are too involved to be traced.

When Richelieu became Prime Minister, Father Joseph became
his unofficial chief of staff for foreign affairs. In those days that
meant he supervised the spy network, another strange occupation
for a missionary friar. The Spaniards tried to corrupt him; funds
would be provided for any good cause he cared to mention. 'It
was the classic temptation, reserved for souls of quality.' He did
not fall. He wanted France to be powerful, he wanted his policies
to be powerfully implemented. His own power lay in his renuncia-
tion of it. The temptation to which he fell was in abandoning a
higher for a lower duty. We are each of us our own Satan, and
he is 'always exactly proportionate to the intelligence, sensibility
and spirituality of the individual in whom he is at work'. Father
Joseph fell to the temptation of believing that a disagreeable task
must be good because it is disagreeable. That was Huxley's
solution to the riddle of the friar's conduct. He groaned under
the burden of political responsibility—and that, for a man of
Father Joseph's quality, was the greatest temptation of all. Again
Huxley contrasts the friar with Richelieu, strengthening his interpretation of his central character by comparison with a greater
one.

Richelieu and Father Joseph served Huxley well for comparisons but in their work together they were admirably complementary. In times of stress and momentary weakness Father

Joseph was able to support Richelieu, for he had the will of the self-abnegated person which was 'a great river of force flowing through him from a sea of subliminal consciousness'. Again, a little later, Huxley refers to the mental training by which 'the conscious will had been systematically aligned with the subconscious' so that 'the power inherent in reality' flowed steadily through his whole being and he was able to give Richelieu the strength he needed. Quite simply, it seems to us, it was a matter of values. His values never changed, his training saw to that, so his will never weakened. He had accepted Richelieu's foreign policy, to unify France under an omnipotent monarchy and break the power of the Hapsburgs for the simple reason that it would make his own foreign policy possible. Together they framed a policy which would drag on the Thirty Years War.

Richelieu's policy was disastrous to Europe and its consequences are a good example of Huxley's thesis that it is quite impossible for statesmen to foresee 'the results of any course of large-scale political action'. Germany and the Rhinelands lost a third of their population, and their material losses were so great they fell into economic decline. Political power was taken over by autocrats and the rule of autocrats through an efficient bureaucracy became the traditional form of rule. The power of Austria was broken, which meant that when Germany at last united it was a purely Teutonic nation with consequences we know well. France, meanwhile, had made war on everybody and everybody had turned on her. She was a wasted and a ruined land; the ground was prepared for the Revolution. Huxley has an interesting comment on historical judgements—it goes with the comments of H. G. Wells on historians' sense of values. He speaks of the 'curious time sense of those who think in political terms'. Richelieu is held to be a great statesman because he increased the power of the Bourbons for a brief time. What he did to the peoples of France and Germany in the long term is forgotten, and he is not blamed for the resulting catastrophes of the nineteenth and twentieth centuries. Historians, when they talk of success, are thinking in terms of brief periods.

Father Joseph is held to be more guilty than Richelieu. He was not like an ordinary politician. He was able to go some way towards union with God. His teacher, Lallemant, recommended the least amount of action until the soul had been trained to give

itself completely to God. Therefore action was not safe except
for proficients in the art of mental prayer. St John of the Cross
had put it bleakly a little earlier: people who have not acquired
through contemplation the power to act well accomplish little
more than nothing, sometimes nothing at all, sometimes harm.
'Good', says Huxley, 'is a product of the ethical and spiritual
artistry of individuals; it cannot be mass-produced.' Yet Father
Joseph, insufficiently prepared by contemplation, went into
power politics, convinced that lasting benefits would result for
the people of France, which calls from Huxley a pessimistic
comment: 'political action is necessary and at the same time
incapable of satisfying the needs which called it into existence.'
It is as if he recognised that all his arguments for right political
actions in *Ends and Means* were vain things.

Huxley seems to argue that if priests go into politics, it is as
well that they should have lived long enough to have an experienced set of values. And this surely would be useful for all who
enter political life. Our ancestors, when life was simple, sought
the wisdom of age and experience in their politicians; now, when
life is so complicated that no one can hope to control it sensibly,
we lean towards youth and inexperience. It is one of the mis-
fortunes of our technological progress that political action is
necessary. We must try to cope with our machines and Mass
Man. In *Ends and Means* Huxley noted that war made totalitarian
rule inevitable. Now he notes that our industrial progress has
made it equally so. Totalitarianism is becoming necessary for
economic efficiency. Middle men thrive absurdly under our half
total English system; only under total control could our English
middle-mania be disciplined to serve us all.

Huxley writes to give himself opportunities for these beguiling
digressions. He returns to Father Joseph to note that as he worked
for Richelieu, his spiritual authority disappeared. Huxley bridged
his path from digression to theme with a note on the kind of man
most valuable in keeping a community sane, moral, efficient. He
is the theocratic saint and he has the necessary force because:
'His actions and all his dealings with the world are marked by
disinterestedness and serenity, invariable truthfulness and a total
absence of fear.' In fact, the kind of man who gets nowhere at all
in our great organisations. The working priests in France come
nearest in practice to what Huxley is advocating; it will be by

humble and anonymous efforts that the ordinary man will remain sane in our acquisitive societies.

Father Joseph came to be regarded with general horror. The end was inevitable. In May 1638 he had a stroke. He returned to his nuns; and the narrative of the quiet stoicism of his last days is modulated in accents of threnody. Eventually there was another stroke and he died. The final judgement on his work came from a saintly priest who was General of the Oratory, Charles de Condren. When he was asked to deliver the funeral sermon he answered 'that he could not, with a good conscience, praise a man who had been the instrument of the Cardinal's passions, and who was hated by the whole of France'.

Huxley chose his themes, we said, for the opportunities they gave him to range over his wide interests. There are two discussions in *Grey Eminence* which are so relevant to his subject that they are hardly digressions. One is art criticism, a brief appreciation of Callot's etchings of scenes in the Thirty Years War, which is a good way of showing the results of Richelieu's policy. As art criticism, it goes with the later 'Variations' in *Themes and Variations*. The etchings, like the later and much greater Goya ones, are first-rate reporting. There is an imperturbability in Callot's style, a 'steady preoccupation with formal elegance' which gives sincerity to his record of atrocities. He had the talent, Huxley says, to give his work sincerity: 'A man without talent is incapable of "honestly" expressing his feelings and thoughts.' What a bitter world it is; even honest expression is a gratuitous grace.

The other 'digression' is a much more considerable one and, like the first, is relevant to his subject at every stage. It is his first essay on mysticism. He will revise his views later, when he has studied the oriental texts more but here, five years before the publication of *The Perennial Philosophy*, he develops the interest which we found latent in *Proper Studies* and touched on in the later chapters of *Ends and Means*. Ultimate reality and ultimate truth exist and every man has the means within himself of getting in touch with them. At this stage, he is mainly concerned with the contribution the contemplative can make to society. At the end of the book he speaks of the 'antiseptic and antidotal functions of the theocentrics' and quotes Eckhart, a mystic who always returned to the world to preach. When Huxley has studied the

oriental texts he will catch their 'holy indifference' to social concerns, while he still betrays a western eagerness in his pursuit of
transcendence and the unitive knowledge of God. Here he is
concerned with mystics within the Catholic Church, whose
teaching was that: 'Once the contemplative has fitted himself to
become... "a man of much orison" (capable of self-transcendence) he can undertake work in the world with no risk of being
thereby distracted from his vision of reality, and with fair hope
of achieving an appreciable amount of good.'

There is another interesting difference between the views
stated here and those he developed later. Here he says that: 'The
nineteenth century could tolerate only false ersatz mysticism' and
goes to the nature mysticism of Wordsworth for an example.
Later, in his essay on Maine de Biran, a contemporary of Wordsworth, he speaks of nature-mystical experience with applause,
and confirms that view two years later in *The Devils of Loudun*
when he describes the recovery of Surin through experiences of
this kind. The road through nature is the most usual road to self-
transcendence and Huxley eventually accepted it.

The central figure in Huxley's essay on contemplation is a
Tudor priest in Essex, the Capuchin friar, Father Benet of
Canfield. He was a friend of Bérulle, an old schoolfellow of
Father Joseph, who had recently published a *Brief Discourse on
Inward Abnegation*. Father Benet's own *Rule of Perfection* owed
much to the medieval English *Cloud of Unknowing*, in which we
find the whole medieval development of Dionysian mysticism,
through which the early Christian Church learned of Hindu and
Buddhist mystical teaching. Father Joseph received his initiation
into the inner life from Father Benet, the master of the masters,
and all through his life he remained his disciple. His teaching was
traditional; that a spark exists in the soul, a divine element of
which man can become aware if he chooses to die to self. Through
this divine element he knows God, who remains Other. That is
the Christian view. The Hindu belief is that the creature, when he
is fit, becomes part of the One.

Huxley provides a close analysis of *The Cloud of Unknowing*
and *The Rule of Perfection*. *The Cloud* is not a beginner's book.
It is a handbook of mystical practice for experienced contemplatives, who must begin with a long-drawn process of moral
amendment, discursive meditation and training of the will. This

should be noted by those who expect any easy chemical access to mystical experience. The contemplative must train himself in abstraction from all creatures, above all from his own feelings and wishes. He may then proceed either to active or passive contemplation; in the active sort he beats upon the cloud of unknowing; in the passive sort, God is the agent and visits the subject. Huxley compares them to the higher and lower *samadhi* of the Hindus. The author of *The Cloud* assumes that his reader has sufficiently mastered his passions and has learned to shut out the operations of the discursive intellect which would only get in the way of any experience of reality. A further difficulty remains; 'distractions', which are irrelevant and pointless thoughts which cloud the sight of reality. Huxley, like all intelligent men who attempt the contemplative life, or even try to pursue a line of logical thought, was plagued by distractions. So his discussion is long and sensitive. Our psycho-physiological machine, he says, grinds away all the time, and all the time it throws up waste products which are nothing but imbecilities. For mystics, they are serious difficulties, intruding between them and reality. These inner distractions correspond to the outer distractions of the world, news, gossip, telephones, casual social contacts, 'all the diversified irrelevances whose pointless succession constitutes the vast majority of human lives'. Huxley eventually becomes so worked up about distractions—'Between congenitally distracted individuals and their distracting, imbecile environment there is set up a kind of self-perpetuating resonance'—that he breaks into verse. Not all his verses are effective. He was probably right to take T. S. Eliot's advice and stick to prose, but these verses are revealing. They show the strength of his desire to achieve the contemplative life. After speaking of man as a frivolous baby at the mercy of distractions, he speaks of

> *A longing to enquire*
> *Into the mystery of this heart which beats*
> *So wild, so deep in us.*

The enriched harmony of verse tells us more of the writer's personal feeling than any prose expression.

We have more distractions to contend with than Father Benet had in his time but human psycho-physiological processes have always been so involved that we have little excuse on that score

for not being able to achieve the 'one-pointedness' at which these
early English mystics aimed. We may claim that our education is
at fault. We produce healthy bodies these days, but we are
increasingly neglecting the training of the mind. Education is
largely in distractions, rather than the dedicated cultivation of
a disciplined intelligence. In the hierarchy of body, mind and
spirit, how shall we train the spirit to one-pointedness if the mind
is not a disciplined instrument? The solution for distractions is
some system of spiritual exercises.

One excellent rule, to avoid distractions, is never to recall past
sins. It should be taken that they are repented and the errors will
not be repeated, so to dwell on them is useless and in fact encourages egotism, which is the root of evil. 'Sin is the manifestation of self.' The teaching of *The Cloud* is that 'All men have
matter of sorrow, but most specially he feeleth matter for sorrow
that knoweth and feeleth that he *is*.' Is-ness is a barrier between
the spirit and God. What is needed is a selfless concentration
upon the experience of knowing God. It is a humbler view than
the Indian: not for us to become part of ultimate reality, but we
can lose awareness of self in our awareness of God.

This completes Huxley's consideration of *The Cloud* and he
returns to Father Benet and his *Rule of Perfection*, at that time
only available to Huxley in an Italian translation of 1667. The
book is about techniques for losing the self in awareness of God.
The desire of the mystic is to lose himself in the will of God. As
the book was then so hard to come by, Huxley examines it in
great detail. It reflects the English gentleness and joy in the
search for awareness of God. 'God's will must not be done in a
grimly stoical spirit, but in full inclination and a sense of joy and
peace.' In the charming Catholic saying: 'The saints were merry.'
There is nothing at all in the book about a whole class of very
important actions; those which individuals perform for nation,
church, political party, for business or family. It is there that
moral problems become difficult and Father Joseph, when he
studied *The Rule*, got no guidance.

Father Joseph clung to the idea of annihilation, which is 'the
final, consummating stage of the long-drawn process of getting
rid of self-will'. As we have seen, he struggled to perfect this
difficult technique so that he could clear his mind of all his
political concerns and be able to contemplate the divine essence.

There are two kinds of annihilation, says Father Benet, passive
and active. In passive annihilation God comes to us while we are
in meditation. It is the active sort which concerned Father
Joseph, for it meant being dead to the world while working in it.
The right relationship between man in time and God in eternity
'is discussed at length and with great subtlety'. The contemplative
at this advanced stage must not shrink from working in the
world. Once he has gone through the early stages of training and
achieved awareness, he can and should fulfil his life in the ordinary
world. For God is everywhere. The experienced contemplative
'must live continuously in the abyss of the divine essence and in
the absolute nothingness of things'. This, says Huxley, is 'probably
the most difficult and exacting of human tasks'. The reward is
'the experience of living simultaneously in time and eternity,
among men and in God; the peace and bliss, here in this earthly
life, of the beatific vision'. He claims that oriental mystics agree
that this is the most perfect condition to which the human being
can attain. We have seen that Father Joseph found it beyond him.
The excitement of his political distractions would come breaking
in. It would seem in practice that the contemplative can return
to the world to offer simple service to his fellowmen, but to enter
fully into the complexities of modern life would be to attempt too
much. There are limits to the extremes at which men can live.
The contemplative is under no obligation to return; he makes
sufficient contribution to society by the quality of his life.

At one point Father Benet leaves traditional mysticism, and it
is here that Father Joseph most gladly followed him. He has the
specifically Catholic idea of meditating on the sufferings of Christ.
Father Benet, a true mystic, turns back from ultimate reality
towards a particular moment of time. Father Joseph followed him
when he wrote his *Introduction to the Spiritual Life*. Both books
were forgotten, but the teaching was spread widely by Bérulle;
and there were Father Joseph's Calvarians. Huxley could never
be sympathetic to this addition to traditional mysticism. He had
already shown how repulsive the idea of atonement was to him;
what kind of God would require atonement? He was attracted to
mysticism as a non-Christian, free of dogmas 'contingent upon
ill-established and arbitrarily interpreted historical facts'. He was
for the Dionysians, who had ceased to be specifically Catholic
and who said, through the author of *The Cloud*: 'Virtue is naught

else but an ordered and measured affection, plainly directed unto God Himself.' Huxley concludes that the result of Bérulle's teaching was disastrous. Mysticism disappeared from the Church until the end of the nineteenth century.

Father Joseph, then, did not do very well. His public policies were disastrous for Europe and his religious teaching was disastrous for the nuns. Not a hero; and not a success story. But what an opportunity for a writer to reconstruct moments in the European savagery, to philosophise over history, to discuss some etchings and to write a short treatise on European mysticism. As usual, his presentation is brilliantly successful. The prose takes on the necessary pace and tone for biography, historical narrative, art criticism, religious and mystical exposition. He has notably extended the range of his character drawing. When he returned to biography eleven years later, taking for subject incidents in a small town just mentioned in *Grey Eminence*, the story ends not in disaster but in triumph. All men have the spark which enables them to be fired with the knowledge of ultimate reality, he says in *Grey Eminence*. In *The Devils of Loudun* Surin recovers from the knowledge of great evil to awareness of ultimate reality.

The Devils of Loudun

The characters in this second biography are much less important people, so Huxley is able to give it the fine quality of those studies of the human condition which take an Olympian view. Detached, and from a great distance, the narrator looks down on the human scene, focuses on a tiny place at a particular moment and describes the obscene human antics that are going on. The book was written when we had become intensely aware of the evil in the human condition. When the German concentration camps were uncovered, we learned that we were no better than we had been in the Thirty Years War. Our liberal illusions were destroyed, and we were in a mood to examine human depravity again so that we should know the worst. It took many years for the ugly passions of war to be brought under control. Enlightened men everywhere struggled that the better part of man should prevail, and Huxley devoted his efforts to this study of Good-and-evil in which he shows how man case rise out of evil to transcendence. Man can stand with his feet in the sewer and his head among the stars.

The Devils of Loudun tells the life stories of two Jesuit priests in the early seventeenth century and of the Prioress who so deeply affected their lives. Their relationship was a triangle of a very strange kind. The first half of the book concentrates on the story of Urbain Grandier, parish priest of Loudun, who was eventually tortured with horrifying ferocity and burned alive because of the false witness against him of the Prioress and her nuns. The nuns suffered from the hysteria which is endemic in any closed community of females, aggravated by the attentions of exorcists and this is enthusiastically described in the first half. The honest critic can only commend the reader to consider before he begins this book how much vivid description of human depravity and torture he can endure. The compensation is the gradual change of atmosphere after the death of Grandier, when the interest focuses on Jean-Joseph Surin, who had been his fellow student with the Jesuits. When Surin became the spiritual director of the nuns, he set about saving them from the quack-priests who had cultivated their demoniac states. The cost was high; the exorcists died one by one of their own satanism and Surin very nearly died of their contaminating influence. He lay paralysed by psychosomatic disorders for ten years, and then recovered when the cruel treatment of the insane of those times was replaced by the compassionate encouragement of a friendly priest. As he had saved the nuns, he in his turn was saved. Surin proceeded to the kind of transcendence Huxley described two years earlier in his essay on Maine de Biran, a kind which by that time appealed to him strongly, and which is familiar to us in Wordsworth. It was an experience of complete at-oneness with Nature, visions of a unitive knowledge of Nature, and through Nature of God.

At that time the Church denied nature, regarded it as evil, thus making a difficulty for itself which the religions of the Middle East and Far East had avoided. The solitude and silence of the desert or the remote Himalayas cleanse the spirit and open it to divine communication. For solitude is a fullness, not isolation. It may be that the desert and the high remote mountains induced a more spiritual communion, but it was of the same order as the experience of Boehme, who was aware that we need not go anywhere to find the Eternal, it is here and now. The landscapes of western Europe have been the ambience of our condition until we denied ourselves the support of nature by living in cities; and it has usually been through contemplation in natural surroundings that our mystics have found a unitive knowledge of God. The most moving description in this book is of Surin rising from his sick-bed on an autumn day after many years and managing to walk into the garden and trail through the fallen brown leaves. It is an eloquent recantation of the statement in *Grey Eminence* that Wordsworthian mysticism is ersatz.

The longer biography, of Grandier, is an account of worldly life. This parish priest was vain, quarrelsome and lecherous, and by malign influence he suffered torture and death for mistakes he had never made, and sins he had never committed. This study of his life and death is a description of rank evil and it is soaked in an atmosphere of psychological depravity. Huxley, as usual, has found a subject which will exercise his skills. He has found a group of people whose actions are beyond the range of fiction. When he was quarrying happily in Brémond's *Histoire Littéraire du Sentiment Réligieux en France* for material for *Grey Eminence* he came upon a story which led him to the curious literature of the happenings in Loudun in the 1630s. There he found enough material on which to develop his three characters, and more than enough to supply digressions on the manners and beliefs of the times.

So he is able to give us a meticulously careful structure of narrative, description and reflection. The first two chapters are the life of Grandier, introduced as Father Joseph is introduced in *Grey Eminence*, but without the short story bravura. He is riding into Loudun to his new home. A little cloud no bigger than a man's hand is painted into the scene. We are reminded that he was living in the grey dawn of the Era of Respectability, whereas for centuries before it was recognised that clergymen were thoroughly disreputable. Grandier meant to enjoy his parish work which included enjoying pretty women. He was handsome, the women liked him; but from the first the men had grudges against him. They had wanted a local man for priest; Grandier introduced his relations to sinecures; aristocratic doors were soon open to him, so envy exacerbated the grudges. He never made any effort to conciliate enemies; he even irritated Richelieu by claiming precedence in a local procession. The pattern of his existence was eloquent preaching, consoling pretty widows, evenings with intellectual friends, and quarrelling with an ever-widening circle of enemies.

The end of the first chapter describes the seduction of a young girl and her ruin. The second chapter opens with her father becoming an implacable enemy. Then, for relief, there is a description of an apothecary's shop which dissolves into another love story, equally familiar in kind. The seducer falls in love with the girl he wants to seduce and we have the curious secret marriage ceremony, in which Grandier is at once priest and husband. His enemies combine against him, he is arrested but the case is not successful. The chapter ends with Grandier in much more serious difficulty. He was acting as local governor for a friend D'Armagnac, when Richelieu wanted agreement to raze the local castle, and he had the temerity to refuse permission. To strengthen the central power Richelieu was eliminating local strongholds. In Loudun he soon had his way and made a note that the local priest must be dealt with when occasion offered. Fate is moving on Grandier from all sides as in the oriental game of chess, when one player slowly and inexorably paralyses and smothers his opponent.

The book would fall into separate parts if the story of Grandier was concluded at once, so chapter three is given to Surin, who arrived in Loudun years after Grandier's ashes had been scattered to the winds. Surin is a completely contrasting figure. As an acolyte, he had had a vision of the essential nature of God and he spent his life resisting the joys of the flesh and seeking to attain Christian perfection. We have a long digression about the urge to self-transcendence, which marks a stage in Huxley's thought between *The Perennial Philosophy* and *The Doors of Perception*. It is on the theme that obscurely we know who we are and we have a passionate desire to escape from the imprisoning ego. At the beginning of the seventeenth century Jesuits were encouraged to seek this escape through quiet meditation. Surin studied the necessary exercises under Lallemant and they were both drawn to an extreme ascetism, which helped them to obtain extraordinary graces. At this stage, non-human nature had no place in Surin's philosophy, and this was characteristic of his time and country. Nature was the source of wickedness, whereas in England at that time, men already approached God through nature, as we know from the meditations of Traherne. Huxley quotes Gabriel Marcel for our modern view: 'It is not God's will at all to be loved by us *against* the Creation, but rather glorifed *through* the Creation, and with the Creation as our starting point.'

The second half of the chapter is devoted to a discussion of the subliminal self, leading to a discussion in the next chapter of the demoniac possession of the nuns of the Ursuline Convent of Loudun. The treatment of their obsession depended on a complete ignorance of the subconscious. In the seventeenth century men could not believe in the innate evil in man. If men and women were very wicked, they were possessed by devils which had to be exorcised. We now believe in the subliminal mind as a repository of septic rubbish, the locus of Original Sin. It also contains the divine spark by which we can become aware of ultimate reality; and while the Freudians think of the sub-conscious as the place of Original Sin, Jung and his followers think of it also as the place of Original Virtue. It is this belief, that at the centre of our being there is the light of divine love and wisdom, which fascinates Huxley and he acclaims Surin as being aware that 'he was eternally united with the divine Ground of all being'. Surin was equally aware that he was eternally damned and: 'In the end, as we shall see, it was the consciousness of God that prevailed.' It is the old trick of the writer, to hint at developing interest so that we are compelled to go on. We certainly require encouragement, for the next chapter is about the obscene hysterical obsessions of the nuns.

The creative work in this book lies in the organisation of the material. There is imaginative work in describing the thoughts and feelings of the characters at moments of crisis, but the creative imagination is fully exercised in shaping the great amount of written material which Huxley unearthed. He presents a drama of interplay and stress, in which tragedy is succeeded by the calm of mind which accompanies illumination. Chapter four begins the study of the nuns of the Ursuline Convent under their Prioress, Jeanne des Anges, who is a little hunchback, strongly sexed, expert in spirituality and a bovaristic extrovert. In the hysterical atmosphere of their enclosed lives, these women sifted the local gossip, and the stories of M. Grandier's amorous exploits took on heroic proportions. The Prioress invited him to become their spiritual director and, when he refused, she chose one of his enemies. She proceeded to dream that M. Grandier tempted her, and her dreams were enthusiastically discussed by the nuns. Other manifestations followed which encouraged Canon Mignon, the spiritual director, to see an opportunity. These were devils and they were sent by M. Grandier. The stories were so silly that Grandier paid no attention to them, but Canon Mignon soon required help with his exorcisms; he enlisted Canon Barré, whose 'parish was so full of devils there was never a dull moment'. Very soon the Prioress and nuns were in a state of sexual excitement which became so chronic that the young nuns were incapable of talking about anything else. The suggestions of the exorcists were forced upon young women who should have been producing families; the result was they were soon behaving like performing apes. The Canons had a further purpose; Grandier would be accused of sorcery and magic and, twenty years before, when that accusation was sustained against a parish priest near Marseilles, the priest had been burned alive.

The narrative pauses in the fifth chapter for a discussion of the law at that time on witches and sorcerers. They were as badly off as the Jews under Hitler or Communists in the States at the time when Huxley was writing. Trials were absurdly unfair, and once again Huxley is pointing out that we are not much better today. Chapter six returns to the narrative and describes how an attempt was made by men of power and reputation to get sense into a situation which had got quite out of hand. They looked like succeeding when chance came in again. Prince Condé arrived in Loudun and expressed a desire to see the show. The nuns were put through the indignities of their circus show once again and the accusations against Grandier were kept alive. He was further accused at this point, of being the author of an anonymous pamphlet against Richelieu. That brought in Father Joseph who, like Richelieu, would have liked to reopen the Inquisition in France and saw in the events in Loudun an excuse for a trial run. A notorious lawyer, Laubardémont, who could twist and distort any evidence, was sent to investigate the facts of the possession of the nuns. The effort to revive the Inquisition failed; it could only be justified by belief in a spiritual fifth column which the sceptical seventeenth century could not be persuaded to believe in. But the persecution of Grandier succeeded. He was arrested, imprisoned and tortured.

Again there is a pause, a suspension of the lurid narrative. The reader would become overheated and the book would burn itself out if the horrible events were described one after another in a plain, straightforward tale. So historical and philosophical exposition is used to insulate the reader from overheated narrative. Chapter seven describes 'the frame of reference within which the men of the seventeenth century did their thinking about human nature'. Robert Burton provides a useful guide; his chapters on the anatomy of the soul express the general belief before the time of Descartes. They believed that the soul is an atom, one and indivisible, and that is important in understanding the exorcisms. If good women, like these nuns, behaved and talked so outrageously, they must have been possessed by alien spirits. They could not say with Huxley: 'Practically all of us are capable of practically anything.' We believe in a wide range of subconscious mental activity and that one mind can influence another on that level. The nuns were hysterical, and their hysteria was exacerbated by the treatment for possession. At various times the nuns agreed that they had accused Grandier wrongly, but by that time the Cardinal was so involved that he could not abandon the case and the nuns had to go on going down into the subhuman world of their grotesque displays. The chapter ends with a vivid description of their degradation.

In the eighth chapter the crowds of tourists collected for the burning even before the trial opened. Everyone but the accused knew the outcome. Huxley's skill is exerted to involve the reader in the crime, so we feel as involved in the treatment of this innocent man as we did in European concentration camps. The victim's fear and his pain are dramatised.

There is a ghost of a breath of relief when an old friar somehow got into his cell and confessed him. The old man knew what to do. He contrived to make Grandier feel that God was there, with him; and all Grandier's words and his deportment from then on are the embodiment of human dignity and compassion. The old friar was soon expelled and the overwhelming effect of the description is horror. It ends with a recital of the psychologically violent deaths of some of his enemies; a grim dénouement asserting a balance in natural justice.

Huxley must now bring the book from darkness into light. Not too suddenly, so we are told how Surin was sent to Loudun to

be spiritual adviser to the nuns. The facts arrange themselves
with artistic propriety. The devils were kept alive by the exorcists,
and when Surin saw an exorcism he believed the devils were real
and in possession. When the Prioress had a ghost pregnancy, he
believed that also. He became so involved that he began to be
possessed himself. Who can concentrate his attention upon evil
and not suffer? And Huxley cries out: 'At the present time the
destinies of the world are in the hands of self-made demoniacs—
of men who are possessed by, and who manifest, the evil they
have chosen to see in others.'

For a long time Surin battled with the Prioress and sought to
attract her devils to himself for her relief. And all the time she
disliked him, for he made this bovarist see herself and recognise
that she was half actress, half unrepentant sinner, and wholly
hysterical. Then she fell in love with him. She agreed to try
mental prayer, and was tied down so that she could not run away
while he whispered healing words into her ear. His ardour infected
her. She went in for austerities. A makeshift grille was put up in a
quiet place so that they could communicate without interruption.
Surin now took her seriously as an ecstatic, and believed her first
miracle, which to a normal observer must have seemed a dubious
affair. She was moving towards a desire for canonisation while
still alive, as more pleasing to Surin than her demoniac reputation.
She achieved stigmatisation; nothing could stop this woman,
whatever course she pursued, but Surin broke down completely
and was recalled to Bordeaux. Eventually, the last of her devils,
Behemoth, agreed to leave her if she could go on a pilgrimage
to the tomb of St Francis, and if Surin could accompany her.
The churchmen then were as little able to cope with a determined female as any men at any time, and she got her way. They
met at the shrine, after proceeding there by different roads. The
exorcists were withdrawn from the convent, and at once the
devils left also and never returned.

The tenth chapter describes the triumphant progress of the
Prioress round France, into the presence of Richelieu, of the
Queen, of the King himself. Huxley permits himself a comment
on these great personages with whom he had become familiar
while writing *Grey Eminence*. Their lives, he says, were a long
effort to persuade themselves and one another that they could
'overtop the limitations of organic existence'. They wanted to be

the offices they held, to be as grand as their positions. They liked
to feel as superhumanly energetic as Rubens painted them. The
comment dissolved into a quick narrative sketch of the last days
of the Prioress, and a brief historical note. She went back to her
convent, tried one more miracle which got so poor a response
from her public that she never tried another. She went on writing
to Surin and others about the state of her soul: 'The soul that
goes on talking about its states thereby prevents itself from
knowing its divine Ground.' She died in January 1665, and the
memorial paintings and the distribution of relics are described in
a spirit of farce.

The final chapter is about Surin. After leaving Loudun, he
was too ill for concentrated study but he could climb into the
pulpit and 'discharge his heart like a trumpet'. He became so ill
that he was almost totally paralysed and at the same time his
mental interest shifted to the contemporary notion of God and
of nature. To us it seems evident that the infinite must contain
the finite; that God and nature are one. We have always regarded
Paradise as nature suffused with the presence of God, and therefore, as Huxley says, 'it is only through the *datum* of nature that
we can hope to receive the *donum* of Grace'. In the early seventeenth century, as we have seen, nature was held to be evil,
separate from God, as a consequence of the fall of Adam and
Eve. 'Hate nature', said Surin, 'and let it suffer the humiliation
God wills for it.' Nature was totally depraved and God could
only be known through a transfiguring union. Surin thought the
infinite was outside the finite. He abhorred his environment and
became incapable of physical action. He felt exiled from God
and man: he was convinced he was a sorcerer. He was deranged,
and was treated with all the systematic cruelty which was meted
out to the insane at that time. He was rescued by an old priest,
Father Bastide, who treated him compassionately as a physically
and spiritually sick man. Gradually Surin recovered.

In October 1655, his confessor told him he would die in peace,
and three years later he was so recovered that he was able to walk.
In October 1660 he was visited by a relative and when it was
time for him to go, Surin was able to get up and accompany him
to the door. When he had gone—it is one of these little scenes of
a moment which Huxley describes so well—Surin was able to
take a few steps into the garden and then beyond, trailing un-

steadily through the autumn leaves. He was cured. He had been alienated from nature, and so much the victim of verbal fantasies and theological notions, that he had attempted to commit suicide. That was all past, but Huxley records the strange contradiction that remained in his thinking. He quotes some of Surin's writings on nature, and particularly a passage in which the doors of perception were cleansed and he seemed, as he walked in the college gardens in Bordeaux, to be surrounded by divine light and: 'I seemed to myself to be walking in Paradise.' Yet he still agreed with his teacher Lallemant, that there was nothing in nature worth looking at or wondering at.

What he experienced as his health improved was a series of extraordinary graces, and as time went on these experiences crowded upon him. Father Bastide warned him that they were not enlightenment, or a means to enlightenment. Eventually, the graces grew less and less and 'he was free to be aware of the proximity of total Awareness, he had achieved the possibility of enlightenment'. The quotations go on, eloquent and consoling evidence that in his last years Surin found peace: 'The last barrier had now gone down and... the Kingdom had come on earth.' So when he died in 1665, there was no necessity for him to go anywhere; he was already there.

The Appendix points the moral to the tale. This story of physical and psychological horror in a little French town more than three hundred years ago, is used for a sermon on our conduct as individuals, and in the mass. It first of all discusses our individual urge for self-transcendence, and the substitutes men have always used for it. Few of us are able to get outside ourselves into awareness of the pervading spirit which most of us believe in; but most of us want that awareness, that is, we want to know about ultimate reality. We should like certainty. Since we fail, we use drugs to escape from ourselves. Alcohol is the most common and has always been used. Vegetable drugs like curare come next, and the means of extracting these drugs has been greatly improved. Recently, chemists have been able to manufacture synthetic drugs and Huxley unwittingly played a part in extending their use. Use leads to excess when there is a sense of inadequacy and aloneness; anything becomes acceptable which will give us, even for a moment, a feeling of liberation from aloneness. At the addict stage, the drugs not only produce sickness and despair, but they deprive us of an essential quality, integrity, as Gabriel Marcel argues in his *Existential Background to Human Dignity*. Integrity he defines as that essential virtue by which man is master of himself and remains in complete possession of himself. Instead of escapism we should seek the fullness of solitude, which is quite other than aloneness, and we can do this best by the patient cultivation of awareness. For most of us, this is most easily done in the countryside, as we watch the progress of the seasons, everything changing all the time so that life can rise out of death or, as we say, awareness comes from stillness. To feel that we are part of nature, of an unending natural process which is a triumphant progress of life through time-space as Surin felt in this book, and as Maine de Biran felt in the previous book, is a release which is followed, in the experience of both these men, by something 'far more deeply interfused', the presence of God.

Huxley turns from the ego to crowd hysteria; to a detailed discussion of crowd delirium as used in religion and politics. Herd-intoxication has become one of the horrors of life as totalitarianisms have flourished. It is a downward transcendence, which all too easily leads to maniacal violence. It is a herd instinct that is both frightening and repulsive. In an elementary form in this book it killed Urbain Grandier; in its developed form, it led to the mutilation, permanently damaging, of our European civilisation. Nothing has frightened us more than the power of the herd to toss up leaders which will destroy it. It is so easy with modern transport to collect a crowd, so easy with lights and megaphones to hypnotise it, so easy with radio and television to multiply it a hundred-fold.

Huxley names free, compulsory education again as the greatest of our social inventions and the most dangerous aid to demagogues. Prepare the crowd with daily newspapers, then expose it to the band music, the bright lights and the oratory and in no time 'you can reduce them to a state of almost mindless subhumanity'. Batter the people by all these means all the time, and the political leaders need never fear that the people will begin thinking. They will suffer stress and strain and anxiety subconsciously; but their conscious lives will be an existence in a state of incipient hysteria. This is Mass Man, the substance of our loudly praised democracies.

Huxley proceeds to describe briefly other methods of reaching the same infra-personal state, rhythmic movement and rhythmic sound. A private road of a similar order is the *mantram*, the repeating of a word to produce trance. It is much used by mystics, but it can be used for downward transcendence equally. Innocently, it can induce sleep.

In *Brave New World* Huxley solved all these problems by supplying the soma drug, which solved the problems of aloneness as well as of crowd hysteria, for it removed identity and the possibility of relationships with anyone else. Promiscuity was all; personality and all that goes with it was dissolved. In *Island*, the *moksha*-medicine increased enlightened awareness; and it could do this because the subconscious had been purged of evil.

The Appendix ends by noting that the power of religious organisations to do evil has visibly declined over the last two centuries. The Church, he suggests, should promote horizontal self-transcendence, which is nothing more than losing ourselves in work, or in some close relationship with another human being as in married love. This has always been the practical way of escaping from the mob, or from evil communications or from depression or anxiety. It would hardly satisfy Huxley, this circumspect and contemptuous withdrawal from the race, for he is a natural preacher and proselytiser; but for those of us who would run our race modestly there is no other course. We can do what he finally exhorts us to do in this Appendix, we can pursue truth with charity, identifying ourselves with the pursuit of knowledge as well as seeking the ground of all being. He has effectively cleansed us, in this Appendix, of the pervasive evil he resurrected when he recreated the devils of Loudun.

The Doors of Perception
and Heaven and Hell

HUXLEY had a late flowering in his early sixties in three short pieces, *The Doors of Perception, The Genius and the Goddess* and *Heaven and Hell* as well as in the collection of essays, *Adonis and the Alphabet*. His wide reading, his experience of living, and his technical mastery were at that time in fine balance. His energies were undiminished, at any rate for the short concentrations which these pieces required. The two pieces on drug taking have been blamed for seducing the young; the descriptions of his experiences under the influence of mescalin are so brilliant and so beguiling that readers have wanted to have a try. He gave scrupulous warnings; they were ignored and it was not noticed that he was confessing failure. The drug released no more than was already there. He had hoped for a break-through to ultimate reality, but it did not come.

As far back as *Texts and Pretexts* Huxley had warned (in the section 'Man and Nature') that when we invite these experiences 'the processes of cleansing and improvement cannot go beyond a certain point, and that the effects cannot last for more than a very short time. We are not free to create imaginatively a world other than that in which we find ourselves. That world is given.' The idea that there are chemical keys which will allow us to open the doors of perception into the ultimately real is equally unlikely. Those we call mystics appear to succeed but they have submitted to laborious preparation.

The human desire for heightened awareness is a continuing theme in Huxley's writings, as we have seen. When Anthony Beavis is standing over his chloroformed friend in chapter forty-nine, he speculates: 'The face of one who had made himself free. . . . But in fact, Anthony reflected, in fact he had had his freedom forced upon him by this evil-smelling vapour. Was it possible to be one's own liberator? There were snares; but there was also a way of walking out of them.' In the Appendix to *The Devils of Loudun*, there is an analysis of this human desire for increased awareness: 'From poppy to curare, from Andean coca to Indian hemp and Siberian agaric, every plant or bush or fungus capable, when ingested, of stupefying or exciting or evoking visions, has long since been discovered and systematically employed. The fact is strangely significant; for it seems to prove that, always and everywhere, human beings have felt the radical inadequacy of their personal existence, the misery of being their insulated selves, and not something else, something wider...'

The theme that each man is an island is one to which he was bound to return when he was describing the mescalin experience: 'Always and in all circumstances we are by ourselves... Sensations, feelings, insights, fancies—all these are private and, except through symbols and at second hand, incommunicable... From family to nation, every human group is a society of island universes.' He did not expect to transcend this aloneness by taking the drug, or to become aware of what it feels like to be Falstaff or Joe Louis; he did hope to know 'from the inside, what the visionary, the medium, even the mystic were talking about'. The order of experience he expected is described in chapter twelve of *The Perennial Philosophy*—the two essays may be read as appendices to *The Perennial Philosophy* and the reader will get most out of them by doing so—'Reality is no longer perceived *quoad nos* (for the good reason that there is no longer a *nos* to perceive it), but as it is in itself.' In Blake's words, 'If the doors of perception were cleansed, everything would be seen as it is, infinite.'

When he took the drug, he hoped to be admitted 'at least for a few hours, into the kind of inner world described by Blake and AE'. He was disappointed, and the reasons seem obvious. For one thing, he was a guinea pig, under the careful control of a medical investigator, who not only guarded him against danger but guided him all the time, putting pictures in front of him, playing music, taking him to selected places. But even without supervision the success he wanted was unlikely; he was not like Blake and AE, and if the drug releases the whole mind, what can appear is what is already there. He tells us what the drug did. He saw with the eye of childish innocence and colours became very bright; he didn't want to do anything or worry about anything (surely sufficient explanation of the discovery of the properties of curare and coca and all the others); he had euphoric sensations about existence in the inner and outer worlds of being.

What he actually experienced amounts to not much more than that. Colours were much more vivid and excited him more. When music was tried, instrumental music was not sufficiently exciting, but madrigals by Gesualdo induced intense reactions. When he heard Alban Berg's *Lyric Suite*, he thought Berg might do better than be so sorry for himself. Sensations might be heightened but judgement was not impaired. There was only one moment which carried him further. He found himself on the brink of panic as he was looking at a chair. 'The fear, as I analyse it in retrospect, was of being overwhelmed, of disintegrating under a pressure of reality greater than a mind accustomed to living most of the time in a cosy world of symbols could possibly bear.' This was his one moment of the kind of truth he was seeking and no doubt the investigator saw the danger and diverted him.

The danger was that he might have too much of a good thing. He might be brought 'suddenly, face to face with some manifestation of the *Mysterium tremendum*'. This was what, too greatly daring, he had hoped to experience. He wanted greater awareness in two realms. The first was suggested by Bergson: 'Each person is at each moment capable of remembering all that has ever happened to him and of perceiving everything that is happening everywhere in the universe.' This is Mind at Large and if our sensations were exposed to it all at once we should be destroyed. The brain and nervous system act as a transformer, reducing the impact. In Huxley's homelier image: 'Mind at Large has to be funnelled through the reducing valve of the brain and the nervous system.' The drug could cut out this mechanism and expose the mind to all that is. The other realm was ultimate Reality, and he was never threatened with awareness of it while under the influence of the drug. He says that he was never a visualiser, and it is the visualisers who become visionaries under mescalin. It seems likely that he had no hope of succeeding because he had not undertaken the arduous training which the mystic undergoes.

What he did find, in reaction to the release from responsibility which the drug brought, was a recurring concern about social responsibility. He could not get away from himself and his Victorian forebears. There was a tape-recording of what he had said while under the drug, and he found the question constantly repeated: 'What about human relations?' and: 'How could one reconcile this timeless bliss of seeing as one ought to see with the temporal duties of doing what one ought to do and feeling as one ought to feel?' That carries him into a defence of contemplatives. They sit quietly, and if all men did that the sum of evil would be greatly reduced. They are not likely to be 'gamblers, or procurers, or drunkards; they do not as a rule preach intolerance, or make war; do not find it necessary to rob, swindle, or grind the faces of the poor'. What soothes his conscience most is the idea that the contemplative can go about his ordinary business without being so besmirched with what Traherne calls 'the dirty Devices of the world' that he cannot return to the world of contemplation.

Later, he makes a plea for the use of drugs as an escape. He attacks vigorously the permitted evils, alcohol and tobacco, and puts the case for a harmless drug if it can be found. That may frighten us now, when we have seen what addiction can do. But Huxley is asking that we try to discover a harmless drug, and he said that long before in *Brave New World*. The idea of the soma drug did not frighten us then, any more than the *moksha*-medicine in *Island* frightened us afterwards. 'What is needed is a new drug which will relieve and console our suffering species without doing more harm in the long run than it does good in the short.' He is compassionately asking for something for Mass Man, who should be encouraged to mind his own business as quietly as he can, as the legions of the forgotten dead have done before him. He is asking for release from the wearisome condition of humanity.

He speaks very differently about the few who try to use drugs for revelation and enlightenment. 'The full and final solution can be found only by those who are prepared to implement the right kind of Weltanschauung by means of the right kind of behaviour and the right kind of constant and unstrained alertness.' They

G

cannot rely entirely on drugs: 'I am not so foolish as to equate
what happens under the influence of mescalin or of any other drug,
prepared or in the future preparable, with the realization of the
end and ultimate purpose of human life: Enlightenment, the
Beatific Vision.' If a harmless drug can be found, its use will be
for chemical vacations; anything more would be a gratuitous
grace.

His own experiment was thoroughly disheartening. With his
absolute honesty he tells us that the investigator asked him to
look at what was going on inside his head. Huxley looked and
everything he saw was shoddy and trivial; as if one was below
decks in a five-and-ten-cent ship, he said. 'And as I looked, it
became very clear that this five-and-ten-cent ship was in some
way connected with human pretensions. This suffocating interior
of a dime-store ship was my own personal self; these gimcrack
mobiles of tin and plastic were my personal contributions to the
universe.' If that is a chemical vacation, we had better cultivate
our gardens. Unless we are prepared for the long necessary preparation, such as Aquinas undertook. Huxley refers to the Angelic
Doctor at the very end; he will not give up hope of piercing the
mystery. He reminds us that Aquinas, while he was writing his
last book, had a revelation, and after that could write no more.
Aquinas had spent his life seeking the greatest good; he was ready
for the revelation.

Two years later, Huxley published another short essay on the
same theme, *Heaven and Hell*. It is an impersonal discussion
instead of a warm description of a personal experience. It is
intellectual rather than sophist. It is short and it is followed by
eight very short and rewarding appendices. The title again comes
from Blake, who got it from Swedenborg, while refuting the
Swede's view, the common one, that evil should be eliminated in
the interests of good. Blake regarded good and evil as necessary
opposites if progress is to be made; they provide that vital opposition which sustains life, an idea to which Huxley subscribes. We
recall the striking quotation from Bagehot in chapter nineteen of
The Perennial Philosophy: 'We could not be what we ought to be,
if we lived in the sort of universe we should expect.'

The purpose of the essay is to examine the methods by which
visions may be obtained. Huxley's analysis reminds us that during
our knowledge explosion we have learned that life and happiness

is very much a matter of chemical constitution. The line between sanity and insanity, health and malaise, may depend on the presence or absence of a trace element or a vitamin in our food. Huxley's concern here is not with the body in normal conditions but with the spirit when the body is tuned to allow it to explore 'the not too distant Virginias and Carolinas of the personal sub-conscious and the vegetative soul'. The exploration can be made in various ways, by the use of drugs and hypnosis among them.

As usual, he warns that this may be the door to paradise for some and for others it may be the door to hell. In a demurely hilarious appendix he reminds us that in the Middle Ages there were considerable natural aids to visionary experiences. Everyone was short of vitamins in the long winters. Ascetics had Lenten fasts to follow; a great help. 'Ecstasies and visions were almost a commonplace. It was only to be expected.' These visions had a regular pattern. Light is the first common feature; then a height-ened sense of colour; wonderful landscapes in wonderful islands were common, like all the legends of golden islands in literature, East and West. Gems appear in visions just as much as islands and 'precious stones are precious because they bear a faint resem-blance to the glowing marvels seen with the inner eye of the visionary'. Like *The Doors of Perception*, this essay is a concen-tration of skill and experience. It is wonderfully suggestive, a fine example of the intellectual function of seeing hitherto unsuspected relationships.

When the climax comes, it is a rehearsal of what he had previ-ously written on these topics: 'Of those who die an infinitesimal minority are capable of immediate union with the divine Ground.' The essay is the most compressed and mordant of his explorations of the mental phenomena by which we become conscious of a farther world. It reflects his immoderate hydroptic thirst for learned support from all ages and all civilisations; but it never grows heavy and it never grows dull. It illuminates a fascinating subject.

The Essays

Introduction

To BE an essayist a writer must have one gift, style. To have
a style he must be a character, and to be a character he must
have wisdom. Huxley added knowledge, gained from much travel,
immense reading and constant meeting with intelligent people.
He had a full mind and an unquenchable spirit of enquiry. He was
on the side of Faraday and his grandfather, T. H. Huxley; he
was on the side of Blake and Keats. His essays are relevant to the
situation in his time and ours, a time of revolution and upheaval,
and therefore a time for steadiness founded firmly on unalterable
values. It was a time of a knowledge explosion and the nature of
an explosion is to throw people about. Therefore steadiness is
sought and poise is the quality most envied. He had the good
fortune to believe that behind all the appearances there is reality,
and for him the reality was the unitive knowledge of God. All his
work leads to that, and the essays record the search and the
affirmation.

In his own preface to his *Collected Essays*, he says that: 'Essays
belong to a literary species whose extreme variability can be
studied most effectively within three poles of reference.' The first
is the personal and autobiographical, which he exploited only in
brief bursts of confidence; travel replaced it as a lead into his
themes. But though he did not exploit autobiography lavishly, it
comes in constantly, always appropriately, always modestly, an
essential grace of the essay form as he used it. The second is the

objective, the factual, the concrete-particular, and under that
heading we can place the pamphleteering essays about the bomb,
and drugs and the two cultures. The third is the abstract-universal,
and that with him comes late. Montaigne and Bacon offer gnomic
wisdom all the time; it is natural to the French language rather
than to ours, and Huxley quotes Valéry to demonstrate it in a
modern. With Huxley, it was a fine flowering of his late essays.

Most essayists succeed best in one of the three poles, perhaps
in two. Huxley was always a person, at any rate after the early
collection *On the Margin*. He is always an amusing and bracing
intelligence. He has the discursive quality native to the form. He
begins anywhere; anything will start him off and, however trivial
it is, we know we shall proceed without any jerks or jumps, but
by sheer persuasive guidance to a serious consideration of one of
the many subjects which absorbed him. This is how he noted the
quality in Montaigne: 'Free association artistically controlled—
this is the paradoxical secret of Montaigne's best essays. One
damned thing after another—but in a sequence that in some
almost miraculous way develops a central theme and relates it to
the rest of human experience.' Huxley is always easy to read—
well, nearly always, for sometimes he expects close attention to
an abstract argument—and he is never trivial. The world and the
times are too wonderfully exciting for anything but the white
light of seriousness. Generalisations are made to be modified, and
we remember happy little essay pieces, which are gay and light as
a short story. And the endings; they may be a rounding of the
subject into a calm finale, or an unexpected flash of wit or a jest.
The final gesture was part of his style.

Huxley's essays span the forty odd years of his writing life and
they give us a rich view of the intellectual life of Western Man
during these very exciting decades. The knowledge explosion was
bringing forward so much that was old and had been forgotten,
as well as what was altogether new and revolutionary. He describes
their range himself: 'Essays autobiographical. Essays about things
seen and places visited. Essays in criticism of all kinds of works
of art, literary, plastic, musical. Essays about philosophy and
religion, some of them couched in abstract terms, others in the
form of an anthology with comments, others again in which
general ideas are approached through the concrete facts of history
and biography.' Then the proud claim, made with justice: 'Essays,

finally, in which, following Montaigne, I have tried to make the
best of all the essay's three worlds, have tried to say everything
at once in as near an approach to contrapuntal simultaneity as the
nature of literary art will allow of.'

On the Margin

The first collection of essays gives us nothing very remarkable.
It is a bundle of short pieces from *The Athenaeum*, with two
longer pieces on Chaucer and Ben Jonson. These, and the very
delightful piece on Edward Lear, must still be useful as they
follow the old critical theory that you write about what you have
greatly enjoyed, in the hope that others will share your enjoyment.
There is nothing better in such brief space on Chaucer and Ben.
We find references to Chaucer throughout his work, admiration
of his psychological insight and his imperturbable good sense.
For the rest, we can cull from these agreeable pieces quotations
which bring back the attitudes of the twenties. The chill breath
of change was already with us: 'In no century have the dis-
illusionments followed on one another's heels with such un-
intermitted rapidity as in the twentieth, for the good reason that
in no century has change been so rapid and so profound.' He was
speaking of boredom in an essay on Accidie and in another, on
Pleasures, he returns to the subject, discussing the ready-made
amusements that were beginning to take the place of active pas-
times: 'With a mind almost atrophied by lack of use, unable to
entertain itself and grown so wearily uninterested in the ready-
made distractions offered from without, that nothing but the
grossest stimulants of an ever-increasing violence and crudity can
move it, the democracy of the future will sicken of a chronic and
mortal boredom.' This prophecy of a future which has already
arrived will be repeated at greater length in his next collection,
Do What You Will.

Huxley was in his late twenties when he wrote these essays and
he enjoys a young man's pleasure in throwing his weight about:
'The subject of any European government today feels all the
sensations of Gulliver in the paws of the Queen of Brobdingnag's
monkey—the sensation of some small and helpless being at the
mercy of something monstrous and irresponsible and idiotic.'

Strong, but true. In the next piece, on Tibet, he has a swing at
three usual targets of the time, speaking of 'the depression into
which the Peace, Mr Churchill, the state of contemporary literature, have conspired to plunge the mind'. The mood is not always
youthfully derogatory; he can offer a ringing defence of an old
ideal we do not hear much about in these days of Mass Man:
'Wren was a great gentleman: one who valued dignity and restraint
and who, respecting himself, respected also humanity; one who
desired that men and women should live with the dignity, even
the grandeur, befitting their proud human title; one who despised
meanness and oddity as much as vulgar ostentation; one who
admired reason and order, who distrusted all extravagance and
excess. A gentleman, the finished product of an old and ordered
civilization.' As we go through the volumes of essays we shall find
that this is the background against which his judgements are made.

Do What You Will

Many will find this his most sympathetic book, for he is celebrating the pagan joy of living. He is writing at the end of the
first and most prolific decade of his creative writing. He is
ebullient with energy and looks on the world in one mood as a
fascinating creation which he must enjoy as much as he can, and
in another as wholly deplorable and clearly getting worse while
he watches it. We can enjoy the book as a comment on the novels
and short stories of the decade and particularly on *Point Counter
Point*. We can enjoy it as a vigorous wholehearted acceptance of
the world, Huxley as a Life-Worshipper. It is a splendid defence
of Paganism, the Renaissance fullness, exhorting us to explore all
possible worlds of experience. We can enjoy it far otherwise, as a
study of man's mental sickness, especially in the essays on Swift,
Baudelaire and Pascal; and as a study of our social sickness, for
we live in a quantitative civilisation, called democracy, in which
man is being corrupted by the machines and by mechanical
amusements.

The book is a declaration of belief at a moment when he is
about to modify his views profoundly. He is about to turn cynical
in *Brave New World*, in which free, creative man is overcome by
his own mechanical and chemical skills. Meanwhile, he will begin

to develop his interest in the world beyond our world and seek to
break through the barriers at the frontiers of normal sense per-
ceptions. He was never entirely successful, as we have seen, but it
is most interesting to read in the Pascal essay that he had already
had experiences of the kind he sought in *The Perennial Philosophy*,
The Doors of Perception and *Heaven and Hell*. 'I too have sometimes found myself in other worlds than those familiar to the
positivist, I too have chased the absolute in those remote regions
beyond the borders of the quotidian consciousness.'

Perhaps the most satisfactory way of tackling the book—it is
the most difficult of Huxley's books to capture in the mind—is to
leave the essay on Pascal for separate treatment, as a long restatement of the problems he has been dealing with throughout the book.

The opening essay gives us the thought behind the early novels.
He is against masochism and asceticism. They are restrictive, they
starve one side of man's nature, whereas the human mind naturally
believes in both diversity and unity. The saints were 'drearily
lacking in variety'. They represented only the spiritual side of
life. By contrast, the Greeks enjoyed a much more complete life
and embraced in their way of life the instincts as well as the spirit,
'the passionate energies' as well as the reason, 'the self-regarding'
as well as the altruistic side of our nature. And so did the people
in the twenties, so did the characters in his novels. In a lyrical
passage a little later he says that 'the human spirit is mainly
nourished by the multiplicity of the world' and asserts with a
jocund pastoral note that it is the same with the mind as with the
body: 'These fields of potatoes and cabbages, these browsing
sheep and oxen, are potentially a part of me; unless they actually
become part of me, I die.'

Some philosophers reduce the food supply of the mind and
ascetics go further, they starve their souls. This is wrong; the
principal food of the soul 'is the direct, the physical experience
of diversity'. It is the creed of youth; let us try everything, let us
learn everything. Our thirst is immoderate, and there is more
available than we can ever hope to enjoy. Later, Huxley, like the
rest of us, will think more of unity than of diversity and accept
the law that unity is found by concentrating the energies on what
we most desire, which means neglecting so much and so much.
Meanwhile, the young man can conclude his essay in a dithyrambic
call for a new religion, which will have many gods: 'Many; but

since the individual man is an unity in his various multiplicity, also one. It will have to be Dionysian and Panic as well as Apollonian; Orphic as well as rational, not only Christian, but Martial and Venerian too; Phallic as well as Minervan or Jehovah-istic. It will have to be all, in a word, that human life actually is...'

In a diminished mood, in 'Spinoza's Worm', he quotes Blake: 'Do what you will, this world's a fiction' and reminds us 'it is no less inescapably *our* world'. So how do we make the best of it? Let us concentrate on living as fully as we can, here and now: 'The only thing in our power is to do our best to be men, here and now. Let us think about the present, not the future.' The reader who comes to this book from the later essays will notice that a very little shift brings us to his later position. A shift of emphasis in the sentences just quoted from the physical to the mental, and we have Boehme's word that we do not have to go anywhere to find the world of the spirit, we are in it now. We are in the eternal present. But in the wearisome condition of humanity, under the rules of time, it is only when we look back that we dis-cover that we were enjoying a glimpse of the eternal happiness. This is a stage further than Huxley goes in his present argument, which is for a full appreciation of the pleasures our world offers. He quotes Pericles, who held that men should accept their natures as they found them. The mind, the senses, instincts, passions, imagination, they must all be exercised: 'Man is multifarious, inconsistent, self-contradictory; the Greeks accepted the fact and lived multifariously, inconsistently, and contradictorily.' Huxley wanted us to avoid the asceticism of the contemplative and equally the asceticism of the dedicated businessman, and be like the Greeks who refused to sacrifice the body to the spirit, and even more emphatically 'refused to sacrifice both body and spirit to the Bitch Goddess—success'. He is facing one of the problems of our age, how can we reconcile our human birthright and our ever-closer association with our machines? 'The vital problem of our age is the problem of reconciling manhood with the citizen-ship of a modern industrialized state.' This is where inconsistency becomes vital; we must live parallel lives. We must accept the human condition of double-think. If we struggle for consistency, the result will be 'the imposition of subhuman insanity. From madness in the long-run comes destruction. It is only by culti-vating his humanity that man can hope to save himself.'

That is as far as he goes in 'Spinoza's Worm' but a little later, in 'Wordsworth in the Tropics' he says: 'The only satisfactory way of existing in the modern, highly specialized world is to live with two personalities.' It is not easy to reconcile this solution with his round assertion: 'If one would live well, one must live completely, with the whole being', for that would seem to imply a unitary approach. It isolates the weakness of the all-embracing approach to life; eventually, it is unsatisfactory. But in the beginning it is good, just as it is good to make a large hole if you want to dig deeply with any comfort.

If a good deal of the book is given to discussing the nature of virtuous living in our mechanised societies, much more is given to the discontents and disorders which trouble them. It was these considerations which formed the background of his thinking while he was composing *Brave New World*. In 'Spinoza's Worm' he asked what were the dangers that threatened our modern world, and his first answers were monotheism and acquisitiveness.

The third danger is the machine. In 'Revolutions' he says that the industrial system 'makes life fundamentally unlivable for all'. He has already admitted that the machines are here to stay, but 'they inflict on humanity an enormous psychological injury that must, if uncared for, prove mortal'. He had special objection to the mechanisation of leisure. In 'One and Many': 'Machines relieve him, not merely of drudgery, but of the possibility of performing any creative or spontaneous act whatsoever.' He speaks of boredom again in 'Revolutions', where mechanical amusements 'are spreading an ever intenser boredom through ever wider spheres'. He was detecting a disease that has become distressingly common in our new towns. When he came to his *Brave New World* he recognised that very few by that time were capable of creative leisure, so he mercifully provided the soma drug.

He is writing in the twenties, so in one of his warming autobiographical glimpses, he opens 'Holy Face' with: 'Good Times are chronic nowadays... The fine point of seldom pleasure is duly blunted. Feasts must be solemn and rare, or else they cease to be feasts... Me personally the unflagging pleasures of contemporary cities leave most lugubriously unamused.' The outcome of it all he foresees in the climax of 'Revolution': 'It will be a nihilist revolution. Destruction for destruction's sake. Hate, universal hate, and an aimless and therefore complete and thorough smashing up of everything.' The words are prophetic; a decade later Europe did her best to smash up everything. It was the winter of our discontent, and out of it we are enjoying the spring of a new age, in which we value the help of the machines to make life tolerable for everyone, and may even learn from the machines that the sane way to live as a social animal is to work hard for others.

Despair and disgust is the other side of the bright picture of the future which our knowledge explosion warrants. Huxley notes that the Greeks were profoundly pessimistic and found the world finally deplorable. That was while they were enjoying the first great European knowledge explosion. That comes in the 'Baudelaire', which is an analysis of a man who 'took pains to make the world as thoroughly disgusting for himself as he could'. It is interesting to compare Huxley's essay with T. S. Eliot's; Eliot, the scrupulous scholar, assembling a formidable array of information and interpretation about a body of writing: Huxley developing a study of a fascinating human aberration, a satanist, with sympathy and penetration, illuminating the poems, and at the same time adding notably to his studies of the world we Europeans have made for ourselves. Modern man, he says, will find in *Fleurs du Mal* 'all his own sufferings described with incomparable energy'.

The first study of a mentally sick man is of Swift. He belonged to a sub-species of horror-lovers, those 'who deliberately seek out what pains and nauseates them for the sake of the extraordinary pleasure they derive from the overcoming of their repulsion'. This was the sub-species to which St Francis belongs, and he is mentioned here in one of those cross-references common in *Do What You Will*. They cumulate until this book becomes one of Huxley's major studies of a favourite theme, human mental nastiness and unhealthiness. St Francis got a rapturous sensation from kissing the diseased hand of a leper; Swift got his pleasure from his own disorders.

St Francis in Huxley's study was a man of power, who failed ignominiously when he tried to be a soldier, so became determined to be famous and powerful in the Church. As for his humility, look at how he addressed the Pope, who was trying to persuade him to model his policy on the old monastic orders: 'do not speak to me of the rule of St Benedict, of St Augustine, of St Bernard, or any other, but only of that which God in His mercy has seen fit to reveal to me.' As for his love of birds and animals, look at the story of the pig—and whoever reads right through Huxley will look at it often enough—in which one of the brothers, sick, expressed a great longing for a pig's trotter, so out goes another and cuts one off a living pig. St Francis was struck by the thoughtfulness of the brother for his sick companion, but showed no concern for the pig. Huxley's conclusion, after his study of St Francis, is that we are born with certain elements and if we suppress any of them, there is atrophy, then decay and we end up with 'a kind of spiritual blood-poisoning'. The Grigory in the essay is Rasputin and there is very little about him. He preached salvation through sin; God loves repentance, so sin that you may repent.

Two essays are concerned with pitiful human weakness. 'Paradise' is almost a short story. It is a glimpse of a Riviera hotel in the off-season, full of old, lonely, middle-class English-women, huddled together for warmth and cheap living, pathetic as an Eventide Home. 'Revolution' embraces the human race in its pity. Life is pointless and intolerable. The slaves in the ancient world were better off than the industrial wage-slaves in England in the last century. A slave was property and, like cattle, was worth treating well: 'Wage-slaves were worked to death at high speed; but there were always new ones coming in to take their places, fairly begging the capitalists to work *them* to death too.' Our historians are just beginning to give us a picture of the lives of poor people in this island down the centuries. Huxley's con-clusion about our present state is that: 'The real trouble with the present social and industrial system is not that it makes some people very much richer than others, but that it makes life funda-mentally unlivable for all.' The deadening prospect is that when the turbulence is at last ended, Mass Man will settle down to something like *Brave New World*.

In the end, it is not useful to think of the Mass or to discuss it. Life is an individual experience and whatever our surroundings each individual human being develops a personality and an aware-ness of further possibilities in being; the self and the other. So when he comes to discuss Pascal, it is to help him in a psycho-logical exploration. The essay, he tells us, is not about Pascal at all, 'but this psychological landscape. Pascal is really only an excuse and a convenience.' He is following up his thesis in the opening essay (he will pursue it again nearly thirty years later in the opening essay of *Adonis and the Alphabet*) that 'every man is a colony of separate individuals'. Pascal was a mathematical genius, who was trained as a Jansenist, but enjoyed for a time the more elegant upper-class pleasures. Then he had one mystical experience, turned ascetic, and gave his life to combating scepticism, the Pyrrhonic scepticism of Montaigne. As T. S. Eliot noticed, Montaigne beguiled him unawares and afterwards Voltaire produced a classical reply to Pascal's arguments. A generation later, Maine de Biran produced another reply which became the subject of Huxley's finest essay. Here, against the background of the life and writings of Pascal, Huxley will rehearse the views he has been expressing in this volume of sceptical essays. 'Never has the case against life been put with such subtlety, such elegance, such persuasive cogency, such admirable succinctness. He explored the same country as I am now exploring; went, saw, and found it detestable.'

Huxley was examining himself: 'I try to be sincerely myself' and he rather proudly assesses himself against these great masters of the European debate on scepticism and belief; Montaigne, Pascal, Voltaire, as well as Maine de Biran who was nearer his own condition. Huxley himself at this stage was sceptical, but he had doubts about his scepticism and there is the single reference to a mystical experience, much less clear than Pascal's reference to the experience which changed his life.

If Pascal was beguiled by the Pyrrhonist Montaigne, Huxley was beguiled by the ascetic Pascal. We find Huxley combating ideas which he himself will very soon accept. There is even a parallel with Pascal's thirst for peace and order (because he lived during the religious wars which Huxley will describe in *Grey Eminence*) and Huxley's despairing appeal for peace during the decade after the invention of nuclear weapons. The tensions in Pascal's thought, between 'a kind of positivistic Pyrrhonism' and dogmatic Christianity which flatly denied it, between the intellectual desire to be Hellenic and the smothering Jansenist asceticism corresponds to Huxley's own range of experience.

In other things, there was no correspondence. Pascal hated sensuality and with it poetry, art, the theatre. He was a sick man which, according to Huxley, is the Christian's natural state. 'Those of us who are blessedly free of these diseases will refuse to accept

Pascal's neuralgia-metaphysic.' When he discusses 'Pascal and Death' and says that Pascal's 'chronic revelation was of darkness, and the source of that revelation was not the God of Life; it was Death', when he says in the next section that Pascal's vision of eternity was of 'huge and frightful problems' because he saw eternity through the death-darkness, we are reminded that Huxley concerned himself in his last years, when he knew that he was dying, to represent death as a bright approach to the Clear Light. Here, Huxley is already for that view; he quotes Pascal saying that those who disregarded death and infinity found the hand of God laid upon them in anger. Huxley will not have that; the hand touches them 'encouragingly, helpfully'.

This comes at the opening of the third and final part of the long essay, and from this section fourteen to the twenty-third, which is a 'Summary of the Life-Worshipper's Creed' we leave Pascal for Huxley's Hellenic, rapturous worship of life: 'the God of Life lays his hand upon men and gives them power not to think the thoughts they do not want to have; he bestows the grace of life upon them.' He will not have the Aristotelian mean, 'a perpetual state of compromise'. Nothing 'of any significance has ever been achieved by a man of moderation and compromise'. And when we bring forward the argument that man has extended his knowledge and increased his vision by concentration, he is ready for us: 'Living excessively only in one direction, the world-mover has been reduced from the rank of a complete human being to that of an incarnate function.' Like the dons and geniuses in Huxley's later fiction.

He spends pages on the praise of the Life-Worshipper: 'The Life-Worshipper lives in the eternal present.' The argument proceeds like a torrent, like the extempore utterance of an inspired orator.

He was beguiling us in this spate of oratory into belief of his belief in the Hellenic plenitude of intellectual life, which was for him the chrysalis stage of belief in the Eternal Present. He sums up the Life-Worshipper's creed in the long twenty-third section. It is a comprehensive creed; the Life-Worshipper is prepared to be an optimist and a pessimist, a positivist and a mystic: 'Pessimism is no truer than optimism, nor positivism than mysticism.' He is arguing for perpetual choice: 'The Life-Worshipper suggests that man shall make use of all his keys instead of throwing all but one of them away.' That is all very well, but eventually we must make a choice. If we accept Huxley's metaphor, we shall note that Montaigne and Pascal and Voltaire used the keys to go into a room in which they could settle down and work, and did not spend their days unlocking doors. This life-worshipping is a desirable early stage in a satisfactory life, but it is suitable only for youth. Huxley was leaving his youth behind as he wrote this philosophy for youth. It was an eloquent argument for a stage in life which he had almost outlived.

Having completed his apology for youth, he returns to Pascal and paints a repellent picture of a sick man with distorted thoughts. Pascal wanted men to throw life away. He invokes the Jansenist God to support his ascetic view that man should be consistent and undesiring; he brings men 'into paralysing contact with death and infinity; he demonstrates the nothingness, in the face of this darkness, these immensities, of every thought, action, and desire'. Page after page the denunciation proceeds, to this climax: 'All his writings are persuasive invitations to the world to come and commit suicide. It is the triumph of principle and consistency.' The essay is a defence of the pagan joy which is the theme of the volume, and it ends with a musical conclusion: 'the harmony of life—of the single life that persists as a gradually changing unity through time—is a harmony built up of many elements. The unity is mutilated by the suppression of any part of the divinity. A fugue has need of all its voices.' It is magnificent; but we read it now as a magnificent farewell to a Pyrrhonic youth by one who was on the way to becoming a Perennial Philosopher.

Music at Night

Music at Night was published between *Point Counter Point* and *Brave New World* and its main interest is that it canvasses the ideas in these novels. The most important essay in the book, 'On Grace', supplements these ideas and deals with a problem at the centre of human affairs; the fact that Nature does not make all things equal and we are not always wise in attempting to make them so. The book is divided into four sections; the first dealing with aesthetics which makes a useful commentary on *Point Counter Point;* the second is philosophical and is one of the seedbeds

Huxley laid down for all his later work; the third is on sex and dull; the fourth is on social questions and looks forward to *Brave New World*. He ends with a delicious piece on cats, one of these virtuoso performances in the comic spirit which Huxley managed so well, and which he enjoyed using as a coda to a serious collection.

The opening essay is a discussion of the novel, which deals with the whole truth while tragedy, in the nature of things, imposes limitations. We have seen how this idea of presenting the whole truth grew in Huxley during the twenties until in *Point Counter Point* we have the whole range, from the ugly to the beautiful and from the detail to the philosophical view. It was the fashion, he says: 'However different one from the other in style, in ethical, philosophical and artistic intention, in the scales of values accepted, contemporary writers have this in common, that they are interested in the Whole Truth.' He returns to the question in *Vulgarity in Literature* when he is defending his novels. In the next essay there is an illuminating comment on his intention in countering the points of the novel: 'the implied or specified "counter" which, in the novel, tempered, or at least was intended to temper, the harshness of the "points" '. He notes that the play based on the novel was curiously hard and brutal, which was exactly the impression of the television version. It was Huxley's gift of style, a kind of grace as he would put it, that tempered his presentation of the Whole Truth.

The essay 'Music at Night' gives the title to the collection because it offers unaffectedly the essence of what Huxley believed. In discussing a Madonna by Piero della Francesca he speaks of 'the greatness of the human spirit, of its power to rise above circumstances and dominate fate' and says that Paradise is regained 'in those deserts of utter solitude where man puts forth the strength of his reason to resist the fiend'. His social cynical guard is down; we are glimpsing the Whole Truth. As again, in his comment on the introduction to the *Benedictus* in the *Missa Solemnis*, 'a statement about the blessedness that is at the heart of things'. From that seed of belief comes the central quest of his life.

The essay 'On Grace' is about the apparent heartlessness in the nature of things. One person, by his chemical constitution, is naturally cheerful, another misanthropic. One has a good brain,

another is stupid. The discussion is important today because
world society seems to be determined to make all men appear
equal. This readiness to pretend equality, brings upon us the
dull grey socialist levelling down. To fly in the face of nature
leads to sorrow and disaster. Huxley goes right back to Job and
accepts his analysis of the nature of things as 'the final word on
this disquieting subject'. It is impossible, Huxley says, 'to justify
the ways of God to man in terms of human morality or even of
human reason'. When Job attempts logical answers based on
human reason and morality, he comes up against the overwhelming forces of nature: 'Behemoth and Leviathan are more convincing than the most flawless syllogisms. Job is overwhelmed,
flattened out; the divine logic moves on the feet of elephants.'
Karl Jaspers, exploring these questions at the end of the war,
spoke of God's demand for unconditional truthfulness and says
that this involved us in asking questions of God which are directed
against God: 'This impulse runs through European thought from
the time of the *Book of Job*.' A few years later, C. G. Jung published his fascinating study, *Answer to Job;* the debate is eternal.

The history of the human race is the story of how man has tried
to get round the profound inequality in the nature of things. We
have learned to develop nature sufficiently to support us and now
we are concerned to develop our own minds so that we can continue to exist as a species, and do so a little more competently.
We must learn to face the Whole Truth, the 'divinely appalling
and divinely beautiful inhumanity' of Grace, which by our human
standards 'is utterly unacceptable'. Meanwhile, the chemists and
the philosophers and all other men of good will, struggle on with
the problem of too many human beings of too many kinds being
too close together. At the end of his essay Huxley says we want
incompatibles, justice as well as grace. He commends us to laying
them side by side, without any vain attempt to reconcile their
contradiction.

In practice, they can be reconciled by love. 'Some men and
women have a special talent for love; they are as few, I think, as
those who have a special talent for mathematics.' Humanitarians
have been trying to teach this talent: 'It is an art very difficult
to acquire, and the successes of its Christian and democratic
teachers have not been considerable.' This is echoed by Erich
Fromm in his recent tract on *The Art of Loving;* it requires three

difficult things, discipline, concentration and faith. Huxley remains unhopeful right to the end. Love would reconcile the claims of grace and justice: 'But in this actual world, where so few people love their neighbours, where those who have not envy those who have and where those who have despise, or, more often, simply ignore, simply are unaware of, those who have not—in this actual world of ours the reconcilement is difficult indeed.'

In the essay on Beliefs and Actions he tackles the problem in another way. Ideas, he says, give us courage and determination. We can't go on feeling all the time, but ideas persist. It is the other side of his thesis that physical vices eventually bring exhaustion, but mental vices grow stronger. He asks what ideas move us most now; not Christianity, not nineteenth-century liberalism, not progress or humanitarianism, they are on the wane. Not even scepticism, because finally it is intolerable and is of no use to the masses who must believe in something. We have given up these transcendental things, he says in 1931, lost faith in them. The accent is on personality, the right of everyone to happiness and self-expression. 'In other words, we claim to do what we like, not because doing what we like is in harmony with some supposed absolute good, but because it is good in itself.' This is very much the spirit of the characters in the early novels, very much the spirit of the twenties; and very remote from the Huxley and his characters by the end of the next decade.

These subjects, especially with Huxley, always end up in a discussion of the population problem. Accordingly, in the next essay, 'Notes on Liberty', we find him observing that all liberty is at the expense of others, because there are so many of us, and the only solution is fewer people selectively bred. They will avoid excess and so be free of the law of diminishing returns which operates in every sphere of human satisfaction. The suggestion is repeated in the essay 'On the Charms of History'. We have seen democracy and universal education and we want to get back to natural inequality which gives us an aristocracy. It will be at its best if it is eugenically evolved. We get a strong whiff of *Brave New World* when he speaks of a new caste system based on breeding, and when we are told that education in that society will be exclusively for social function. Eventually, the lower castes would be eugenically abolished. He does not explain how we shall do without them.

The third section is about sex, and as all he asks for is now permitted, it makes dull reading. The fourth section is again in the mood of *Brave New World*. Mass education has made 'highbrow' a term of contemptuous abuse. The intelligent and educated feign stupidity, for education is no longer respected. As soon as the mass became educated, they discovered that education was no longer a distinction, because everybody had it. The stupid were as badly off as before; the talented got the rewards. It is fortunate, says Huxley, with a slightly raised eyebrow, that the masses have not taken to the things of the mind. If they had, our economy would collapse. If men sat at home and read, they would not be rushing about in cars buying things. So highbrows, 'being poor consumers, are bad citizens'. Sour wit, we may think now, about a pitiful situation: from which we have not found any escape.

The next essay, 'The New Romanticism' carries us forward once again to *Brave New World*. Revolutionaries a century and a half ago were democrats and individualists. The reformers of 1832 were out for individualism and freedom. Our modern revolutions, those of Lenin and Ford, are 'the exact antithesis of the revolutionary liberation preached by Godwin'. We are becoming more and more creatures of the machines.

One more essay, 'Wanted, a New Pleasure' is worth noting and again because of its relevance to *Brave New World*. The best dream-come-true in *Brave New World* is the harmless soma drug, and Huxley writes about the need for something of the kind in this essay. What we need is 'a more efficient and less harmful substitute for alcohol and cocaine. If I were a millionaire, I should endow a band of research workers to look for the ideal intoxicant.' He grows lyrical about its benefits because he believes it would make life on earth a paradise. It would 'abolish our solitude as individuals, atone us with our fellows in a glowing exaltation of affection and make life in all its aspects seem not only worth living, but divinely beautiful and significant'. This was the spirit in which, twenty-five years later, he approached the new drugs.

It has been a strenuous book, but it ends with an agreeable bit of nonsense created out of nothing but Huxley's abundant inventiveness, wit and good humour and his most enviable gift of style. It is advice to a young novelist—buy a pair of siamese cats and watch them.

'Vulgarity in Literature'

The essay, 'Vulgarity in Literature' was first published as a
Dolphin Book in 1930 and is now reprinted with *Music at Night*.
It has the characteristic ebullience of his writing at that time.
The vulgarians he deals with at length are Balzac, Dickens and
Poe. Even more interesting is the defence of his own writing
when he turns to a general treatment of vulgarity in writing. This
is reprinted conveniently in the compressed version of the essay
published in *Collected Essays*. He had been attacked for his descriptions of love-making. He replied here that it is a necessary part of
rendering the Whole Truth to describe what he called 'physiology'
in deference to ageing Edwardian readers. Many readers then regarded it as vulgar or downright wicked. He turns on his attackers,
calling them stupid and morally reprehensible. They force him
to try to shock them more, and he hopes the result will be to
reform and educate these stupid criminals until they enjoy considering the truth about sex. He had this natural ambivalence
between strong sensual feeling and transcendence, he enjoyed
describing sensuality in his early novels as much as he enjoyed
the other extreme of experience in the later ones. He had the
usual human urge to defend morally what he enjoyed doing. The
Victorians had to distort their imaginative pictures of life by
leaving out 'physiology'; Huxley was one of the pioneers in telling
the truth, and he got away with it because of his gift of style.

He develops his theme of expressing life as wholly as we can.
He takes an example of a writer who was never vulgar; Flaubert.
Flaubert was an ascetic of letters, who resisted images and all
literary adornments. Few can do so. Huxley's own feelings were:
'An image presents itself, glittering, iridescent; capture it, pin it
down, however irrelevantly too brilliant for its context. A phrase,
a situation suggests a whole train of striking or amusing ideas
that fly off at a tangent, so to speak, from the round world on
which the creator is at work.' Could there be a better description
of his own most vigorous writing through the previous decade?
For example, of that concluding essay on cats in *Music at Night*?
He proceeds to another aspect of his problem. We have this wide
range of human activity to bring into imaginative writing. If we
do it badly, as best selling writers obviously do, we are vulgar. To

do it well is a matter of style or, as he puts it: 'Sincerity in art
... is mainly a matter of talent.' In this unequal world so few of
us have the talent to write.

'The Olive Tree'

'The Olive Tree', published in the same year as *Eyeless in Gaza*,
and a year before *Ends and Means*, has very little to do with the
thought developing in these books. Instead, it is a collection of
untroubled essays mainly on two of his interests, travel and
writing. The title essay is a short piece of inspired travel writing;
neat descriptions, amusing scholarship. It could be part of an
anthology of Huxley's Mediterranean pieces. His descriptive gift
is innocent, quite detached from his interest in people, sex,
religion. It is a holiday from these responsibilities; it is the
happiest sort of communion with Nature.

In 'In a Tunisian Oasis' he is content to be descriptive and
amuses us most when he sketches little boys and their various
ways of getting money from tourists. For comparison, we go to
Norman Douglas, whose prose was more highly wrought without
being mannered: Early Colloquial, whereas a little later, in the
twenties, The Colloquial came into its own. The mob of well-
educated men who wrote with ease. Douglas never gave the
impression of being a tourist. He was the wandering scholar, who
gave his days and nights in long sequences to a place before he
wrote about it; while Huxley was ready to supply travel journalism
of a quality which retains its freshness and delight. 'Waterworks
and Kings' is a very slight piece of that kind, describing the
terraced water-gardens in Kassel, Hesse.

There are a few more slight pieces and a couple of innocently
ebullient essays on sex which we may discuss before we come to
the literary essays, first, 'Crébillon the Younger'. When one
writer discusses another he is willy-nilly telling us about himself,
and that may be the chief interest of his piece. Huxley on
Crébillon tells us about Huxley. The opening is directly valuable
material on *Brave New World*, for he talks about Utopias and
H. G. Wells' prophetic books: 'prophecy is an expression of our
contemporary fears and wishes'. Crébillon was a very minor
eighteenth-century French novelist whose interest to Huxley was

H

his gift for analysing the psychology of love. 'With the dry intellectual precision of his age, he describes and comments on his characters, analyses their behaviour, draws conclusions, formulates generalizations.' While our modern method is to give the facts 'in a so-to-speak raw state, leaving the reader to draw his own conclusions from them'. Huxley supposes, as we should, that the best method of presentation will be a combination of the two. Then comes a phrase which sums up neatly Huxley's own method: 'expansive implication and suggestion.' He directs us back to eighteenth-century French novels to study love, which is always a mixture of the sacred and profane, the intellectual and the physiological. Aristocratic eighteenth-century France, unlike our Victorians, understood its dual nature and 'Crébillon *fils* is one of the acutest, one of the most scientific of the students'.

In splendid contrast with this fastidious discussion is the intellectual romp called 'Justifications'. It is a delicious example of Huxley's ebullient enjoyment of human hypocrisy. His subject, the Reverend Henry James Prince, a popular preacher and leader of an extravagant sect in the nineteenth century, gives him the kind of opportunity he enjoyed in his longer biographies. It gives him a chance to develop a subject which no novelist could use, a subject too good to seem true. Here is truth that is stranger than fiction, and Huxley finds the greater energy needed for its full enjoyment. His subject is justification, and he records actions which the normal person would not expect anyone to justify. He is studying extreme examples of double-think. 'Justifications have to be made in terms of the philosophy which condemns the acts or thoughts that it is desired to justify.' The Puritans contrived to combine Christianity and Capitalism; Thomas Schucker, a Swiss Anabaptist, in 1527 cut off his brother's head in front of witnesses who permitted the murder because Schucker declared he had been ordered by God to do so. Then we come to Prince, who discovered in himself a faculty for dominating people, and used it over women to get control of their money and on occasion to enjoy their persons. His personal magnetism was so great that he was able to have carnal communication with Sister Zoe on a sofa in the chapel, as a climax (and what a striking one) to a religious service he was conducting in his Agapomone or Abode of Love.

He leaves his case notes to end with a generalisation on the nature of God. Belief in a personal God, he says, clearly heightens energy and strengthens will. But belief in a personal God makes the believer think he is 'justified in giving rein to such all too human tendencies as pride, anger, jealousy and hatred, by the reflection that, in doing so, he is behaving like God who is a person'. This should make us 'extremely chary of accepting belief in a personal deity'. It will be easy for him after this to develop the idea of the unitary knowledge of God in his later writings. But how his mood has changed; from the amused Pyrrhonic aesthete who told the story of Prince, to the sober thinker speculating on the nature of ultimate Reality; from the younger to the mature Huxley.

The essays which remain are the introductions to R. B. Haydon's *Autobiography* and to D. H. Lawrence's *Letters*; and the opening essays on words and on writing. We have come to literature again. The Haydon essay was published in 1926 and is exactly in the mood of the short story, 'The Tillotson Banquet' which it must have inspired. It is written with a delicate relish and is uncompromising on Haydon's lack of talent. Huxley is amazed at this man's belief in himself. Poor Haydon: 'the epitome of every failure, he believed in himself extravagantly.'

The D. H. Lawrence piece was written in a very different mood. Here, Huxley is exerting himself to recapture for the reader his memories of a friend who had died, a fellow-craftsman for whose genius he had a very great respect. In the huge corpus of writing about Lawrence, one of the pieces which everyone should read is Huxley's Preface to the *Letters*. Huxley is able to write with complete sympathy about Lawrence. They were writers within the same ambience; even when he quoted Lawrence on his 'belief in the blood' he is not inconvenienced. Lawrence felt at home in his darkness; and rejected the light of science. And still Huxley is full of understanding. When Lawrence argued from his solar plexus, Huxley merely avoided further discussion of science. He proceeds to an exposition of Lawrence's immediacy in writing, which helps us greatly to understand what Lawrence felt. The *numen* had to speak through him and when it did, it would have been disloyal to tamper with it. 'Art, he thought, should flower from an immediate impulse towards self-expression or communication, and should wither with the passing of the impulse.'

It may be that as the critical commotion settles we shall find
that Lawrence's short stories and the travel sketches best survive.
The world is still full of people who knew him and one story is
of his pacing the room telling his short stories out loud; and then
writing them down while their immediacy was still about them.
'If he was dissatisfied with what he had written, he did not, as
most authors do, file, clip, insert, transpose; he rewrote. In other
words, he gave the *daimon* another chance to say what it wanted
to say.'

When he turns to Lawrence's religious beliefs, Huxley is
equally understanding and illuminating. Lawrence thought, inevitably, that man was 'the locus of a polytheism'. This polytheism was a democracy: 'all gods had an equal right to exist.'
From this belief came two rather surprising doctrines, one onto-
logical, the other ethical. First comes the Doctrine of Cosmic
Pointlessness, and he quotes Lawrence: 'There is no point...
to drag in the idea of a point is to ruin everything.' The ethical
counterpart is insouciance. Lawrence advised his sister: 'Don't
meddle with religion. I would leave all that alone.' It is better
to occupy oneself fully in the present—and so once more we
come to the revelation of the mystics: there is only the present
and we are always there.

Huxley distinguishes the essence of Lawrence's novels. Lawrence
had a scientific approach; he analysed his characters down to the
atoms of which they were composed. He analysed their behaviour
so far that 'they cease to have characters and reveal themselves as
collections of psychological atoms'. When Huxley turns to discuss
how the possession of this gift and his loyalty to it affected his
life, a new interest runs parallel to our interest in Lawrence; for
this may be Huxley's view about himself. 'He knew by actual
experience that the "real writer" is an essentially separate being,
who must not desire to meet and mingle and who betrays himself
when he hankers too yearningly after common human fulfil-
ments. All artists know these facts about their species.' Lawrence,
according to Huxley became a voice crying in the wilderness of
his own isolation.

Again, when he speaks of Lawrence's wanderings, we hear a
personal note. 'His travels were at once a flight and a search', a
search for a society in which he could establish contact, a flight
from the responsibility of living in his own island. It is a most

pleasant relief to be abroad and not be responsible for the people we meet and the crowds we move among. The amused Pyrrhonic aesthete and the Puritan genius; it is a fine description, and it achieves one of these miracles Huxley said was impossible. Unlike most descriptions of Lawrence, it makes us like the man, as we like the portrait in *Point Counter Point*. In the last few pages, Huxley does his duty as introducer handsomely. He makes us want to read the letters, and he gives us a general view of their effect before we busy ourselves in their detail. The essay is a model of its kind.

'Words and Behaviour' is a contribution to Huxley's anti-war writing, and goes along with his work in the *Encyclopaedia of Pacifism* and the chapter on War in *Ends and Means*. It is related to Orwell's essays on the careful use of words and the avoidance of *Crimestop* and *Doublethink*. It is part of the war against ignorance and stupidity which frustrate men at all times and in a knowledge explosion make them incapable of realising great advantages.

Huxley's argument is very reminiscent of Orwell's arguments later; the gist of it is that we must think. We still 'boast and swagger' for our country, we still 'hate, despise, swindle and bully for it', and no doubt we shall go on doing so until we get rid of our otiose diplomats and rewrite our school history books. He ends with: 'Politics can become moral only on one condition: that its problems shall be spoken of and thought about exclusively in terms of concrete reality; that is to say, of persons.' No more double-plus-good quack-speak; those speeches and journalism composed entirely without passing through the critical intelligence. It is not easy to give up our engrained habits of public utterance. It needs self-denial not to rouse the mob. It needs all the energy that thinking requires. Huxley says the effort must be made: 'To think correctly is the condition of behaving well. It is also in itself a moral act; those who would think correctly must resist considerable temptations.'

The opening piece, on 'Writers and Readers' is about the power of the written word, and opens typically with a list of figures; the number of books published annually, the amount of newsprint consumed in a year. Writers and readers: 'when the two come together, what happens? How much and in what ways do the readers respond to the writers?' Huxley distinguishes three kinds of writing; the first is an anodyne; the second is propaganda; the third is imaginative literature. Popular scientific exposition, a kind in which his family made such distinguished contributions, comes under propaganda. Huxley's treatment seeks to produce more responsibility in the development of this unique gift of man, communication by elaborately arranged sounds.

He reflects sadly that we have lost our old imaginative guides, the literatures of the Jews and Greeks. We have lost the common ground of all western cultures. Our new guides will come from the knowledge explosion. It may be generations before all the new knowledge is absorbed into a metaphysic, so meanwhile we must rely on the scientific expositors, remembering that they can only supply the raw material on which our minds must work: 'science is knowledge, not wisdom; deals with quantities, not with the qualities of which we are immediately aware.' It is not easy or comfortable to discover a metaphysic during a knowledge explosion like ours, but the scientific expositors are able to give us more help than Huxley indicates in this essay. He will do better in the next, which is about his grandfather.

T. H. Huxley's scientific work has been absorbed and overtaken; he survives as a prose artist. 'Science is soon out of date, art is not.' So Aldous approaches his grandfather's writings entirely as a literary critic, more precisely, as a rhetorician, eager to analyse the writings and find out the rules for writing good expository prose. 'The observable facts of literature are words arranged in certain patterns. The words have a meaning independent of the pattern in which they have been arranged; but it is the pattern that gives to this meaning its peculiar quality and intensity; that can make a statement seem somehow truer or somehow less true than the truth.' As the Scottish rhetoricians used to say, the prose unit in English is the phrase.

He distinguishes three kinds of writing in grandfather's work: purely descriptive, philosophical and sociological, and the controversial and emotive. In the first, he sought order and clarity: 'Huxley's scientific papers prove him to have had a remarkable talent for this austere and ungrateful kind of writing.' The philosophical writings give the critic more scope: they have much higher potentialities of beauty. Rhythms can be heightened, as he demonstrates.

In the writings of the third division, controversial and emotive,

'Huxley was severe, but always courteous'. There is greater warmth and penetration in the analysis of the prose in this division, and at the end comes the admission: 'in point of fact the man of letters does most of his work not by calculation, not by the application of formulas, but by aesthetic intuition.' The prose writer is born, not made; and we should add, he develops by much practice. The Victorian audience accepted a wider range of prose rhythms than our own and we notice that grandfather had a wider range within his smaller vocabulary than Aldous. Grandfather's range was in the colour and weight of his prose texture; Aldous' variety lies in pace and brightness rather than weight and colour. Each was a master in the prose manner of his time; and this tribute is the only study Aldous has left us on prose technique.

'The Art of Seeing'

In 1939 Huxley found that his poor sight was getting very much worse. At the age of sixteen he had nearly lost his sight but it had gradually improved. Now, it became alarmingly bad. He heard of Dr W. H. Bates' work in visual re-education and tried his methods. Very soon he was reading without spectacles and had lost all strain and fatigue. He was so grateful he wrote this short book, a manual foreseeing every kind of visual ailment which could be helped by exercises and faithfully describing these exercises. The style is appropriately expository, flat, simple, direct. The reward of the general reader is that he is meeting the writer who was going to give us *Island* nearly twenty years later. There is the same concern about mental relaxation, about co-ordinating mind and body, the same faith in the *vis medicatrix naturae*. There is the same passionate desire to help his fellowmen. It is essentially a practical manual and as such has little interest, other than this, for the reader concerned with Huxley's literary work.

'Themes and Variations'

The special interest of *Themes and Variations* is the essay on Maine de Biran, his longest essay, certainly among his best, and

new-minted for this 1950 volume. It is a study of a philosopher
who wrote a *Journal Intime*, as Huxley sometimes made a favourite
character do. As a philosopher he was not very distinguished but
he believed in the animal, the intellectual and the spiritual in man
working together, and this Huxley would obviously find sympathetic. The essay develops ideas put forward much earlier in
the Pascal essay. The four Variations are on artists who exposed
in their work the dark places of the subconscious. These studies
are prefaced by a short piece on 'Art and Religion', and followed
by a long piece on the demographic and ecological crisis the
human race was passing through in the late forties and which it
has not yet overcome. This excited and incisive piece on the
population problem seems an odd addendum to the richly cultivated essays on art and philosophy, but it sometimes takes all
sorts to make a volume of essays.

We have come a long way since 'The Double Crisis' was
written in 1949 but the population problem remains. There are
more people than there is food for them, but we can be more
optimistic than Huxley about solutions. We feel ourselves nearer
solutions he touched on, deserts can become fertile with cereals,
fish can be farmed instead of hunted. We can even hope that the
ultra-conservative peasant farmers of the Oriental world may one
day be persuaded to cultivate their land more efficiently. Huxley
was given to pessimism on these subjects; we were running
through our natural resources at an alarming rate: 'this rake's
progress towards human and planetary bankruptcy' he calls it.
Not only were the fertile landscapes becoming dustbowls but we
were consuming oil and minerals irresponsibly. In 1949 our
spirits were low after the exhaustion of war. We are in general
more optimistic now: we believe that human ingenuity gets over
its material problems.

The problems are part of the knowledge explosion. Babies and
old people survive much more than before. Our communications
remind us daily about the plight of the neoliths of the world. He
puts it dramatically: 'Given sewage systems, aureomycin and
plastic dentures, contraception becomes a necessity and the
adoption of a world population problem a matter of the most
urgent importance.' But carry your knowledge explosion a little
further and make it possible to control the sex of a foetus, and the
problem is solved. Tropical neoliths will want men children, and

very soon there will be few females to breed on. Old people will soon be so numerous and hearty in western countries, that the good sense of age will begin to influence policy.

Optimism is more likely to feed and clothe and house the world than brilliant pessimism. And when pessimism says, as Huxley does, that people are going to be more and more stupid and we shall have twice as many defectives by the end of the century, we feel sure it must be wrong. The human race is invincibly stupid, but it is not getting worse. Intelligence has always been rare, but there is enough about at the moment to have produced the greatest knowledge explosion in the history of the race. And if the explosion is great enough to bring the passions under control, the future of the race is assured.

The five essays on art are called 'Variations' and they are word and thought patterns playing on chosen themes. They remind us of what Sir Kenneth Clark said in the memorial volume: 'what he wrote about painting proves him to have been one of the most discerning lookers of our time... Aldous had an astonishing faculty for seeing what an artist really meant.' The variations have a prelude, a brief question and answer on the relationship of art and religion. The answer is that there is none. Man is like a ship, a whole divided into compartments: 'there may be good wine in one compartment, bilge-water in the other.' Our natures do not form a synthesis but a mere collection of opposites.

'Variations on a Baroque Tomb' is a word tapestry on funeral monuments in which he reflects that for two hundred and fifty years death has very rarely been an artistic theme. It has been handled more frequently in literature, and an appreciation of 'The Death of Ivan Ilyitch' follows, a story often mentioned by Huxley and here very adequately praised. Then, as if supporting his conclusion in the last essay, he notes that the baroque artists were working during a time when there was a great flowering of mystical religion, and these mystics rejected emotions because they were impediments to spiritual progress.

Three more 'Variations' follow, and the next is on El Greco, a piece which amply corroborates the words of Lord Clark. Before we go to the Prado and Toledo to look at the El Grecos, we should read this Variation. The theory which it expounds is that El Greco was expressing our capacity for union with the divine. He does so by combining representation with abstraction.

He was a disciple of Titian but he ignores landscape. Like his Byzantine ancestors he ignores the third dimension. These backgrounds are flat abstractions and set against them are bodies which have lost their bony structure and even their muscle systems. 'In these paintings there is no redemption of time by eternity, no transfiguration of matter by the spirit. On the contrary, it is the low-level organic that has engulfed the spiritual and transformed it into its own substance.' It is probably the only occasion on which Huxley has gone to psycho-analysis for an answer; he concludes that El Greco must have been afraid of the wide spaces of the air and dreamed of a place like a womb where he would be secure.

The two following sets of Variations, like this, are explorations of the morbid subconscious. 'Variations on The Prisons', Piranesi's engravings, opens with some thoughts on Bentham devoting twenty-five years of his life on elaborating plans for a perfectly efficient prison. He proceeds to discuss those prisons of the mind 'whose walls are made of nightmares and incomprehensions, whose chains are anxiety and their racks a sense of personal and even generic guilt'. He found these subjects irresistible. *The Prisons* were engraved when Piranesi was a young man, acutely aware of the solitariness of the human spirit and acutely aware that: 'Each living solitude is dependent upon other living solitudes and, more completely still, upon the ocean of being from which it lifts its tiny reef of individuality.' El Greco's backgrounds are an expression of an obscure disease in the human spirit; Piranesi's engravings are one of the great abstract expressions of human aloneness.

The final Variations are on Goya. It might have been expected. In *Grey Eminence* there are eloquent descriptions of Callot's war etchings. Somewhere in Huxley's oeuvre there must be something on Goya and here, appropriately and corrosively, come the Variations. As so often, he approaches the subject indirectly, and this time with a suggestion for an anthology of later works. He defines the title: 'the Later Works of those artists who have lived without ever ceasing to learn of life.' Huxley would appear in that anthology himself and Goya, during the last twenty odd years of his life, produced etchings which could not be foreseen in his early work. This late work was in no way transcendental, it was not directly a study of the subconscious hells. It was a picture of the world he saw, as it became more and more frightful. He saw the Napoleonic hordes in Spain and the worse horrors of civil war afterwards: 'and all the time, like the drone of a bagpipe accompanying the louder noises of what is officially called history, the enormous stupidity of average men and women, the chronic squalor of their superstitions, the bestiality of their occasional violences and orgies.' Passages like these are the essential virtue of these pieces, but they are all clear, accurate guides to the works of art they describe, with useful notes on the techniques involved as well as on the artistic ambience of the times in which they were produced. These variations are a significant contribution to Huxley's examination of the morbid area of the human consciousness.

The long sustained 'Variations on a Philosopher' is in strong contrast to the mood of the Variations. Maine de Biran flourished in the days of the Revolution and of Napoleon. He flourished intermittently, perhaps we should say, for he was a martyr to minor physical frailties. When he was well, he could philosophise, but when his body was a burden he became incapable of thought. He came from Périgord, where he was a squire and enjoyed looking after his people. He lived much in Paris, became Quaestor of the Chamber of Deputies, and spent his time in the social round. The opening of the essay makes all this clear in a short story fantasy very similar in style to the opening of *Grey Eminence*. Biran was not happy about the social round. As a philosopher, he knew it was foolish. As a man about town, he was hypersensitive about all the slights to his inconsequence. Just the subject for Huxley; the whole range from philosophy to social lightheadedness. This man, who in old age would dress up and go to these social occasions, cultivated the inner life and sought perfection. Biran had all the attractions of his weaknesses. His strength lay in the country, where he could, on fair occasion, have visions of the wonder of the world and the essential nature of things, very similar to those Wordsworth was having about the same time. He was no poet, but such experiences were recorded in his diary. Huxley says that his *Journal Intime* is almost unique in the history of philosophy. 'Thanks to its minute and detailed sincerity, we know Biran as we know no other of the great metaphysicians of the past.'

Huxley's purpose is to use this private account to discuss those

aspects of man's nature and destiny which were his constant
concern. The result is a microcosm of all the worlds of thought
which Huxley explored most happily throughout his writing life.
It is the warmest and richest presentation of his views on the
great subjects which preoccupied him, for he has a sympathetic
subject, a man who with sympathetic faults and failings pursued
his search for truth unfalteringly. Biran failed, as Huxley failed,
and as we all fail; but his attempt, as recorded in this private
journal, stirs the heart and the imagination.

Biran dreaded the reading public; he hated the exposure of his
ideas. He had no natural gift for writing; the right word was
always difficult to find. After much searching and much rewriting:
'The product of his labours is a prose that merely permits itself
to be read, never exhilarates or delights.' This gave him a sense
of inadequacy which Huxley notes was balanced by a conviction
of intrinsic superiority. 'I study ideas for their own sake', the
Journal says, 'in order to know what they are, what they imply,
disinterestedly, without reference to self-love or passion. This
disposition makes me eminently fit for the inner life and psychological research, but unfits me for everything else.'

His conclusions as a philosopher were modern and existentialist.
He saw that his happiness depended upon his bodily condition;
that the world of ideas and the processes of thought were not
within his control. He was conscious of the hiatus between language and the data of experience. Words cannot describe the
experiences of the inner man: 'In his essence the inner man is
ineffable, and within him how many degrees of depth, how many
points of view have not as yet been so much as glimpsed!' The
two orders of existence are closely related and are sometimes in
opposition because we are incarnate spirit. The 'I' of our consciousness acts upon a passive and resistant organism. 'Of
necessity knowledge arises through antithesis. For man, everything is antithesis.' When he sought truth, he knew that he was
seeking the unknown, and that no other philosopher could help
him in his search. For: 'The point was salvation, and salvation
consists in the direct knowledge or experience of God.' When he
had such an experience, it was a gratuitous grace. It was the
spring of 1816: 'In the air one breathes at this season of the year
there is *something spiritual,* which seems *to draw the soul to
another region.*' Was it a gratuitous grace, or the result of all his

searching, the just reward of his long endeavours? He was a man of fifty when he made that record. It is worth quoting because it recalls so much that Huxley wrote on this subject: 'it is my *inner light* that becomes brighter and more striking, so that the heart and mind are suddenly illumined by it. I have often detected in myself these sudden and spontaneous illuminations, when the truth emerges from behind a cloud; it seems that our material organization, which was the obstacle in the way of inward intuition, ceases to be resistant and that the spirit has nothing to do but receive the light which is appropriate to it.'

Huxley uses his subject in his usual way; he awakens our interest and sustains it so easily that he can afford to go off on some personal interest, which we see has illuminated the subject when we return. All the great subjects of Huxley's meditations appear in this magnificent essay; of time and transcendence, of the dual nature of man, of man in society and solitary, of the nature of ultimate reality and the possibility of our becoming aware of it in our existential condition. This essay can be used as the most attractive introduction to Huxley's thought.

'Adonis and the Alphabet'

This last collection of essays has the golden touch which his work enjoyed at that time. He had matured his world outlook, he was seeking a unitive knowledge of God serenely, his prose technique was not only adequate to the demands he made on it but he exploited it with a virtuosity which is a constant delight. There are no new ideas in this collection; it is rather a perfect mirror of his thought and expression. It is the word management and shaping of his material which gives us most pleasure, as he confirms his findings on life and the things in it which he most enjoyed. Sometimes he is offering a final statement of his position and if we were choosing pieces for an anthology of Later Works, we should come to *Adonis and the Alphabet*.

The opening essay, 'The Education of an Amphibian' is about education. Huxley liked to describe us as creatures belonging to two elements; he describes us so again in a preface to his wife's book. This and the next essay are not easy reading. They are close-packed and invaluable summaries of beliefs which had been developing over four decades; so, unless the reader is in the mood for sustained concentration, he had better leave the opening essays until later or he may never reach the entirely delightful and easy essays which follow. In this essay; 'The end proposed is the re-discovery within ourselves of a virgin not-mind capable of non-verbally not-thinking in response to immediate experience.' This idea of intellectual virginity comes from Meister Eckhart and for him it is realised by constant and intense self-awareness. This will lead the five selves of man to greater efficiency and once again Huxley cries: 'How grateful I should feel if someone had taught me to be, say, thirty per cent efficient instead of fifteen or maybe twenty per cent!' He defines at the beginning the merging but clearly distinguished not-selves. 'First, the not-self of habits and the cumulation of conditioned reflexes, the region with which psychiatry mainly deals.' Second, the not-self which does the walking, breathing, digesting. Third, the one 'who inhabits the world from which we derive our insights and inspirations'. Fourthly, the world of visionary experience and finally, 'that universal Not-Self, which men have called the Holy Spirit'.

To develop knowledge of these not-selves, Huxley says, we must draw up a curriculum of the non-verbal humanities so that we can train all these senses, from the kinesthetic to spiritual insight. This extends our western ideas of education, and the range and content of his course complies with the traditional oriental training of the disciple. It provides a full life and a healthy one. 'Health is the harmony between self and the not-selves.' We are very much in the atmosphere of *Island* and we experience the same uncertainty. It is not sufficiently convincing; while the oriental regimen, based on thousands of years of experience, is totally satisfying. The end Huxley proposed is only intelligible when we relate it to the states achieved by oriental ascetics. The second essay, fortunately, helps us to understand the first.

'Knowledge and Understanding' is a final statement of Huxley's religious position, of the way of life he thought appropriate to the human condition. He does not reject knowledge. On the contrary, like the Buddhists, he sees that the intellect has its essential place. It is necessary in the practical affairs of the world, and when education loses sight of the necessity for the disciplined accumula-tion of knowledge in the individual and the community, it fails everybody. Later in the essay, he repudiates the Cartesian 'I think therefore I am' in favour of 'Thoughts come into existence, and sometimes I am aware of them.' There are so many thoughts coming into existence he says, that an education in the humanities of two thousand years ago requires supplementing, by training in the humanities of today and tomorrow. In so many ways Greek experience is irrelevant to ours. Our rate of change in the total cumulation of knowledge, is much faster; we have a background of humanitarianism, of which the ancient Greeks knew nothing. Our views on work are more egalitarian because we have no slaves. Our philosophy is different, because we do not base it on language and regard all other tongues as barbarous. We have a sense of the past and knowledge of it, and in that matter the Greeks were childish. It is as well to go through all these simple points again; we are still struggling against the prodigal waste of brain hours on languages and civilisations that have become irrelevant to our lives in our knowledge explosion.

We could base our education on the idea of awareness which Huxley is constantly canvassing. If to know all is to forgive all, we should try to see that our young people know enough to be charitable and so abate the overpowering violence in the minds of men. We seek understanding, and knowledge is preliminary to understanding, although it is separated from it. A man may know a great deal and be deficient in understanding. Huxley argues later that we may have to forget much of our knowledge to attain understanding. We must try to cope with the paradox that 'in order to understand, we must first encumber ourselves with all the intellectual and emotional baggage, which is an impediment to understanding', and then we must subtract. He falls back on Eckhart: 'Virgin... is a person void of alien images, free as he was when he existed not.' This is the attitude of the mystic, 'a son of time present', and it is the mystic who has the understanding of which Huxley speaks.

In reaching understanding, there is a law of reversed effort: 'We cannot make ourselves understand; the most we can do is to foster a state of mind in which understanding may come to us.' It comes when we are totally aware: 'aware to the limits of our mental and physical potentialities.' In this state, distraction cannot interfere, and any idea of approval or condemnation is excluded. In this state of total awareness we are prepared for 'the understanding, moment by moment, of reality at all its levels'.

The essay ends with a recall of the essence of all his teaching: 'For when there is understanding, there is an experienced fusion of the End with the Means, of the Wisdom, which is the timeless realization of Suchness, with the compassion which is Wisdom in action.'

In the Renaissance, in 1487, Pico della Mirandola gave his great oration on the dignity of man. He makes the Supreme Maker proclaim to man: 'I have placed you at the very centre of the world, so that from that vantage point you may with greater ease glance around about you on all that the world contains... It will be in your power to descend to the lower, brutish forms of life; you will be able, through your own decision, to rise again to the superior orders whose life is divine.' In the incomparably richer world of today, Huxley proclaimed the range of man's opportunities in the same proud, urgent way and he has given us, in these two late essays, the most concise account of his beliefs about the high possibilities of the human condition.

We may relax now to look at the charming pieces which make up the volume. 'The Desert' is about solitude and silence and words. We are given glimpses of nature at its most brilliant, caterpillars filling the desert floor, cicadas breaking from their sheaths. Then a glimpse of man's arrangements for nuclear destruction, and the reflection that if we survive that madness, it will be as caterpillars survive, by organic reaction. Our intelligence will fail us but our organic instincts will carry us through. When he comes to words, they 'are the greatest, the most momentous of all our inventions, and the specifically human realm is the realm of language'. He swings violently in these essays between optimism and pessimism, and after abandoning the intelligence he swings to optimism at the end: 'I am still optimist enough to credit life with invincibility... beyond survival is transfiguration.'

'Ozymandias' is a study of the kind of community D. H. Lawrence invited Huxley to join. Huxley, always the enthusiastic student of the human being and his communities, offers here a most amusing description of the Llano del Rio Co-operative Colony founded by a Los Angeles politician in 1914. The colony made every possible mistake, and Huxley suggests from his study of many American experiments, that the best hope of survival for these communities lies in powerful religious ties which will overcome the frictions of communal living. Next best thing is a magnetic leader.

The interest of these experiments is that some of them have contributed significantly to our knowledge of the most difficult and important of all the arts, the art of living together in harmony. They are usually Communist, that is, they hold all things in common; but according to that excellent totalitarian tract, *The Acts of the Apostles*, rather than according to Marx.

'Liberty, Quality, Machinery' is again about population. It is built around the Tolstoy quotation which opened *Science, Liberty and Peace* nearly ten years earlier; machines put more power in the hands of fewer people and they oppress the many. The people the machines have bred turn the earth into cities and spread squalor in them all. He looks forward to the pill to control population and deplores the mass media which enable rulers to suppress the truth, and bully and hypnotise their people. A sudden turn, and he is discussing the little machines which make the 'do-it-yourself' movement. First, the practical world of household upkeep and repairs, and then the world in which amateurs model and paint as a therapy. It helps us to make sense of experience and to impose order and meaning into our lives.

He remains very much in the real world in the next essay, on 'Spoken Literature'. Publishing is becoming so expensive we had better start a do-it-yourself movement to overcome this censorship by economics. Valuable new books lie unpublished, many of our classics are out of print: 'the great silencer, the muffler attached to every channel of intellectual and artistic expression, is money.' It is another area in which it is possible to be optimistic or pessimistic, and Huxley chooses to be gloomy although thanks to paperbacks we probably have more good books available to more people than ever before. Huxley is eager that we should do better. He would make recordings of the best that has been thought and said, and make sure that everybody heard them. Very authoritarian and over-optimistic: for only he that has an ear can hear.

'Canned Fish' shows the essayist at his best. He visits a canning factory, which he describes, and then is off down the illuminating corridors of his well-stored mind. A passage on words—the general theme of the collection—and a horrified glimpse of the lives of ordinary man at any time: 'bruised, galled, strained beyond the limits of organic endurance.' Back to his fish to tell us that

the world of fishes is in a state of revolution; they are turning up
in unexpected places because the climate is changing. Warmth
is creeping northwards, and that leads to a glance at the climatic
possibilities of the world.

'Tomorrow and Tomorrow and Tomorrow' is another piercing
glance across the world into the future, and one that we have
shared with him often before. We are playing the prodigal with
our natural resources; we are living in a Golden Age, squandering
our assets with no thought for our children's children. One
Utopian dreamer after another is discussed, Sir Charles Darwin,
Harrison Brown, Sir George Thomson. They are prophets of
ultimate woe, but we are only disturbed when, towards the end,
Huxley talks again about the population problem. It will be
necessary to have a vast Marshall Plan. We have heard it so often,
we know it will help, but we observe that whatever sensible plan
is tried, man defeats it with his acquisitiveness, his sloth and his
animal determination to live his life in his own way, though he
damns himself in doing it.

When we read 'Hyperion to a Satyr' we feel that all roads in
these late Huxley essays lead to *tat tvam asi*—that art thou;
transcendence; and on the way, the political pattern of the
future, masters and slaves, living in the 'trinity of the Nation,
Party and Political Boss'. Here, the way is through dirt and
disease, and all the medieval and Renaissance literature on dirt
and disease; and from there to sewage systems, the drainage of
great cities, an enthusiastic discussion of 'the merits of activated
sludge', sludge which ends up 'in the form of odourless solid
which, when dried, pelleted and sacked, sells to farmers at ten
dollars a ton'. It is part of our technological revolution that western
man, Mass Man, has been rescued from the dirt that shamed him.
We know from Somerset Maugham and George Orwell that quite
recently the lower classes smelled. Now, there is pride in clean-
liness (with passing student fashions in the other direction) and
soon there will be godliness. The balance of our nature will be
restored.

'Mother' is about another side of our economic revolution. It
is an essay about the manufacture of expendable rubbish for
Mass Man. Long ago, craftsmen made single objects of great
beauty or great ugliness for very rich men. The riches are now
with the masses and millions of ill-constructed, badly-designed

objects are made to take his money from him. He takes the
thriving greeting card industry as an example. It is the answer
for those who hate to write and cannot spell. If Huxley descends
to that level he does not stay there long. He turns to the idea of
the Great Mother as creator and destroyer; of death following
life so that life may renew itself; and talks of reviving the mother
symbol of the cosmic mysteries of life and death. Until recently,
man has had festivals to remind him of these mysteries, but now
Mass Man is protected by distractions from any thought of them.

'Adonis and the Alphabet' is a celebration of the unknown
men who gave us the alphabet, and like all true essays it is about
much else which was on the writer's mind. At the beginning he is
against tragedians, moralists and preachers. He has also had
enough of satirists and debunkers. He is for 'the divine equan-
imity'. The habits of birds lead him to cruelty to animals and,
sure enough, to the follower of St Francis who cut a trotter off a
living pig. When he gets back to the alphabet, it is to remind us
that 'our thoughts, feelings and behaviour are, to a much greater
extent than we care to admit, determined by the words and syntax
of our native tongue'. It is the art of the essayist to hold our attention and concentrate it, while he offers us a travel sketch, a
digression on cruelty to animals, a metaphysic of language and a
final sustained O Altitudo. It is the art of transference of interests
and to the reader who is concerned with Huxley's preoccupation
in later life with the Reality beyond our cosmic appearances, this
essay has a place alongside *Heaven and Hell*, published in the
same year.

Three little travel essays follow 'Adonis', all inspired by the
same trip to the Middle East. A brief piece, 'Miracle in Lebanon'
describes a miracle and analyses the double-crossing secret agent.
The born secret agent can never be relied on. It is obvious to
most of us that he could well disappear with the diplomat. The
shadow of the psychologist falls upon the ending of the essay; the
psychologist in the pay of the politician to condition the people.
'*That* will really be a revolution. When it is over, the human race
will give no further trouble.'

'Usually Destroyed' is the most thunderous sermon on calamity
that Huxley ever penned. We are in Jerusalem. We are tourists,
so we have a guide, a fragile, rather pathetic sentimental figure,
who does not hold our attention for long. The preacher is in full

voice; we have heard it all before, but never with the force of these unfaltering fulminations on the future of mankind. 'I show you sorrow' said the Buddha, and Huxley shows us sorrow past and present.

He would have done better to sit in his garden than go all the way to Jerusalem to wail at the wall. Then there is compensation. From an open window comes the sound of the Fantasia of Bach's *Partita in A minor*. The wailing ceases and we have a most delicate embroidery of words on the nature of time and music. As he listens: 'A tunnel of joy and understanding had been driven through chaos and was demonstrating, for all to hear, that perpetual perishing is also perpetual creation.'

After a few pages of travel embroideries, 'Famagusta or Paphos' becomes an appreciation of Mallarmé, recalling the admiration expressed nearly twenty-five years before in *Texts and Pretexts*. He quotes again 'O si chére de loin'; the ambience is French, and criticism becomes interpretation.

'Faith, Taste and History' is a good example of Huxley's favourite modelling technique, shaping his material from an opening on the easy level of the tourist, to an appreciation of newly discovered art forms, a return to his original subject and an unexpected explosion of merriment for a coda. The visit was to Salt Lake City and the Temple of the Mormons, which was huge and contrived to be completely unoriginal and prosaic. One of the great modern monuments to brute force. For the men who built it had no roads and only ox-wagons for transport to carry the great granite blocks. Dedicated effort to produce a huge ugliness; and so to the relation between art and religion once again. In a dozen pages the gamut from animal vulgarity, to the grace of life expressed in the older polyphony.

'Doodles in the Dictionary' is about the art of Toulouse-Lautrec, and there is absolute concentration on the subject. No distractions, once the opening has been made, the recall of young Aldous spending Etonian Tuesdays manufacturing Latin verses, and the reflection that such useless activity was rather like life for most people; doing things for ever which they do not like. Huxley obtains the Latin dictionary Toulouse-Lautrec used as a boy. It is full of sketches, particularly of horses. A quick biographical sketch and then appreciation of his drawings.

In 'Gesualdo: Variations on a Musical Theme' the echoes are

back to the variations in *Themes and Variations* and to the essay on the Mormon temple in this volume. These strands run through the essays everywhere. The opening of this Variation is an example of the gradual approach which he used systematically. It is the counterpart of the rhetorician's rule that the speaker must first impress himself upon his public. The particular subject will be focused against a general background which will give the subject perspective, appropriate value and interest. We are going to discuss the music of Gesualdo; we begin with a general comment on the exploration of space and time. For centuries we have explored space and every part of the world is known. Only recently have we explored many aspects of time. For instance, until recently we have not explored our European musical inheritance before 1680. The Monteverdi Vespers were forgotten from the middle of the seventeenth century until 1935. So with Gesualdo, whose madrigals were known to Milton, but to no later poets until our own day. We are given a brief biography of this Prince of Venosa and the essay goes on to the madrigal and the intense expressiveness it achieved in those Gesualdo has left us. 'The intricacies of polyphony are made to yield the most powerfully expressive effects, and this polyphony has become so flexible that it can, at any moment, transmute itself into blocks of chords or a passage of dramatic declamation.' The quotation illustrates Huxley's gift; he wrote these critical analyses with perfect clarity and euphony, and like all good critics he wrote to celebrate and share what he loved most.

Adonis and the Alphabet is pulsating with life and eagerness and hope. When Huxley returned three years later in *Brave New World Revisited* to his beliefs and the worries of the world, the magic had gone. In the later volume the eagerness and the courage had seeped away. Anxiety and tension had replaced them. The golden moment had gone. So we must cherish *Adonis and the Alphabet* as almost our last contact in essay form with this rich intelligence in full enjoyment of the new knowledge in the world and the new hopes for man. One remarkable essay was to follow.

Epilogue

Literature and Science

IN HIS LAST DAYS he wrote a valedictory essay which displayed again the rich furniture of his mind and brought an atmosphere of mature reasonableness to the debate on the two cultures. Never had he written more warmly, more persuasively or with a finer tone. Never had his critical appreciation been more sensitive. Never, to echo a phrase he uses so often in this essay, had he given a sense so pure to our sweet English tongue. The contemporary debate on the two cultures is necessary and pressing but the division into two is arbitrary. There is only one culture in England as in other countries, if we take language and moral outlook as its basis. Scientists and artists share that base, and when we build on it we find many arts and more sciences, and that many men have professional status in some of them and are completely ignorant of most of them. It is an inevitable condition of our knowledge explosion. The debate will be finished when we are sure of the base, and Huxley is here concerned with the language part of it. What is necessary to our comfort and advantage is that scientists should be able to use the language efficiently as expositors, and that they should relate their discoveries and technological ingenuity to our moral base. What is necessary for men of letters is that they should be able to understand the scientists and accept the obligation to do so. They must then purify the words of the tribe to meet this new understanding.

This obligation they share with politicians and lawyers and all those who direct our progress towards healthier and more comely lives. It implies endless endeavour in all professional life; discovery followed by absorption into the world view. Endless necessary alternation between discovery and absorption. Endless energy therefore to maintain the balance and Huxley quotes Blake again: 'Energy is Eternal Delight.'

The essential vocation of the man of letters has not changed; to understand and interpret human nature and help us understand our natural surroundings as well as ourselves. He places us in the world and there is a new world to place us in. He must prop our minds, give us steadiness in this flux of knowledge. We have been frightened, Huxley says, by the astronomers, who have destroyed our comfortable beliefs about our planet and our little galaxy. We have been frightened by the psychologists and the psycho-analysts, who have given us a sense of human littleness and a sense of the unutterable evil in our natures. This, says Huxley, is more deadly than the threat of extinction which the physicists and chemists have made so possible and imminent.

Literary men, he says, have absorbed the horrors of space and evil. They have given much less attention to the great additions to the common store of scientific knowledge made by less spectacular scientists like the bio-chemists, the physiologists and the anthropologists. It will be harder for the man of letters to understand these subjects and master their theories so that he can interpret them imaginatively. For these vigorous pursuits he will require the energy which Blake describes: 'Energy is the only life and it is from the Body, and Reason is the bound or outward circumference of Energy.'

There are two areas in which the accumulation of energy has become most notable, youth and old age. We grow daily in respect for youth as it struggles to demolish what is inane and what is insane in our social structures. We shall grow in respect for age since, thanks to our new medical knowledge, western man not only lives longer but retains his intellectual vigour as never before. When the vision of youth and the experience of age—all the notable things in literature have been said for decades now by men who have grown old—when these exert their pressures upon our societies, evolutionary development will look like revolutionary change. Yet, because there are so few of them, young and old, with the necessary intelligence and the necessary

knowledge, all the savants of Europe have urged that we become
a European community so that the intelligent will prevail over
the masses and their seducers.

It is this stimulating dilemma to which Huxley directs our
attention in this valedictory piece. He is a man of letters and he
addresses himself to men of letters, exhorting them to purify the
words of the tribe so that they can convey the clear light of the
new knowledge; so that they can prop our minds as more and
more knowledge is made available and must be absorbed if
humanity is to continue to exist and enjoy the earth. This last
message is as warm and stimulating as anything he wrote. Men
can become frightened when they are discovering so much; their
concern is whether the human mind can accept it all and remain
sane. Huxley was never in doubt. Knowledge leads to understanding, and we must pursue it energetically.

It is here that he draws attention to the remarkable energy
exerted by Ezra Pound and T. S. Eliot in their obscure researches
into earlier European thought. If only Ezra Pound, a consummate
purifier of the words of the tribe, had used his talent to interpret
modern science in a work of high literary art. When shall we
have our Lucretius? Optimism is not easy. The poets are not
interested, perhaps because their education has not given them
ears to hear. There never was a time since the Renaissance when
our poets have given us so little help. Until they are able to catch
up with knowledge and formulate a contemporary world view, it
is difficult to see why we should listen to them. Our interpretations
of moods and actions must be those of contemporary science;
anything else is irresponsible fiction. It is the responsibility of
men of letters to know the rules of nature, so far as scientists have
discovered them. They are in a new world of dazzling brightness
which they must transform down to a synthesis which will help
their contemporaries. They may feel alone in an unfriendly
universe, they may have a paralysing obsession with the oblitera-
tion of mankind, they may be haunted by the appalling possibilities of the imbalance of the conscious and the unconscious
mind. All these things, says Huxley, are challenges to intellectual
combat and spurs to achievement.

This is an inspired vision of a dying writer. He came down to
earth in the rest of his essay, right down to earth, to ecology and
its practical applications. If man hopes to survive, he must learn

to live in harmony with nature; and our city hordes have lost the art. We must understand that 'the world is poetical intrinsically, and what it means is simply itself. Its significance is the enormous mystery of its existence and of our awareness of that existence.' More awareness; knowledge is more awareness. It is a declaration on behalf of the intelligence. It must be prepared to absorb more, to rationalise the new knowledge in relation to the old, and make a new synthesis, to achieve harmony, to cerebrate its way to a new world view. We must do what the mystics tell us to do and live in the eternal present; and not enwomb ourselves in the obscure thoughts of obscure ages.

He ends on a paradox: 'Thought is crude, matter unimaginably subtle.' Language is clumsy and will never be adequate for what the scientist and the man of letters want to say. His last word is sweet reasonable exhortation in this condition: 'Cheerfully accepting the fact, let us advance together, men of letters and men of science, further and further into the ever expanding regions of the unknown.' What courage! It carries us back more than a hundred years to:

> *that which we are, we are;*
> *One equal temper of heroic hearts,*
> *Made weak by time and fate, but strong in will*
> *To strive, to seek, to find, and not to yield.*

A Select Bibliography

BIBLIOGRAPHY:

Aldous Huxley, a Bibliography, by H. R. Duval. New York (1939).
Aldous Huxley, a Bibliography (1916–1959), by C. J. Eschelbach
and J. L. Schober (1961).

PROSE WORKS:

Limbo (1920).
Crome Yellow (1921).
Mortal Coils (1922).
On the Margin (1923).
Antic Hay (1923).
Little Mexican (1924).
Along the Road (1925).
Those Barren Leaves (1925).
Jesting Pilate (1926).
Two or Three Graces (1926).
Proper Studies (1927).
Point Counter Point (1928).
Do What You Will (1929).
Vulgarity in Literature (1930).
Brief Candles (1930).
Music at Night (1931).
Texts and Pretexts (1932).
Brave New World (1932).
Beyond the Mexique Bay (1934).

The Olive Tree (1936).
Eyeless in Gaza (1936).
Ends and Means (1937).
After Many a Summer (1939).
Grey Eminence (1941).
The Art of Seeing (1943).
Time Must Have a Stop (1945).
The Perennial Philosophy (1946).
Science, Liberty and Peace (1947).
Ape and Essence (1949).
Themes and Variations (1950).
The Devils of Loudun (1952).
The Doors of Perception (1954).
The Genius and the Goddess (1955).
Adonis and the Alphabet (1956).
Heaven and Hell (1956).
Brave New World Revisited (1959).
Island (1962).
Literature and Science (1963).

Letters of Aldous Huxley, edited by Professor Grover Smith (1969).

CRITICAL STUDIES:

Aldous Huxley, by Jocelyn Brooke in the *Writers and Their Work* series. (Revised edition, 1963.)
Aldous Huxley, a Literary Study, by John Atkins. (Revised edition, 1967.)
Aldous Huxley, 1894–1963, A Memorial Volume, edited by Julian Huxley (1966).

Index

INDEX TO WORKS